PRAISE FOR
CO-TEACHING FOR ENGLISH LEARNERS

Supporting one of the fastest growing segments of the nation's student population can be challenging, particularly when educators work in isolation. Maria Dove and Andrea Honigsfeld show us how to support English learners through collaborative practices that work. This must-have book draws from the most current research and provides multiple practical examples, protocols, and essential questions to guide us in making collaborative practices a reality in our own particular settings.

—Dr. Debbie Zacarian, President
Zacarian and Associates

Dr. Dove and Dr. Honigsfeld articulated it very clearly when they presented to our teachers of ELLs in Western New York: "You cannot have successful co-teaching without co-planning." Their new book continues the much-needed conversation on how to co-teach by looking carefully at the relationships and the school-based opportunities required for success. All teachers have the need to refine new practices in our profession that lead our students to effective academic outcomes. Dove and Honigsfeld have a unique ability to define with ease the why and the how of tackling effective co-teaching for ELLs. We must change the ways we have always done our work as teachers. There is no going back when we know more because of the work of these two important researchers.

—Denise Gonez Santos, Executive Director
Regional Bilingual Education-Resource Network West

Dove and Honigsfeld have captured the essence of co-teaching through the recommended practice of collaborative teamwork using several models including "Model 7: Multiple Groups Two Monitor/Teach." One example of this model demonstrated how both teachers are engaged in small-group instruction and plan for independent activities where students explore grade-level content with the scaffolding of and modifications to age-appropriate readings. To ensure success when using this co-teaching model, the research shared by the authors demonstrated the necessity of students to be involved in highly engaging activities while discovering new information. This hands-on learning approach allows English learners to develop new language skills through the application of speaking, reading, and writing tasks.

—Susan Brown, English Learner Specialist
Charlotte Mecklenburg Schools

As a large and diverse urban school system, our district needed to create a service model structure to meet the needs of over 15,000 English Learner students (ELs), representing over 120 languages. We selected co-teaching as one of the service models because this model allowed students to remain in the content class with their native English-speaking peers while receiving their required EL services. Co-teaching is an ideal model for our district because it allows for students at all levels of English language proficiency access to the complex grade-level content, tasks, and standards while acquiring productive and receptive language skills. With the support of Dr. Dove and Dr. Honigsfeld, our district is in our second year of implementing the EL co-teaching model. We started by analyzing the data and grouping students based on their language needs and allowing the EL teacher to co-teach in sheltered ELD/English Language Arts classes. In these classes, we saw over 2 years growth as evidenced by text-level assessments. At the middle and high school level, co-teaching expanded to content classes to support English learners through an integrated approach alongside the content teacher. Both models proved to be successful for our district as we added another 29 EL co-teachers this school year. Dove and Honigsfeld's new book provides a deep dive into the advantages and challenges of each co-teaching model along with low-prep strategies for the partners. This is essential in helping the content and EL teacher select the appropriate model for their setting and to implement high-yield strategies in the integrated language and content setting. The authors highlight the importance of collaboration among EL teachers and content teachers to have shared accountability for the academic, linguistic, and social emotional success of ELs.

—Molly Stovall Hegwood, Director of EL Services
Metro Nashville Public Schools

This important follow-up volume is just what we need, just in time! It will invigorate co-teachers of English Learners while urging them to refocus their attention from "just co-teaching" to the truly effectual work of teacher collaboration throughout the entire instructional cycle. At the same time, best practices for student engagement and focused English language development are clearly described within a deep analysis of the seven co-teaching models. Co-teachers will return to this volume again and again for the practical tips and authentic examples to mix and match models to the benefit of their English Learners.

—Debra Cole, MELL Instructional Specialist
St. Louis – Missouri English Language learning

From the get-go, Dove and Honigsfeld present a clear call to action. We have an obligation to provide the best, most consistent, and aggressive support to a growing population with very specific needs. And what better way to do that than by collaborating and co-teaching with intentionality and precision? Offering structures and strategies for each of seven key models of co-planning and co-teaching, the authors have given us all we need to meet our common goals in a compelling, detailed, and inescapably helpful resource. The rest is up to us.

—Pete Hall, Former School Principal
EducationHall

Working in a very large, linguistically diverse school board, where top priorities include the goals of ensuring equity and high expectations for all students, it's exciting to find a text which commits on practically addressing the complexity of co-planning, co-teaching, and co-assessing to support the success of English learners, through and through. It is with respect of educators of the field that the authors have truly demystified how successful partnerships unfold, honoring the power of the whole collaborative planning cycle. By providing in-depth illustrations and real-life scenarios with several variations to highlight a variety of contexts, this book allows for multiple entry points. Honestly, in all my roles in education over the last 22 years, including ESL/ELD teacher, classroom teacher, resource teacher, and even now as a leader supporting over 250 schools to address the needs of ELs, I have never found a resource that does what Dove and Honigsfeld have achieved here. This book is ideal for school teams—teachers with their administrators—ready to roll up their sleeves. I have always believed that supporting linguistically diverse students to achieve academically should not be beyond our reach and would wonder why many districts share the experience that they cannot get there effectively. Dove and Honigsfeld have revealed where the link has been broken. Their research is focused on intentionally orchestrating conditions in classrooms for students to learn the content while acquiring the language of instruction and how all this is to happen in tandem. Now that is true rocket science!

—Zaiba Beg, Instructional Coordinator of ESL/ELD Programs
Peel District School Board

Co-Teaching for English Learners

We dedicate this book to our respective families:
Tim, Dave, Jason, Sara, Meadow Rose, Gavin Joseph, and
Rohnan Xavier; Howie, Benjamin, Jacob, and Noah.

Co-Teaching for English Learners

Learners

A Guide to Collaborative Planning, Instruction, Assessment, and Reflection

Maria G. Dove

Andrea Honigsfeld

CORWIN
A SAGE Publishing Company

FOR INFORMATION:

Corwin

A SAGE Company

2455 Teller Road

Thousand Oaks, California 91320

(800) 233-9936

www.corwin.com

SAGE Publications Ltd.

1 Oliver's Yard

55 City Road

London EC1Y 1SP

United Kingdom

SAGE Publications India Pvt. Ltd.

B 1/I 1 Mohan Cooperative Industrial Area

Mathura Road, New Delhi 110 044

India

SAGE Publications Asia-Pacific Pte. Ltd.

3 Church Street

#10-04 Samsung Hub

Singapore 049483

Program Director: Dan Alpert

Developmental Editor: Lucas Schleicher

Production Editor: Amy Schroller

Copy Editor: Diane Wainright

Typesetter: C&M Digitals (P) Ltd.

Proofreader: Dennis W. Webb

Indexer: Sheila Bodell

Cover Designer: Michael Dubowe

Marketing Manager: Maura Sullivan

Copyright © 2018 by Corwin

Printed in the United States of America

Library of Congress Cataloging-in-Publication Data

Names: Dove, Maria G., author. | Honigsfeld, Andrea, 1965- author.

Title: Co-teaching for English learners : a guide to collaborative planning, instruction, assessment, and reflection / Maria G. Dove, Andrea Honigsfeld.

Description: Thousand Oaks, Calif. : Corwin, A SAGE Company, [2017] | Includes bibliographical references and index.

Identifiers: LCCN 2017023934 | ISBN 9781483390918 (pbk. : alk. paper)

Subjects: LCSH: English teachers—Training of. | English language—Study and teaching—Foreign speakers. | Independent study—Evaluation.

Classification: LCC PE1128.A2 D696 2017 | DDC 428.0071—dc23
LC record available at https://lccn.loc.gov/2017023934

This book is printed on acid-free paper.

18 19 20 21 10 9 8 7 6 5 4 3 2

Contents

Note From the Publisher

The authors have provided access to video and web content throughout the book that is available to you through QR codes. To read a QR code, you must have a smartphone or tablet with a camera. We recommend that you download a QR code reader app that is made specifically for your phone or tablet brand. You may also access the videos and other resources on the companion website at http://resources.corwin.com/CoTeachingforELs.

Preface

Co-teaching for English learners (ELs) is a compromising balance of planning and delivery of instruction among teaching partners. The instructional cycle we explore in this book—collaborative planning, delivery, assessment, and reflection—examines this balance and the interdependence of these components to bring about a successful co-taught class. Many researchers of inclusive education and practitioners in inclusive schools alike emphasize the need to engage in this complete cycle of collaboration (Bell & Baecher, 2012; Friend, 2008; Murawski, 2009a, 2009b; Theoharis & O'Toole, 2011). From our research, in which we continue to examine co-teaching practices specifically with English learners, we strongly concur that there is an urgent need to look beyond the instructional classroom practices of co-teaching. Ignoring three elements of the collaborative instructional cycle—co-planning, co-assessment, and reflection—would significantly disrupt the instructional balance and negatively impact student learning.

For co-teaching to succeed, teachers need time, commitment, and structured opportunities built into the school day for a range of collaborative instructional activities. When collaboration becomes an integral part of the co-teaching initiative, it allows teachers to (a) think deeply about differentiating instruction; (b) gather, evaluate, and respond to student data; and (c) reflect on the teaching–learning process that takes place in the class (Schon, 1990). The practice of teacher collaboration does not always seem readily accepted, as Elena Okanovic, English to Speakers of Other Languages (ESOL) instructional coordinator of the St. Louis Public Schools, ESOL Bilingual Migrant Program, remembers:

> *Just several years ago, when our district began piloting co-teaching for ELs in mainstream classrooms, I could not believe that today I would be the one who would not only promote co-teaching and collaboration for my colleagues but also coach participants to become even more successful in their current co-teaching practices with ESOL and mainstream teachers in grades K–8. I was one of the most reluctant teachers to believe that the co-teaching model would work for my students, for their individual linguistic needs, for my colleagues, and for me as an ESOL educator. Back then, I strongly believed that the optimal way to increase the students' English and academic proficiency was to pull my ELs aside while juggling between preteaching the mainstream curriculum, assisting individual students with completing specific assignments for the mainstream curriculum, and reteaching challenging content concepts while trying to implement the district's newly adopted ESOL curriculum. I have recently realized that my best intentions to help my students were unintentionally creating*

additional barriers for them to access the main curriculum. By the end of my first year of co-teaching, my partner and I had indeed developed a positive model of the 'healthy marriage' in our collaborative practices—we were thinking the same, making the same comments simultaneously, assessing work similarly, and celebrating our successes. Because of the success I experienced with co-teaching as an ESOL teacher, in my current role I am able to guide and support teachers who are just beginning their co-teaching journey.

Elena's reflection is both unique as well as much too common. We have heard from many English Language Development/English Language Learner (ELD/ELL) teachers who did not think collaboration and co-teaching with grade-level/content-area teachers were in their best professional interest, or that they would have positive outcomes for their students. At the same time, we have been fortunate to work with numerous educators around the United States who have fully embraced teacher collaboration and made co-teaching an integral and successful part of their approach to serving ELs. This book was inspired by both groups of educators.

WHY WE WROTE THIS BOOK

As longtime coauthors and copresenters, we ventured into this new project to offer a deeper discussion of the collaborative instructional cycle that we first began in our 2010 Corwin publication titled *Collaboration and Co-Teaching: Strategies for English Learners*, developed primarily for general-education ELD/ELL teachers. This time, our intention is to present a closer look at each of the four components of the collaborative instructional cycle: co-planning, co-teaching, co-assessing, and reflection, with an in-depth examination of seven co-teaching models in K–12 classrooms.

In the past five years, many state and local educational agencies have made a marked shift away from segregated, incongruous instructional services for English learners, either requiring or recommending co-teaching as an optimum way to develop students' English language skills. More and more, co-teaching has become a commonly sought-out option for serving ELs, primarily as a result of the general transformation in overall vision for the academic success of these students. This vision is rooted in the belief that all English learners need to develop their language skills while learning the mainstream curriculum. Leos and Saavedra (2010) have addressed this notion as follows:

ELLs [English language learners] are tasked to develop three distinctly different learning skill sets simultaneously—reading (product) and language development and language acquisition (process)—to become successful lifelong academic learners and thinkers. Educators are tasked to understand how to teach foundational language development skills fused through the lens of language acquisition aligned to the academic content areas at each grade level. (p. 11)

When English learners are included in general-education classes through co-teaching they are supported to acquire rigorous academic content as well as language and literacy skills at the hands of both a content-area expert and a language-learning expert.

WHAT CAN YOU FIND IN THIS BOOK?

This book expands on the foundational co-teaching skills and strategies that our first book addressed. Our purpose with this volume is to offer new ideas and solutions, more extended explorations, greater analysis and details of practices, and lots of fresh examples and new teacher voices from the field. You will be able to refer to this book for the following types of information and resources:

1. An in-depth look at collaborative practices that enhance the co-planning, co-delivery, co-assessment, and reflection of culturally and linguistically responsive instruction

2. Specific guidelines for maximizing teacher expertise for co-planning success, including optimizing time with explicit instructional and co-planning routines

3. A detailed examination of each of the seven co-teaching models with a close look at instructional strategies as well as descriptions and analyses of lesson plans

4. A thorough review of co-assessment practices, including how ELs are assessed and examining student data

5. Practical ways you can implement a collaborative service delivery model for ELs

6. Prompt, accessible answers to critical how-to questions that arise as your school designs and implements collaborative practices to support ELs

7. Access to tools and resources that enhance the collaborative instruction cycle

8. Video clips you can view and analyze via QR codes

9. Insights into dozens of educators' collaborative practice who shared their authentic experiences and successful strategies via vignettes

10. Reflection questions that build on the information in each chapter and help facilitate a collaborative exploration of the book and your own practice

HOW IS THIS BOOK ORGANIZED?

We have organized the book around the essential parts of the collaborative instructional cycle. In Chapter 1, we make a case for the practice of co-teaching for ELs and the importance of the entire collaborative instructional cycle—co-planning, co-teaching, co-assessment, and reflection. Chapter 2 addresses the nuances of co-planning complete with partnership-building strategies and practical tools. The next seven chapters (Chapters 3 through 9) are each devoted to one of the seven co-teaching models, with detailed descriptions and analyses of each class configuration, a review of the advantages and challenges of their implementation, strategies to incorporate when selecting each model for instruction, and variations for arranging classes for co-teaching and ways to combine various models for fluid instruction. Chapter 10 focuses on the purpose of collaborative assessment practices, frameworks for co-assessment, differentiating assessment practices for ELs, and assessment tools for data gathering as well as protocols for sharing data. The final chapter, 11, is devoted to reflective practices between co-teachers or among co-teaching teams, and self-assessment tools for further consideration of program and instructional practices. While Chapters 3 through 9 are more similarly structured (as each unpacks the intention behind each co-teaching model) the remainder of the chapters also include several recurring features that are consistent throughout the book. We present

- a short introduction to the topic of the chapter and then continue with a more in-depth discussion;
- several authentic quotes from educators whose comments capture the essence of the chapter (see the quote from Elena Okanovic above);
- summary charts that offer easily accessible information on key topics;
- diagrams and illustrations to help visualize key points; and
- practical tools such as checklists, rubrics, and templates that may be readied for implementation or adapted for local use.

WHY NOW?

Preparing all teachers to engage in collaborative instructional practices in support of a culturally and linguistically diverse student body has never been more topical than now. The current demographic trends and future projections emphasize the growing diversity and increasing number of English learners, both new arrivals to and those born in the United States. Cultural and linguistic diversity is no longer unique to big cities or urban, inner-city schools. Many rural and suburban school districts face the same challenges in addressing the needs of a multilingual student body. Segregated program models for English learners are no longer favored; instead, an increasing number of schools look to build upon teachers' collaborative expertise and restructure to systemically integrate ELs into the fabric of the school while providing rigorous core instruction along with language support. With the realization of collaborative instructional services, English learners will no longer have to leave to learn! This book will help all educators of ELs to fulfill that promise.

Acknowledgments

Once again, we would like to thank all readers of our previous volumes on the topic, *Collaboration and Co-Teaching: Strategies for English Learners* (2010) and *Collaboration and Co-Teaching: A Leader's Guide* (2015). We so appreciate your interest and commitment to an integrated service delivery for the sake of ELs.

We would also like to express our appreciation to all teachers and school and district administrators, instructional coaches, fellow professional developers, and researchers who have been at the forefront of bringing attention to co-teaching for ELs, taking the challenges on, and championing the need for collaboration. A very special thank you to the numerous educators who generously shared their experiences with us, invited us into their classrooms, and contributed to this book with authentic stories, practical tools, and sincere reflections.

We would also like to thank our critical friends who offered their honest feedback and unwavering support, both of which enhanced the planning and the writing process of this volume:

Dr. Audrey Cohan, Dean, Division of Sciences, and Professor, Division of Education, Molloy College, NY

Kelley Cordeiro, ESOL teacher, Farmingdale Public Schools, and Doctoral Research Assistant, Molloy College, NY

Violeta Gamez, EL Resource teacher at Willow Creek Elementary School, IL

Dr. Margo Gottlieb, cofounder and lead developer, WIDA Consortium, WI

Shalinie Sarju, Doctoral Research Assistant, Molloy College, NY

Elizabeth Stern, UDL coach, Smithtown UFSD, NY

We very much appreciate the patience, guidance, support, and friendship of our dear editor, Dan Alpert. Your equanimity and generosity of spirit were central to the completion of this project. We cannot thank you enough. We would also like to express our gratitude for the entire Corwin team, for their work on the manuscript preparation, videotaping, and production process.

We are particularly grateful for our friends and colleagues in the Division of Education at Molloy College, Rockville Centre, New York, for their ongoing support of our research and publications concerning the teaching and learning of culturally and linguistically diverse students.

We are continually inspired by those educators in the field who work with English learners every day. Thank you for your generosity in opening up your co-taught classes to us and giving us the ability to continue to investigate the realities of collaborative instruction.

And last but not least, our greatest appreciation belongs to our families and friends who never waver in their support of our work and never cease to cheer us on.

About the Authors

Maria G. Dove, EdD, is Associate Professor in the Division of Education at Molloy College, Rockville Centre, New York, where she teaches preservice and inservice teachers about the research and best practices for developing effective programs and school policies for English learners. Before entering the field of higher education, she worked for over thirty years as an English-as-a-second-language teacher in public school settings (Grades K–12) and in adult English language programs in Nassau County, New York.

In 2010, she received the Outstanding ESOL Educator Award from New York State Teachers of English to Speakers of Other Languages (NYS TESOL). She frequently provides professional development for educators throughout the United States on the teaching of diverse students. She also serves as a mentor for new ESOL teachers as well as an instructional coach for general-education teachers and literacy specialists. She has published articles and book chapters on collaborative teaching practices, instructional leadership, and collaborative coaching. With Andrea Honigsfeld, she coauthored three best-selling Corwin books, *Collaboration and Co-Teaching: Strategies for English Learners* (2010), *Common Core for the Not-So-Common Learner, Grades K–5: English Language Arts Strategies* (2013), and *Common Core for the Not-So-Common Learner, Grades 6–12: English Language Arts Strategies* (2013). Their latest volume is *Beyond Core Expectations: A Schoolwide Framework for Serving the Not-So-Common Learner* (2014). The same writing team also co-edited *Coteaching and Other Collaborative Practices in the EFL/ESL Classroom: Rationale, Research, Reflections, and Recommendations* (2012), published by Information Age.

Andrea Honigsfeld, EdD, is Associate Dean and Professor in the Division of Education at Molloy College, Rockville Centre, New York. She directs a doctoral program in Educational Leadership for Diverse Learning Communities. Before entering the field of teacher education, she was an English-as-a-foreign-language teacher in Hungary (Grades 5–8 and adult) and an English-as-a-second-language teacher in New York City (Grades K–3 and adult). She also taught Hungarian at New York University.

She was the recipient of a doctoral fellowship at St. John's University, New York, where she conducted research on individualized instruction and learning styles. She has published extensively on working with English language learners and providing individualized instruction based on learning style preferences. She received a Fulbright Award to lecture in Iceland in the fall of 2002. In the past twelve years, she has been presenting at conferences across the United States, Great Britain, Denmark, Sweden, the Philippines, and the United Arab Emirates. She frequently offers staff development, primarily focusing on effective differentiated strategies and collaborative practices for English-as-a-second-language and general-education teachers. She coauthored *Differentiated Instruction for At-Risk Students* (2009) and co-edited the five-volume *Breaking the Mold of Education* series (2010–2013), published by Rowman and Littlefield. She is also the co-author of *Core Instructional Routines: Go-To Structures for Effective Literacy Teaching, K–5 and 6–12* (2014), published by Heinemann. With Maria Dove, she co-edited *Coteaching and Other Collaborative Practices in the EFL/ESL Classroom: Rationale, Research, Reflections, and Recommendations* (2012) and co-authored *Collaboration and Co-Teaching: Strategies for English Learners* (2010), *Common Core for the Not-So-Common Learner, Grades K–5: English Language Arts Strategies* (2013), *Common Core for the Not-So-Common Learner, Grades 6–12: English Language Arts Strategies* (2013), *Beyond Core Expectations: A Schoolwide Framework for Serving the Not-So-Common Learner* (2014), *Collaboration and Co-Teaching: A Leader's Guide* (2015)—the first three Corwin bestsellers.

1

Teacher Collaboration Is Not an Option

It Is a Must

While researching the practice of co-teaching for English learners (ELs), our biggest "Aha" moment came when we were visiting an elementary school in a suburban district in the state of Virginia, a school that could be considered a 90/90/90 school—90%-plus students were eligible for free and reduced lunch, 90%-plus students were non-White, and 90%-plus students met the standards in reading or another area (Reeves, 2000). At first, we assumed that much of the academic success of ELs in this school was due to the co-teaching practices the principal had carefully established. However, when we visited the classes, we found novice co-teachers still negotiating their roles and responsibilities and ways to configure classes for co-taught lessons. What we soon discovered was that the "magic" was not in the co-teaching per se but in the intricate scheduling of ongoing meaningful professional dialogue among teachers in well-established collaborative teams. We observed their intense focus on aligning instruction to standards, their skillful examination of student data, and their ongoing reflection of their own teaching

School leaders who recognize the value of collaboration seek to provide those opportunities not only for their teachers but also for all members of the school community. Wanda Ortiz, coordinator for Bilingual/English as a New Language (ENL) programs in Brentwood Union Free School District (BUFSD), the district with the second largest EL population in New York State, shared the following:

Collaboration and co-teaching are as important for teachers as for building and central office administrators. At our district, the implementation of this practice has given us the gift of working together as a whole unit. We are no longer isolated departments. The ELA,

Social Studies, Math, Science, Special Education and Bilingual/ENL (English as a New Language) departments co-plan, co-instruct, and co-assess the effectiveness of best teaching practices, professional development needs, and the quality of the curriculum in place. (Personal communication, July 17, 2015)

Collaboration should be the norm, but is it really? Jeffrey Mirel and Simona Goldin (2012) report the findings of a recent study by Scholastic and the Gates Foundation concluding that teachers in the United States spend only about 3% of their teaching day collaborating with colleagues. A lot of American teachers continue to plan their lessons, teach their classes, and examine their practice while working alone. "In other countries, such as Finland and Japan, where students outperform those in the US . . . collaboration among teachers is an essential aspect of instructional improvement" (para. 4).

John Hattie's (2015) latest work has documented a groundbreaking discovery of the importance of collaborative expertise as well as recognizing the power of collective efficacy. He identified that the greatest barrier to students' academic achievement is within-school variability. For this reason, meaningful teacher collaboration—sharing successful instructional strategies, examining student data, reflecting on effective teaching practices, and so on—is key. When teachers collaborate and form high-functioning teams, the whole is greater than the sum of its parts, and their collective efficacy—their effectiveness—is increased (Eells, 2011; Knowapple, 2015). Co-teachers' collective efficacy indicates the shared belief—a new frame of reference—that together they can achieve success with ELs.

VIDEO 1.1: Student Benefits

To read a QR Code, you must have a smartphone or tablet with a camera. We recommend that you download a QR Code reader app that is made specifically for your phone or tablet brand.

http://resources .corwin.com/ CoTeachingforELs

WHY TEACHER ISOLATION IS NOT AN OPTION

English learners are receiving more widespread attention in recent years than ever before (U.S. Department of Education, 2015a). There is increased discussion about this population across schools, districts, and communities: who are they, where do they come from, what cultural and linguistic assets do they bring to the classroom, and what are their unique needs that all teachers must know about and be willing to address with professional competence and compassion? Research on ELs is also expanding: New studies have emerged documenting the most current understanding about the various subgroups of ELs and synthesizing effective practices for them (Bunch, 2013; Kibler, Walqui, & Bunch, 2015). Professional journals, magazines, websites, and conferences are showcasing exemplary practices from around the United States with carefully documented details and promising outcomes for ELs from which all educators can benefit.

Invariably, the work that results in success for ELs does not happen in a vacuum. Instead, collaboration among educators is becoming the norm, though it may take a range of shapes and forms—professional learning communities (PLCs), literacy and language support teams, grade-level and department teams, focus groups, community of learners for special purposes (e.g., technology integration), and so on. Many new teachers are initiated into the profession through professional development opportunities provided by their school districts, including mentoring and peer coaching. However, what often gets them acculturated to and socialized in their chosen profession are the personal learning networks (PLNs) they build. PLNs are gaining a growing importance among educators. Blog posts, Pinterest boards, Twitter chats, and other online social networks are buzzing with ideas, practical suggestions, ready-to-go tips, and opportunities to collaborate on projects as well as mentor one another to aid educators in their daily work with ELs.

Over a decade ago, Zamel and Spack (2004) cautioned about "misunderstandings, unfulfilled expectations, frustration, and even resentment" (p. 13) that may mark English language development/English language learner specialists' experiences if ELs and their teachers continue to be marginalized, if they remain outsiders in a given educational context, and if barriers separate content experts and ELD/ELL specialists. Consequently, it is no longer a viable option for educators of ELs to work in isolation from each other; teachers of ELs need to have access to the general-education curriculum and understand the grade-level academic expectations for ELs. See if you agree with what Rance-Roney (2009) reports as a common state of affairs a few years ago across the United States or if you have seen changes to how teachers approach their work with ELs:

> In many schools, the EL specialist or ESL (English as a second language) teacher goes it alone. The EL classroom is viewed as the one-stop shop for all the needs of English language learners—testing, translating, counseling, editing college applications, and even health care. Mainstream school personnel may abdicate responsibility for the needs of ELs because they believe that the specialist understands these students better. (p. 34)

What we have witnessed over the course of the past ten years since we started researching and training teachers about co-teaching is that more and more educators agree with a need for a critical shift: The shift is that all teachers are teachers of ELs and responsible for supporting their social-emotional well-being, acculturation, language development, and overall school success. All elementary classroom teachers and secondary content teachers must embrace their role as teachers of academic language and disciplinary literacy, and develop the necessary knowledge and skills (Turkan, de Oliveira, Lee, & Phelps, 2014).

School support personnel (guidance counselors, speech language pathologists, social workers) also need to coordinate their services with their teaching colleagues to ensure best placement, highest-quality intervention, comprehensive social-emotional support, and timely academic progression. All educators need to build capacity to develop a shared understanding of culturally and linguistically responsive education and to establish common academic, linguistic, social-emotional, and personal goals for ELs. This is successfully happening through co-teaching in numerous school districts around the United States, such as Arizona (Oracle Charter School, 2016), Colorado (Beninghof & Leensvaart, 2016; Blair, 2015; Goldstein, 2015; Robles, 2015), Georgia (Russell, 2012), Idaho (Wootton, 2013), Illinois (Ponce, 2017), Minnesota (Noble, 2015), New York (Ali, 2016; Garafalo, 2016a, 2016b; Honigsfeld & Dove, 2015a, 2015b; Ocasio, 2016), Oregon (Stratton, 2015), and Washington ("Supporting English Language Learners at Cherry Crest," 2016), just to highlight a few recently reported cases.

WHO ARE ELS?

English learners are one of the fastest-growing subgroups of the K–12 student populations in the United States. Depending on where you live and work, ELs may represent a tremendous variety of experiences. It is important to begin your collaboration with colleagues by taking the time to learn about ELs as a group representing varied backgrounds and to understand individual needs, too. Elsewhere, we have already discussed the complex patterns among this population (Honigsfeld & Dove, 2015a). See Table 1.1 for a summary of the diversity that exists among ELs and Figures 1.1 and 1.2 for two possible completed EL profiles. The first one may be used as a Google form so all team members have access to the student's *Cultural, Linguistic, and Academic Profile* and consider it a living document that can be updated regularly, whereas the second one offers a quick overview of a child's background information in an at-a-glance format. (See companion website for blank forms.)

Table 1.1 Diversity Among English Language Learners

Characteristics of English Learners		
Immigration Status	**Prior Education**	**Linguistic Development**
<ul><li>Recently arrived</li><li>Refugees</li><li>Without legal documentation</li><li>Temporarily living in U.S.</li><li>U.S.-born/citizen</li></ul>	<ul><li>Formal, grade-appropriate education in U.S./other country</li><li>Limited/interrupted formal education in U.S./other country</li></ul>	<ul><li>Monolingual: home language only</li><li>Bilingual: two languages other than English</li><li>Bidialectal, speaking both a standard language other than English and a dialect</li><li>Multilingual in three or more languages</li></ul>
Language Proficiency *in Language(s) Other than English*	**Level of English Language Proficiency**	**Learning Trajectory**
<ul><li>Only receptive skills</li><li>Productive oral skills</li><li>Limited literacy skills</li><li>Grade-level literacy skills</li><li>A combination of the above</li></ul>	<ul><li>*Starting:* Very limited language production</li><li>*Beginning:* Receptive and emerging productive skills</li><li>*Developing:* Basic oral and written skills</li><li>*Expanding:* More advanced oral and written skills</li><li>*Bridging:* Near native proficiency</li></ul>	<ul><li>Typical academic and linguistic development</li><li>Academic and/or linguistic challenges that respond to individual systematic and targeted interventions</li><li>Academic and linguistic challenges that require special attention</li></ul>

Adapted from Honigsfeld & Dove (2015a). *Proficiency levels based on the PreK–12 English Language Proficiency Standards* (Teachers of English to Speakers of Other Languages, 2006).

Figure 1.1	Cultural, Linguistic and Academic Profile for _____

2016 ACCESS Scores

Listening PL 2.3   **Speaking PL 2.9**   **Reading PL 2.5**   **Writing PL 1.9**
Overall Composite 2.3

Languages Spoken (Languages or dialects spoken at home. Who speaks this language?)
Parents—Spanish; Student—English & Spanish

Family Situation (Primary caregivers; parents, siblings, extended family & living situation. Resources & community services available in their home language & culture.)
Student lives with both parents and 2 younger sisters

Educational Background (Prior formal education—type of school; # of years; additional educational experiences)
Bilingual PreK–1st grade

Cultural Background (Dominant cultural background of student & family; important days of celebration; basic beliefs concerning family, education, friends, & religion)
Mother is very supportive of education and attends all IEP meetings and parent/teacher conferences

Personal Interests, Abilities, & Health (Student's interests & extracurricular activities. Notable physical or health conditions that influence learning or instruction (i.e., vision, hearing, food allergies, IEP))
Speech Notes from Bilingual Speech Pathologist: *Received speech services in Spanish last year along with services in English with xx. His dominant language is Spanish, although he is picking up a lot of social English.*
Link to Special Ed Teacher Notes re: Accommodations
(Link to detailed notes inserted here)*

Immigration Status (Parent country of origin & date of arrival or U.S.-born)

Born in United States

*See notes on next page

Developed by Carolina Kazimierski (Willow Creek Elementary) and Violeta Gamez (Goodrich Elementary School), EL resource teachers in Woodridge, IL, based on Honigsfeld & Dove, 2010.

Special Education Teacher Notes

Related/Educational Services:

- *Speech*
- *Access to a Classroom Aide*

Classroom Accommodations—ELL:

- *Use visuals when giving verbal directions in English*
- *Check for student understanding after giving verbal directions by asking him to repeat expectations/directions in his own words using English*
- *Use simple language/vocabulary*
- *Provide explicit vocabulary instruction in English*
- *Allow student the opportunity to write in Spanish for extended writing tasks (will be translated by staff) or to use a scribe in English*

Classroom Accommodations—SPED:

- *Verbal and visual cueing/prompts to stay on task*
- *Model task expectations*
- *Extended time for activities/tasks*
- *Preferential seating close to teacher*
- *Shortened tasks*
- *Check for understanding, especially when multistep directions are given*
- *Use positive reinforcement to promote attending to instruction/task*
- *Read instructions/problems to student when reading skills are not the primary learning target*
- *Provide student a low distraction environment when completing tasks in the classroom*
- *Give student breaks during long academic tasks/work in the classroom*

Assessment Accommodations:

- *Use visuals when giving verbal directions in English*
- *Check for student understanding after giving verbal directions by asking her to repeat expectations/directions in her own words using English*
- *Model assessment expectations*
- *Verbal and visual cueing/prompts to stay on task*
- *Use positive reinforcement to promote attending to assessment*
- *Read instructions/problems to student when reading skills are not the primary skill being assessed*
- *Assess student in a small group with minimal distractions*
- *Give student breaks*
- *Extended time*
- *Allow student the opportunity to write in Spanish for extended writing tasks (will be translated by staff) or to use a scribe in English*

Figure 1.2	An EL Profile-at-a-Glance

Name: Yong-Li D. Grade: 11th Date: 8/15/16 Prepared by Ms. M.

Student Strengths	Student Needs
High levels of organization and attention to detail *Willingness to work beyond the basic course requirement* *Strong grammar skills in writing*	*Expressive language skills lag behind receptive skills, especially oral language use* *Hesitant to participate in class discussions, even in small-group or pair work* *Writing lacks sentence variety*

Academic Goals

To graduate with age-peers

To build more comprehensive knowledge base in Social Studies and English, specifically in U.S. history and twentieth-century literature

Language Development Goals

To communicate with more confidence with peers and teachers both in academic and nonacademic settings

To use more complex sentence structure in written and oral communication

Accommodations or Modifications (if necessary)

Scaffolding tools (language frames, templates, one-pagers, outlines, models)

Flipped learning opportunities (recorded minilessons to be made available, Khan Academy, Discovery Learning, PBS, video podcasts)

Source: Template adapted from Program-at-a-Glance form from Virginia Institute for Developmental Disabilities (2001).

NEW ROLES FOR TEACHERS OF ELS

Understanding ELs and having a shared ownership of their academic, linguistic, and social-emotional development among all educators is essential. Traditionally, the ELD/ELL specialist or teacher was considered to hold the primary responsibility for English learners: their linguistic and literacy development, their acculturation to a new land and a new school, their social-emotional well-being, and more. Many ELD/ELL teachers we know have taken it upon themselves to support their students and their families in ways that go beyond the call of duty or any job description or contract they signed.

With the introduction of rigorous standards for college and career readiness—including the Common Core State Standards (CCSS), Next Generation Science Standards (NGSS), and the College, Career, and Civic Life (C3) Framework for Social Studies State Standards—much has changed for all teachers and students. ELD/ELL teachers' roles have also shifted. To be responsive to the needs of ELs and to be aligned to the new expectations, Maxwell (2013) suggests capitalizing on the expertise of ELD/ELL teachers:

> The nation's roughly 45,000 ESL teachers—many of whom split their time among schools with little chance to co-teach or plan with content teachers—have expertise and strategies that experts say all teachers will need to ensure that English-learners are not shutout of the rigorous, grade-level content. (para. 9)

Based on the interviews she conducted, Maxwell (2013) has found many successful programs and practices, most of which are built heavily on teacher collaboration. ELD/ELL teachers no longer function in isolation, but instead, team up to support ELs' linguistic and academic development.

Although in the past English language development programs were recognized as a stand-alone subject matter, the more current understanding is that language acquisition is not a separate subject but a systematically supported practice situated in the authentic context of the classroom. Integrated language and content learning provides ELs the opportunity to acquire English through content-area lessons. The concept of integrated instruction is a powerful way for ELs to develop both their language and academic skills. For example, writing across the curriculum experts Bazerman et al. (2005) have long noted that writing supports subject area learning and thinking. Further, they remind us that "while the sophistication of the subject matter engagement changes over the course grades, the use of writing to increase understanding, involvement, subject learning, and disciplinary thought remains consistent" (p. 38). Whereas English learners in yesteryear were exposed to programs that emphasized understanding and speaking for beginning-level students devoid of content area study, and reading and writing were slowly introduced, it is now widely recognized that developing all four skills—speaking, writing, reading, and listening—simultaneously with content-area study is pertinent to their academic success. Accordingly, this emphasis on language and content instruction necessitates ELD/ELL and content experts to coordinate their efforts to teach ELs.

Diane Staehr Fenner (2013b) synthesizes the findings of a TESOL work group on the changing roles of ELD/ELL teachers and concludes that they "should be recognized as experts, consultants, and trainers well versed in teaching rigorous academic content to ELs" (p. 9). More specifically, it has been agreed that ELD/ELL teachers

(1) have specialized expertise in understanding and teaching academic language;

(2) should support content-area teachers in integrating content with language goals as they collaboratively analyze the academic language demands of their content areas; and

(3) design lessons that not only address academic language and content simultaneously but also build on ELs' funds of knowledge, home language, and culture.

Similarly, Valdés, Kibler, and Walqui (2014) also discuss the changing roles and responsibilities and make a strong case for a systemic shift in the type of instruction teachers should design for ELs. They suggest inviting

students to engage in rigorous cross-disciplinary activity from their first class, and both ELD/ELL and content-area teachers must design and enact disciplinary teaching that simultaneously develops grade level conceptual understandings, academic practices, and the language required to do so. (p. 25)

For this type of instruction to happen, consider what conditions must be in place:

- Language is recognized as dialogical—it is developed through meaningful interaction with others.
- Students must participate in activities that allow for authentic language use.

- Content and language are integrated; language is not a goal in itself but a vehicle that helps ELs make reasonable progressions toward mastering grade-level content.
- Appropriate background knowledge for student understanding and successful task completion is provided.
- Learning tasks should contain all four language skills (speaking, writing, reading, and listening) with particular emphasis on the productive skills of speaking and writing.
- Lessons must be scaffolded to break down language and content information without watering it down.
- Lessons must be relevant and connect with ELs' lived experiences.

As a result, ELs will experience instruction characterized by the following:

- Curriculum continuity with clear goals and objectives
- Instructional consistency that supports content and language development
- Reduction in fragmented, disjointed learning experiences
- More integration and less student isolation

In a recent report from Montgomery County, Maryland, schools, Marietta and Brookover (2011) describe a diminishing role for pullout programs for ELs and an increase in push-in, plug-in, and co-taught classes. In our work, we consistently avoid using terms such as *push in* and *plug in*, which generally refer to programs in which the ELD/ELL teacher supports and assists the work of the grade-level/content teacher without much or any coordination of instruction. However, we must recognize that these types of programs exist in the United States. In contrast, we advocate for co-teaching, specifically referring to the following type of service delivery:

> In co-teaching, there is no distinction between the EL teacher and the general education teacher; both work with the entire class on mastery of content and language-acquisition objectives. Some grade level teams have arranged for the EL teacher to teach a whole-class language-oriented lesson once a week to build the language skills of all students, regardless of their EL status. (Marietta & Brookover, 2011, p.12)

THE COLLABORATIVE INSTRUCTIONAL CYCLE

There are many misconceptions about the practice of co-teaching. First and foremost, co-teaching does not work as a process in itself. The simple placement of two teachers in the same classroom does not constitute an instant teaching partnership. Many researchers of inclusive education as well as practitioners in schools with collaborative school cultures emphasize the need to engage in a complete instructional cycle of collaboration, which consists of four interrelated phases: collaborative planning, instruction, assessment, and reflection (see Figure 1.3). All four phases together will maximize teacher effectiveness and impact on ELs' language acquisition, literacy learning, and content attainment.

Disregarding or neglecting any of the four phases will disrupt the balance and continuity of the cycle and negatively impact student learning. While the co-teaching itself or other collaborative or integrated instructional practices might receive substantial attention, teachers need time and structured opportunities for the other three components of the collaborative instructional cycle in order to

Figure 1.3 The Collaborative Instructional Cycle

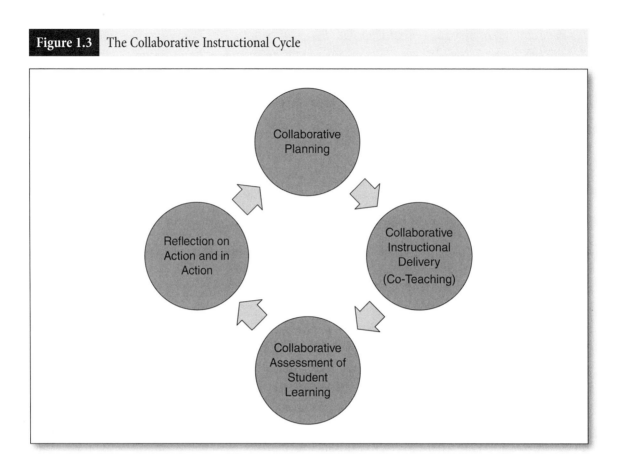

(a) deeply think about differentiated unit and lesson planning,

(b) gather and assess formative student data, and

(c) reflect on the teaching-learning process that took place in the class (Schon, 1990).

Agatha Vitale, high school ELD/ELL teacher from Brentwood, NY, defines co-teaching as "an honest, comfortable, trusting partnership; accepting and respectful of different styles of teaching and respectful of different areas of expertise. There is no more mine/yours . . . only ours!" (personal communication, September 27, 2015). What Goldenberg and Coleman (2010) suggest for effective ELD/ELL instruction is likely to be successfully achieved through collaboration and co-teaching:

> Effective second-language instruction provides a combination of (a) explicit teaching that helps students directly and efficiently learn features of the second language such as syntax, vocabulary, pronunciation, and norms of social usage and (b) ample opportunities to use the second language in meaningful and motivating situations. (p. 68)

For successful co-teaching to take place, a multitude of opportunities for collaboration must also be established. Among others, Pappamihiel (2012) found that a necessary prerequisite of successful co-teaching is shared planning and administrative support. See Table 1.2 for a summary of instructional collaborations along with the goals and outcomes of these practices, each of which is best implemented with administrative support.

Table 1.2   Opportunities for Instructional Collaborations

Collaborative Practices Aligned to Instruction	Goals	Outcomes
Joint Planning	• Establish attainable yet rigorous learning targets • Share instructional routines and strategies • Align instructional content • Design appropriate formative and summative assessment measures	Shorter- and longer-term plans (daily lesson plans or unit plans) reflective of the following: • Language and content objectives • Strategically selected instructional accommodations and accelerations • Differentiated instruction according to students' academic and linguistic abilities
Curriculum Mapping and Alignment	• Plan and align instruction for a longer period of time • Create an overall guide for joint planning, parallel teaching, and co-instruction	• Rigor, relevance, and research-informed approaches infused into the curriculum • Instructional intensity in the planned and taught curriculum for ELs
Parallel Teaching	• Accelerate ELs' knowledge and understanding of mainstream curricula • Ensure that what happens during ELD/ELL lessons parallels general class instruction	• Coordination and sharing of lesson goals and objectives • Established content for the ELD/ELL teacher to preteach or reteach
Co-developing Instructional Materials	• Scaffold instructional materials • Select essential materials that support accelerated learning	• Differentiated, tiered, teacher-made resources • Chunking of complex materials or tasks into manageable segments • Selection of essential learning tools
Collaborative Assessment of Student Work	• Jointly examine ELs' language and academic performance • Analyze student data and identify areas that need improvement or targeted intervention	• Shared formative and summative assessment measures • Co-developed assessment tasks • Joint goal setting for ELs using assessment data
Co-teaching	• Co-deliver instruction through differentiated instruction • Use various models of instruction to establish equity between co-teaching partners and students	• Coequal partnerships • Shared ownership for learning • Engagement in the entire collaborative instructional cycle
Joint Professional Learning (See Table 1.3 for details)	• Enhance pedagogical knowledge, skills, and dispositions about ELs • Establish a shared understanding about ELs' needs, best practices, and effective strategies • Explore new and emerging directions in ELD/ELL education	• Sustained engagement in learning with colleagues • Application of new learning to teaching • Reflection of new learning • Opportunities to showcase new learning

Creating ongoing possibilities for collaborative work allows teachers to share their knowledge and expertise with one another. It opens instructional pathways for ELs by developing a consensus of what students need and what actions should be taken to meet those needs. It assures the development of curriculum guides for the sake of ELs as well as ways to build programs for them that have continuity and consistency. Nevertheless, the knowledge base of faculty and school administrators when it comes to working with ELs also must be advanced, cultivated, and honed. For this reason, we have identified various ways for professional learning to occur in Table 1.3.

It is during the shared professional learning opportunities that teachers reflect on their own beliefs, pedagogical knowledge and skills, and areas of growth. It is also during these times that teachers can develop some essential capacities: trust, collaboration and communication skills, and collective efficacy.

Table 1.3 Joint Professional Learning Opportunities: Approaches and Benefits for ELs

Joint Professional Learning Practice	How to Do It	Benefits for ELs
Collegial Circles	Meet with colleagues on a regular basis to discuss common questions and concerns, offer solutions to frequently experienced problems, and explore appropriate instructional techniques.	Teachers' knowledge-base about ELs' needs increase, leading to consistency and continuity of instructional practices.
Peer Visitations	Visit one another's classes to observe the teaching-learning process and EL participation as well as demonstrated learning outcomes in the classroom.	ELs may be shadowed, informally assessed, while teachers can collect data on the most effective strategies for them.
Collaborative Coaching and Mentoring	Support each other's practice through modeling effective instruction and providing ongoing student-centered classroom assistance for one another.	ELs receive instruction that is supported by multiple teachers' input through informal and formal observations and opportunities for practice.
Research and Development	Collaboratively study and review research related to an instructional approach for ELs, and plan and implement lessons based on your exploration.	ELs' needs drive the shared research project, thus building teacher capacity for working with ELs.
Collaborative Inquiry (Action Research)	This is a more in-depth exploration of an overarching concept that deals with ELs' language acquisition or instructional needs—also known as *teacher research* or *action research*.	Teacher research will yield authentic data about ELs' academic or linguistic development and lead to research-informed decisions.
Lesson Study	Jointly plan a lesson in response to a study question or goal that you establish in collaboration with your colleagues. Engage in several lesson observations and discussions, and revise the lesson so it could be retaught and observed in other classes by your peers.	Teachers will polish their lessons and have access to a collaboratively developed pool of lessons.

Joint Professional Learning Practice	How to Do It	Benefits for ELs
Professional Learning Communities (PLCs)	Participate in PLCs that are commonly created as a structure for improving schools by focusing on a collaborative school culture and a collective purpose for learning.	Teachers in a PLC will establish a shared purpose and specific goals for ELs.
Professional Learning Networks (PLNs)	Develop your PLNs—online communities for learning—and take advantage of the opportunities social media provides for sharing and telling your success story.	ELs will experience instruction that is based on their teachers' success stories.
Collaborative Learning Teams (CLTs)	Form CLTs—through shared goals, regular meetings, and an organized approach—to engage in professional learning focused on effective instruction.	ELs will receive instruction that is informed by research and careful joint reflection.

TRUST

Trust is an unyielding requirement of collaborative relationships. Without it, any efforts to build meaningful partnerships will inevitably fail. Bessette (2008) suggests "The development of a trusting relationship over the life of a co-teaching partnership may be the most critical issue of all" (p. 1394). As trust develops and grows between the two partners, their co-teaching becomes more productive—fully focused on the needs of the students rather than on uncertainties and insecurities of their work relationship. It is that focus that keeps the co-teaching partnership moving forward.

Trust comes from sustained opportunities for collaborative conversations in which co-teachers learn to value one another. Davison (2006), who studied collaboration between ELD/ELL and content teachers with a special emphasis on developing collaborative and co-teaching relationships, coined the term *partnership teaching* and emphasized the difference between cooperative teaching and partnership teaching:

> Co-operative teaching is where a language support teacher and class or subject teacher plan together a curriculum and teaching strategies which will take into account the learning needs of all pupils, trying to adjust the learning situation to fit the pupils. Partnership Teaching is more than that. It builds on the concept of co-operative teaching by linking the work of two teachers, or indeed a whole department/year team or other partners, with plans for curriculum development and staff development across the school. (pp. 454–455)

To create a thriving co-teaching partnership, teachers must earn each other's trust and nurture it. O'Connell and Vandas (2015) suggest a learner-centered approach to building TRUST between teachers and students. We adapted their acrostic to be applicable to the co-teaching partnership:

Talent: Discover each other's assets for learning

Rapport + Responsiveness: Establish a professional connection and forge a co-teaching partnership based on mutual respect for each other

Us Factor: Move from the "I" to the "we" and recognize each other's contributions

Structures: Set up mechanisms and routines that help develop a shared ownership of the teaching-learning process for all students

Time: Spend time and take the opportunity to nurture the co-teaching relationship (adapted from O'Connell & Vandas, 2015, p. 15).

Partnership teaching deeply depends on the respect teachers build for each other while they have strong communication skills, practice openness, and demonstrate flexibility. Table 1.4 summarizes some key elements of trust building among co-teachers.

Trust is not something that can be taken for granted. In his best-selling publication *The Speed of Trust,* Stephen M. R. Covey (2008) suggests that

> trust is a function of two things: character and competence. Character includes your integrity, your motive, your intent with people. Competence includes your capabilities, your skill, your results, your track record. Both are vital. (p. 30)

Covey also likens building trust to maintaining a bank account. While expanding relational trust, you deposit into the trust account you have with different people, and when needed, you withdraw from it. See if this analogy applies to your collaboration and co-teaching practices with your colleagues—what is your trust account balance, and how do you maintain it for a thriving, respectful, personal, and professional relationship? Our answer to building and maintaining a trusting relationship is to foster collaboration and communication skills.

COLLABORATION AND COMMUNICATION SKILLS

Much has been written about what leads to effective collaboration. We borrow and adapt the 6 C's of collaboration (conversation, coherence, collegiality, conflict, control, and celebration) from

Table 1.4 Key Components of Trust Building

What it is	What it looks like
Shared goal setting	Co-teachers agree on goals for themselves as teaching partners as well as their students; unit goals and lesson objectives as well as instructional targets are jointly developed with attention both to language and content.
Shared decision making	Both teachers participate in every phase of the collaborative instructional cycle; one does not dominate or control the territory.
Joint risk taking	Teachers feel comfortable or are at least willing to experiment with new strategies or co-teaching models; or one teacher supports the other's idea for a new initiative.
Fostering high expectations for each other	Teachers maintain a high level of professionalism and understand that each will "carry his or her weight."
Relying on each other	Teachers can count on each other to come prepared for the lesson at hand, support one another's teaching, and be flexible when plans for instruction change.
Overcoming fear of vulnerability	Teachers lower their guards and do not fear embarrassment or failure in the presence of the other.

Wink (2013) to illustrate some key dimensions of teacher collaboration with a special focus on the needs of ELs:

Conversation: Talk openly and honestly to your co-teachers about ELs' needs and what you can offer to support them. During these collaborative conversations, make sure you engage in active listening, show empathy for each child, and be supportive of each other. One way to engage in an honest conversation with your co-teachers is to openly share what expertise you bring to the partnership and what discipline-specific, general, or language- and literacy-building strategies you would like to work on. See Figure 1.4 for how Lisa C. Mead and Mary Amodemo—two teachers from Brentwood UFSD, NY, who were just beginning to collaborate—prepared to engage in a professional dialogue by jotting down their strengths regarding skills they have and strategies they are good at employing in the classroom, as well as what professional and pedagogical skills they would like to build. Notice that some of the strengths (classroom management, technology) of one teacher happen to be the skills that the other teacher would like to build. At the same time, there are some common areas of needs (depth of knowledge [DOK], Spanish) that the two teachers agreed to develop together while supporting each other on that journey.

Figure 1.4 Strategies Exchange Cards Developed by Two Co-teachers

Card #1

What I am good at	What I would like to learn or improve
Science and technology	Spanish
Making up songs on the spot	Crafts
I am very patient and experienced with students who struggle	DOK questioning
Upbeat: "Look on the bright side"	Vocabulary development strategies
Flexible	Teaching basic reading and writing
Open to new ideas	Classroom management
	Spelling (I am dyslexic)

Card #2

What I am good at	What I would like to learn or improve
Classroom management	Technology
Verbal discussions	DOK questioning
Organizational strategies	Spanish
Flexible, nurturing personality	Stress management (my own stress)
I make things work	
Creative	
Planning	
Relationships with parents	
Learn from my mistakes	
Behavior management	
Welcoming others into my room	

Coherence: Establish roles, responsibilities, and expectations for each member of the co-teaching team. Together, you need to build a clear understanding and consistency about what to expect from ELs as far as their linguistic and academic performance, as well as express those expectations with one voice. See Figure 1.5 for select sketches by Elizabeth Choi, ESOL teacher, Farragut Middle School in Knoxville, Tennesee, depicting how she perceives her various co-teaching roles.

Figure 1.5a   Centers

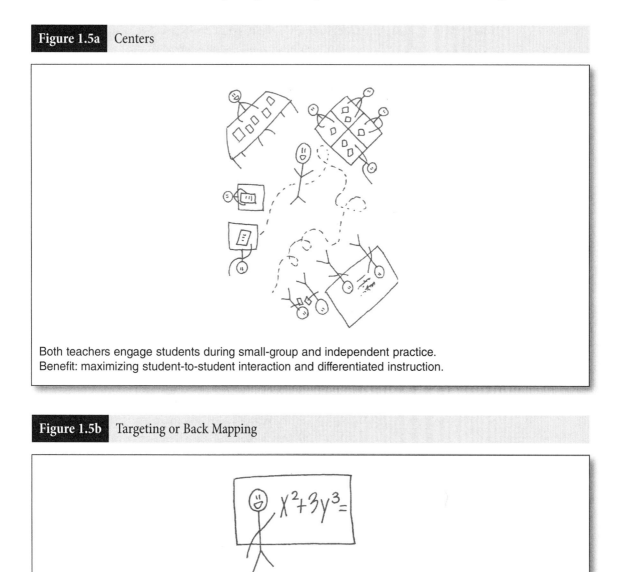

Both teachers engage students during small-group and independent practice.
Benefit: maximizing student-to-student interaction and differentiated instruction.

Figure 1.5b   Targeting or Back Mapping

Both teachers teach groups based on student proficiency level. Benefit: offering targeted intervention and maximizing differentiated instruction.

Figure 1.5c Paralleling

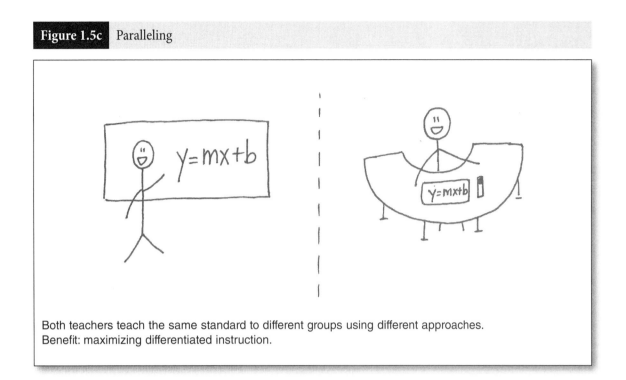

Both teachers teach the same standard to different groups using different approaches.
Benefit: maximizing differentiated instruction.

Figure 1.5d Supporting

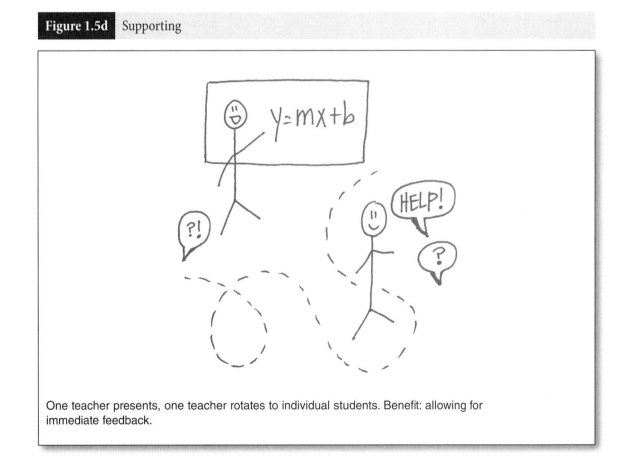

One teacher presents, one teacher rotates to individual students. Benefit: allowing for
immediate feedback.

Figure 1.5e	Modeling

One teacher leads, one teacher questions, writes notes, or models. Benefit: using multiple modalities to enhance comprehension.

Collegiality: Ensure that cooperation is the norm. As co-teachers, you may or may not have developed friendships outside the classroom, yet your professionalism is critical to the success of your work. You might disagree about pedagogical matters and may have different skill sets and varied levels of expertise when it comes to working with ELs. Collegiality will help sustain a cooperative interaction between and among each member.

Conflict: Recognize that growth does not happen without constructive conflict—productive disagreement that results in mutually beneficial outcomes. Differences of opinion are inevitable; however, when you respect each other's beliefs and experiences, the process of working through conflict results in mutual understanding and consensus building.

Control: Agree to share control by jointly establishing the norms of collaboration. One strategy you can try with your co-teacher is to jot down three to five nonnegotiables (your deepest philosophies of education) and then negotiate your nonnegotiables. (See Figure 1.6 for such a list shared by Ryan Zak, middle school language development coach of Kildeer Countryside School District 96, IL). The process of sharing and openly discussing your pet peeves is vital.

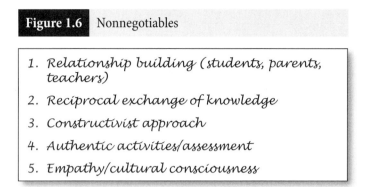

Figure 1.6 Nonnegotiables

1. Relationship building (students, parents, teachers)
2. Reciprocal exchange of knowledge
3. Constructivist approach
4. Authentic activities/assessment
5. Empathy/cultural consciousness

Celebration: "Teams that celebrate together accelerate together" (Wink, 2013, para. 7). Remember to acknowledge your big and small achievements as well as setbacks and challenges (and how you have overcome them). Starting collaborative planning meetings with celebrations (both personal and professional ones) invites a positive mindset into the partnership.

To engage in collaborative reflection, individually and collectively, collaboration skills must be developed. Conderman, Johnston-Rodriguez, and Hartman (2009) suggest that co-teachers practice a range of communication strategies. See Table 1.5 for these practices adapted for ELs.

Table 1.5 Communication Strategies

Communication Strategy	Purpose(s)	What it sounds like
I-message	• To indicate ownership of your feelings about what happened • To indicate what you have observed, how you feel about the event, and the concrete effect that event had on you	*I really appreciate that you are willing to work with all students, not just the ELs.* *I would like to revise our co-planning routine. I think we can be more effective with our time if we follow a set structure.*
Oreo Technique	• To share a sensitive issue or concern (situated between two other statements) • To share an issue and invite collaboration	*I noticed how committed you are to help Juanita. I think she seeks your help (or mine) more frequently than before, when in fact we could expect her to be better socialized by now. I wanted us to discuss ways in which we can help her interact with her peers more.*
Paraphrase	• To check the accuracy of the content of a conversation	*So in other words, we are going to both address both the language and content objectives for each lesson rather than assigning specific roles to ourselves.*
Summarization	• To highlight main points of a longer conversation or meeting	*Let me see if I can summarize what we have just agreed to: We will plan six learning stations—you design three and I design three—and we will use 2 days to make sure all students can rotate through every station.*

(Continued)

Table 1.5 (Continued)

Communication Strategy	Purpose(s)	What it sounds like
Open-Ended Question	• To solicit others' opinions, thoughts, or views	*How do you think today's lesson went? I am wondering how we can differentiate instruction based on student language proficiency levels and their interests.*
Closed Questions	• To establish agreement on factual information or seek closure on details	*Can you translate this note into Spanish, please? Did you create a tiered version of the activity sheet for the beginning ELs?*
Seed Planting	• To indicate the need to visit with a parent or colleague at a later time. • This skill is used when the issue is not of critical concern.	*I realize you are on your way out, but I noticed that you seemed a bit distracted during our team meeting today. Could we talk about this when we have more time—how about tomorrow at lunch?*
Response to Affect	• To empathize with someone • To check your perception of someone's feelings	*You seemed rather frustrated and upset when Ron did not hand in his homework today.*
Literacy Devices	• To communicate using an analogy, simile, or metaphor • To relate to co-teacher via shared experiences	*We really rocked today's lesson! Teaching with you today felt like synchronized diving! We certainly jumped into the deep end, but we seemed to be fully in sync the whole time.* *Working with our students is like cooking: We tried a new recipe today, it did not quite work out the way we planned it, so we really need to work on our ingredients a little more.*

Adapted from Conderman, G., Johnston-Rodriguez, S., & Hartman, P. (2009). Communicating and collaborating in co-taught classrooms. *TEACHING Exceptional Children Plus,* 5(5). Retrieved from http://files.eric.ed.gov/fulltext/EJ967751.pdf

COLLECTIVE EFFICACY

A shared purpose, a mutual cause, and the ability to bring about change through joint action are essential elements for positive group efficacy. Coupled with a collaborative school culture, collective efficacy can bring about effective school change. According to Goddard (2001), collective efficacy among educators contributes significantly to student academic achievement. By combining a group of educators' concerted knowledge and abilities, members can collaborate to share responsibility for the instruction of English learners. Positive outcomes depend on how well the group can put ideas into action. As reported by Hattie (2015b),

> the greatest influence on student progression in learning is having highly expert, inspired and passionate teachers and school leaders working together to maximise the effect of their teaching on all students in their care. There is a major role for school leaders: to harness the expertise in their schools and to lead successful transformations. (p. 2)

When services for English learners are offered in a collaborative way, the areas of expertise and the collective strengths that teachers bring to the classrooms are amplified. However, a movement away from isolated interventions to a concerted effort for the sake of ELs must be carefully orchestrated by administrative and teacher leaders.

INSPIRATION FROM THE FIELD

**VIDEO 1.3:
Supporting
Teachers**

http://resources
.corwin.com/
CoTeachingforELs

Read what colleagues—ELD/ELL specialists and classroom teachers as well as building and district administrators—shared with us from around the United States. We have found them inspirational and affirming. See how they reflect your own experiences or add to your understanding.

Consider Dr. Alla Gonzalez Del Castillo's reflection on the role of district-level leadership support. As the director of the K–12 ELD/ELL Bilingual Migrant Program at St. Louis Public Schools, Missouri, she notes:

While much of our work on developing co-teaching practices in our district has been focused on building teacher capacity, for both the ELL teacher and the mainstream teacher, I cannot underestimate the influence school leadership teams have on the success of the co-teaching initiative. Intentional clustering of ELs and teacher support cannot happen without school leaders' awareness and commitment to this collaborative work. Inviting school leaders to become part of the planning stage of the co-teaching initiative was extremely helpful. Their input on teachers' ability to have release time from school to participate in training guided the approach we took on the PD structure, offering each PD session three times. Such structure allowed schools to minimize the number of subs needed for classroom coverage on co-teaching PD days. Inviting school leaders to learn about co-teaching for ELs through a training session was also helpful. The training established a common context and a common language for co-teaching teams and school leaders to use as they plan, implement, and reflect on co-teaching practices in their schools. As we develop co-teaching as a district instructional practice, we continue to grow as educators and leaders.

Read the following summary written by Merita Little, principal of Steele Creek Elementary School, Charlotte-Mecklenburg Schools, North Carolina, on how she helped create the path to success with co-teaching for ELs at the school building level.

The systematic approach that I took in planning for the co-teaching practices in my school center around many hours of preplanning with my core team, which consists of my administrative, ELL, and EC (Exceptional Children) teams. We collected teacher survey and verbal data to launch their understanding, willingness, and professional development commitment to the process. After securing the data, we carefully mapped out the necessary goals that would be implemented by weekly and quarterly goals, which were linked to planning, professional development, and cohort reflection. We also created a master schedule with co-teaching in mind. After creating the documents, we shared the information with the staff for feedback and created a professional development schedule. Our co-teaching teams have been videotaped by the district, and we were asked to serve on a district panel due to the success of our program. Many of our students are growing academically, and all teachers even outside of the ELL classroom are learning more about cultural and linguistic diversity.

See Mara Barry's suggestions on how to get the most out of a co-teaching relationship. As a language development coach at Prairie School, Kildeer Countryside School District 96, Illinois, Mara co-teaches with five classroom teachers and must navigate relationship building with several colleagues.

Take the time to build your relationship with your co-teachers and the classes you are co-teaching in. Co-teaching is truly a marriage! My co-teachers and I often joke that we are over the courting phase and truly into the "heart" of our relationship. Don't be afraid to share what you are feeling. If things don't feel right for you, they probably are not right for your co-teacher either. Take the time to make a partnership agreement. Talk about what is working and what isn't. Adjust what needs adjusting—whether it is the planning, the teaching, or the reflecting. Be open and honest with one another, just like in a marriage. You need to trust the relationship and believe in one another. We are committed to co-teaching and doing what is best for our Culturally and Linguistically Diverse students.

Finally, consider the steps to success shared by Deborah Harpine, EL teacher from William Walker Elementary School, Beaverton, Oregon.

We are successful because we work to actively communicate with each other, and although we sometimes have differences of opinion, they are never tied to our competence as a teacher. I feel the keys to our "success" so far lie in the steps we have taken to get to this point, although as collaborators this is a continuous process.

Steps to our success:

1. *Administration buy-in, leadership, and support*

2. *Setting aside protected time to plan "units of study" in several long blocks of time to be spaced out how the team decides*

3. *Common planning time to set up weekly or biweekly meetings to do the nuts and bolts of matching model choices to lesson plans*

4. *Planning the daily schedule around needs of the grade-level and teacher assignments. For example, if a teacher works with more than one teacher in a grade level, or multiple grade levels, the time for teaching the units of study must not be at the same time of day.*

5. *Setting a weekly or biweekly meeting time for teachers to plan with their co-teaching partner(s)*

6. *Teach for a while to settle in*

7. *Reevaluate whenever necessary*

We all work to be active communicators. We listen. We think about the other's perspective. We take time to appreciate each other. We recognize that we won't agree all the time on everything.

We are OK with not being the "teacher in charge" all the time. We respect each other's expertise. And we don't take each other for granted or expect that every day or lesson will be perfect, or that we will always be having a great day. We are flexible and are constantly working on our collaboration. In education, as in life, nothing stays the same. But we can, and do, use that to our advantage.

TAKEAWAYS

In this chapter, we have established the foundation for the essential collaborative practices that are needed to provide integrated instruction for ELs. We have identified why teachers should no longer work in isolation, the new roles that ELD/ELL teachers are being asked to assume, and why co-teaching is only a part of a collaborative instructional cycle that can positively affect the academic achievement of ELs. Yet no doubt you still need the answer to one very important question: *How* can collaborative instruction best be implemented? In the chapters that follow, we explore in great detail each part of the instructional cycle and offer clear, practical solutions for its implementation.

QUESTIONS FOR FURTHER DISCUSSION

1. What would you consider to be the most important personal and professional prerequisites of successful teacher collaboration and co-teaching? How can teachers further develop these skills?

2. What have you found to be the most important contextual or external factors necessary for successful teacher collaboration and co-teaching? How can they be improved or enhanced?

3. What is the role of administrators and instructional leaders, such as coaches and department chairs, to ensure that collaboration and co-teaching are viable service options?

2

Co-Planning

Co-planning is undeniably the most important component of the collaborative instructional cycle. Co-teaching does not happen without it, so when teams of teachers enter a classroom without ample preparation, it may at best be described as shared real estate or "push in." The success of any true co-teaching practice depends on the success of co-planning. The benefits of co-planning are numerous—teachers bring their unique expertise together, examine their own philosophical beliefs, learn new strategies from each other, design lessons that are differentiated and scaffolded, address all learners' needs, and expand their focus on their students. In a blog post, Tiffany Ko (2014) shares why co-planning is fundamental to co-teaching:

> Co-planning is one of the essential ingredients of successful co-taught classrooms. It allows co-teachers an opportunity to discuss topics such as classroom expectations, discipline, procedures, and pet peeves. It also ensures that lessons are differentiated and individualized to meet the needs and characteristics of both the students and the teachers. Moreover, co-planning allows teachers to deliberately select the best co-teaching approach to deliver the curriculum, the content, and instructional strategies. (para. 3)

In addition, the synergy that often occurs between people as they collaborate creates a combined effect that often sparks innovative ideas, strategies, and solutions as compared with when an individual plans alone.

Briana Cajamarca is a high school English to speakers of other languages (ESOL) teacher who has been collaborating and co-teaching with many content-area teachers for the past eight years in Glen Cove, New York. She has established a "make it work" attitude toward co-teaching, emphasizing the need for co-planning, identifying what she needs from the planning process to be effective, and clearly defining her role as a co-teaching partner:

> *Even when the [English language development/English language learner] ELD/ELL teacher is the same and the student population is similar, the routines and models we use and the dynamics that exist vary widely between classrooms. When we plan, communicating*

through e-mail is highly practical and effective, but I also solicit unit information through a request form. I need key information such as essential questions, unit objectives, and vocabulary, so I can begin to create and gather supplemental materials, which can include a reference sheet for each unit—an effective tool in supporting student learning and organizing the target content. I also research bilingual materials that may be useful for clarifying new topics. If lower proficiency students cannot independently complete homework in English, these bilingual materials can provide support and act as alternative homework assignments.

**VIDEO 2.1:
The Co-
Planning
Process**

http://resources
.corwin.com/
CoTeachingforELs

Co-planning is most frequently focused on a unit of study or lesson, and it involves planning between two or more educators. Before you get down to mapping out a unit, discuss what you bring to the table. Identify your top five teaching skills and other areas of specializations that all students and your colleague will benefit from. Are you skilled with SMART Board technology or other computer-based tools? Are you trained in Kagan cooperative structures or other strategies that support flexible grouping? Do you have expertise in designing rubrics, creating formative assessment tools? Have you practiced differentiated instruction? Do you include scaffolding or tiering in your lessons for English learners (ELs)? Remember to share what your professional needs are as well, such as possible skills you would like to develop or what you would appreciate learning more about. Wlazlinski (2014) concludes that successful co-teachers

> forge a teaching philosophy that is based on a strong commitment to aligning the content and language curricula, meeting the needs of EL students, effecting differentiation and engaging in reflective practice because of a shared goal and vision. (p. 23)

In this chapter, we also recognize and address the challenge of co-planning when less-than-adequate time is made available. We stress the need for systemic support for collaboration for leadership teams, commitment from both co-teaching partners, and the establishment of routines and co-teaching schedules that support this practice.

COLLABORATIVE PLANNING

Careful preparation for co-teaching includes sustained conversations around the following dimensions of shared instructional beliefs and practice:

1. Establishing a partnership and laying the foundation for collaboration

2. Examining student data to make instructional decisions

3. Planning instruction by integrating both professionals' expertise

4. Expanding impact on student learning through systemic efforts for collaboration (Chapman & Hyatt, 2011)

Let's examine each of these four points as they relate to the co-planning experience for ELs.

Foundations for Co-Planning

As co-teachers—whether you self-selected your partners, volunteered to serve as co-teachers, or were matched up by administrators—your willingness to enter into a long-standing professional relationship and commitment to continuously strengthen your partnership will be critical (Pawan & Sietmann, 2007). Since co-teaching is a relationship that depends on successfully connecting with each other personally and professionally, we strongly recommend that you don't shy away from having an honest conversation about your *needs and wants*. Start by discussing questions with each other such as the following:

- What are our expectations for this partnership? What are our expectations for our students?
- What are our *nonnegotiables* and how can we negotiate them? (See Chapter 1.)
- What are some key ground rules we should establish for ourselves for collaborative planning, instruction, assessment, and reflection?
- What are some key tools we agree to use for collaborative planning, instruction, assessment, and reflection?
- How can we ensure parity so neither of us dominates instruction and ends up feeling like an assistant?
- How might we best proceed to learn about each other's areas of expertise?
- How might we share classroom space? What materials and resources should be shared?
- What plans might we have for classroom management?
- Who will be responsible for assessment and grading?

Completing and discussing the outcomes of a co-teaching inventory will also contribute to establishing a partnership. Try the short inventory in Figure 2.1 and feel free to add additional questions at the end to customize the experience

Maximizing Teacher Expertise

During collaborative planning, respect for each other and a full recognition of the range of talents, knowledge, skills, and experiences each teacher brings to the table are critical. While Table 2.1 shows fundamentally different knowledge and skill sets, our purpose is not to dichotomize the two teachers' backgrounds. We certainly recognize that the two teachers share a range of common skills based on their teacher preparation and experience. Instead, we wish to highlight how enriching it may be for both teachers as well as all their students when two professionals combine their professional backgrounds. We have also found that after years of collaboration (also conceived as job-embedded, ongoing professional learning), the partners acquire each other's knowledge and skills, and occasionally are indistinguishable in the co-taught classroom.

We invite you as co-teachers to see what you can do to maximize your expertise and support each other, since co-teaching typically is limited to one or two class periods a day for many ELs. See Table 2.2 on how two elementary teachers have combined their content and ELD knowledge as they mapped out what the classroom teacher can do whether the ELD/ELL teacher is present or not. The left side of the chart lists most of the subjects that Ms. Herring teaches each day. The right column lists tips and strategies that Mr. Barnes thinks will be helpful to their EL students.

Figure 2.1 Co-Teaching Interest Inventory

Name: _____   Date: _____

1. What is/are your certification area(s)?
   _____

2. What grades/subjects/courses have you taught? What grades/subjects/courses have you **co-taught**?
   _____

3. What are your favorite subjects or topics to co-teach? Why?
   _____

4. What subjects or topics are difficult for you to co-teach, and what makes them challenging?
   _____

5. What subjects, units, or topics make you work the hardest?
   _____

6. Rate the following instructional strategies/practices according to your level of comfort and readiness to implement:

   1 = very comfortable, 2 = somewhat comfortable, 3 = not very comfortable (yet)

☐ Anchor Charts	☐ Graphic Organizers	☐ Project-Based Learning
☐ Anchor Activities	☐ Grouping	☐ Scaffolding/Tiering
☐ Bilingual Resources	☐ Hand-Held Devices	☐ Technology
☐ Differentiated Instruction	☐ Hands-on Learning	☐ SMART Board
☐ Flipped Learning	☐ Learning Stations/Centers	☐ Vocabulary

7. What are your favorite (go-to) strategies for working with ELs?
   _____

8. What are your greatest successes with ELs?
   _____

9. What are your greatest successes with co-teaching?
   _____

10. What are three things you are most concerned about regarding co-teaching for ELs?
    _____

11. What are three things you would like to get out of the co-teaching experience?
    _____

12. What question(s) would you like to ask your co-teacher?
    _____

Table 2.1	Teacher Expertise

ELD/ELL Teacher	Core Content Teacher
Second-language acquisition theories and methodologies Instructional models to build English language proficiency Knowledge of linguistics, such as language variations Standards for English language development Methods and techniques for literacy and language teaching Cultural understanding	Core content knowledge Specialized methods and techniques for teaching content areas Core content standards Core content curriculum with grade-level expectations Well-organized knowledge of concepts and inquiry procedures Standardized assessments in the core content area

Table 2.2	Mr. Barnes and Ms. Herring's Collaboration for the Week of October 19–23

Morning Work	• Notebook routine (same every day for consistency)
Read Aloud	• More explanations • Stop and sketch/act/talk/add a movement • Scaffold vocabulary with explanations/simpler definitions
Shared Reading	• More explanations • Stop and sketch/act/talk/add a movement • Scaffold vocabulary with explanations/simpler definitions • Sentence starters/frame
Minilesson	• Pictures! Graphics! Add more visuals to anchor charts
Reader's Workshop	• Read with a partner—Discussion starters, "Something I noticed . . ." • These are things good readers do . . . Independent reading—give a strategy of the day/week • Try to have two different ways for students to learn • Vocabulary words (Tier 2; words with multiple meanings) • Always build background (explain vocabulary) • Two stations a day
Writing (opinion writing)	• Completed in steps: Start with— • Key words for the concept • What is a leader? Give examples of leaders, characteristics of leaders. What do you think about these? I think a good leader is _____. • 1 minute prewrite; tea party—everyone get up and share their ideas; minilesson; writing time (pull small group; checking work; sentence frames for YE; paragraph frames for EM, DM, etc.); read/share with others
Math	• Teach vocabulary explicitly (pictures, hand motions, and anchor chart) • Visualization

Systemic Support

Time for collaborative planning is the most frequently cited challenge. Villa and Thousand (2005) observe that

> although many incentives appeal to specific individuals, the one incentive that is common to and highly valued by everyone engaged in education and educational reform is time— time for shared reflection and planning with colleagues. (p. 65)

Discuss with your leadership team how collaborative planning time may also be utilized for curriculum planning (such as curriculum mapping and alignment) or building and participating in professional learning communities (PLCs) (DuFour & Eaker, 1998; Fisher, Frey, & Uline, 2013). Co-planning will support standards-aligned curriculum while allowing general-education teachers and instructional specialists to coordinate and refine their plans for instruction and assessment. Creating the logistical support for collaborative planning must be a top priority: Administrators must consider all the creative ways they can provide time for teachers to work together for a sustained amount of time, on a regular basis, with clear goals and agendas in place. In describing restructuring a high school that placed collaboration at its core, Franco, Petrie, Ready, and Donovan (2014) note that "continuous improvement is ongoing, and change—whether mandated or embraced—is inevitable" (p. 39). For change to be sustainable, teachers cannot be expected to rely merely on found time to co-plan. Collaboration must be part of their daily routine, and co-planning time must be protected time to ensure professional preparation for the joint class sessions. See a sample elementary schedule (Figure 2.2) and a secondary schedule (Figure 2.3) that indicate co-planning times available to teachers. Please note these examples are from New York State, where the designated program is referred to as ENL (English as a new Language).

This is how Kelley explains her schedule:

> This schedule is for integrated and stand-alone ENL services provided for four sections at the kindergarten grade level. My prep periods are scheduled so that I have common time each day with one or more of my co-teachers. The two teachers with whom I have the least prep time (J.G.—2 periods, K.M.—3 periods), are teachers with whom I have co-taught previously, where we have established a strong professional relationship and instructional routines. I have four common prep periods each week with the two teachers with whom I am co-teaching for the first time (L.M., L.O.) Every Wednesday, my prep period is shared with all of my co-teachers. We meet formally for a group grade-level meeting every other Wednesday during this period, and informally as needed during all other prep periods. I also share a common lunch period with all of my co-teachers daily. This allows us many opportunities to co-plan, reflect on lessons, and discuss student progress. The proximity of our classrooms also allows us to check in with each other throughout the day. The integrated instructional periods were scheduled to allow as much consistency as possible with daily routines. When I arrive in a classroom, the classroom teacher and I are able to transition students directly into our co-taught lesson, so as not to waste any instructional time. This consistency also helps students to have a clear understanding of the routines and expectations of our time together.

Figure 2.2	Kindergarten ESOL Teacher Schedule

ESOL Teacher: Kelley Cordeiro

School: Saltzman East Memorial, Farmingdale Union Free School District, NY

Year: 2016–2017

Period/ Time	Monday	Tuesday	Wednesday	Thursday	Friday
1 8:42– 9:22	K Stand Alone Room 7	K Stand Alone Room 7	K Stand Alone Room 7	K Stand Alone Room 7	K Stand Alone Room 7
2 9:24– 10:04	Integrated Room 111 Co-teacher: L.M.	Integrated Room 111 Co-teacher: L.M.	Integrated Room 111 Co-teacher: L.M.	Integrated Room 108 Co-teacher: L.O.	Integrated Room 111 Co-teacher: L.M.
3 10:06– 10:46	PREP ENL Teacher: K.C. Co-teacher: L.O.	Integrated Room 108 Co-teacher: L.O.	Integrated Room 108 Co-teacher: L.O.	Integrated Room 111 Co-teacher: L.M.	Integrated Room 108 Co-teacher: L.O.
4 10:48– 11:28	Integrated Room 108 Co-teacher: L.O.	PREP ENL Teacher: KC Co-teachers: L.M., K.M., L.O.	PREP ENL Teacher: KC Co-teachers: J.G., L.M., K.M., L.O.	PREP ENL Teacher: K.C. Co-teachers: J.G., L.M., L.O.	PREP ENL Teacher: K.C. Co-teachers: L.M., K.M.
5 11:32– 12:12	Integrated Room 1 Co-teacher: K.M.	Integrated Room 1 Co-teacher: K.M.	Integrated Room 1 Co-teacher: K.M.	Integrated Room 1 Co-teacher: K.M.	Integrated Room 3 Co-teacher: J.G.
6 12:16– 12:56	Integrated Room 3 Co-teacher: J.G.	Integrated Room 3 Co-teacher: J.G.	Integrated Room 3 Co-teacher: J.G.	Integrated Room 3 Co-teacher: J.G.	Integrated Room 1 Co-teacher: K.M.
7 1:00 – 1:40	LUNCH ALL Kindergarten teachers & ENL teacher	LUNCH ALL Kindergarten teachers & ENL teacher	LUNCH ALL Kindergarten teachers & ENL teacher	LUNCH ALL Kindergarten teachers & ENL teacher	LUNCH ALL Kindergarten teachers & ENL teacher
8 1:42 – 2:22	K Stand Alone Room 7	K Stand Alone Room 7	K Stand Alone Room 7	K Stand Alone Room 7	K Stand Alone Room 7

Figure 2.3 Secondary Schedule

Teacher	7:40 – 8:21 Period 1	8:25 – 9:08 Period 2	9:12 – 9:53 Period 3	9:57 – 10:38 Period 4	10:42 – 11:23 Period 5	11:27 – 12:08 Period 6	12:12 – 12:55 Period 7	12:59 – 1:40 Period 8	1:44 – 2:25 Period 9
Margaret Mitchell	Prep	English 11R ENL Co-teach	ENL Emerging 9/10	English 11R ENL Co-teach	Lunch	ENL Entering 9/10	Professional Prep	Duty	English 11R ENL Co-teach

This is how Margaret explains her schedule:

Currently, I am co-teaching three periods of English 11. Periods 2 and 9 I co-teach with Mr. Biondi. The groups are a mix of different language levels, with the majority of the students at the advanced level. Our only common planning time is 1st period, but we only meet when I am not screening new admits. For example, tomorrow I have to meet a newcomer, so we won't be able to co-plan face-to-face. Period 4 I co-teach with Mr. Mediate. The group is a mix of Emerging and Transitioning (Intermediate) students. We usually co-plan face-to-face during my lunch break, which is 5th period. With both of my co-teachers, we take advantage of technology to keep in touch and exchange materials. We e-mail, use Google share, or text. Since it is our second year together, we also reuse lesson materials from last year, which makes our workflow smoother.

CO-PLANNING ESSENTIALS

It has been well established that it can no longer be ELD/ELL teachers' sole responsibility to address ELs' linguistic and academic needs in the classroom. Santos, Darling-Hammond, and Cheuk (2012) conclude that all teachers need to know how to respond to students' needs by addressing:

1. Language progressions—How students learn language, both in terms of general language acquisition and in terms of the acquisition of discipline-specific academic language;

2. Language demands—What kinds of linguistic expectations are embedded within specific texts and tasks with which students are being asked to engage;

3. Language scaffolds—How specific representations and instructional strategies can be used to help students gain access to the concepts as well as to the language they need to learn; and

4. Language supports—How classrooms and schools can be organized to support students in continually building a deep understanding of language and content. (p. 4)

These four concepts may serve as foundational knowledge for collaborative teachers to explore

- Monitoring students' language development jointly will help set attainable goals.
- Examining the language demands embedded in each lesson and unit will raise linguistic awareness and aid in developing language objectives or language learning targets for ELs.
- Scaffolding learning for ELs will help make the grade-level content accessible.
- Collaboratively creating a supportive classroom environment will empower ELs to participate in learning.

In addition, for effective teacher collaboration, co-teachers should be prepared to share with each other

- expertise of content, knowledge of literacy and language development, and pedagogical skills;
- instructional resources, technology tools, and supplementary materials that are scaffolded, tiered, and differentiated;
- instructional strategies that represent research-informed and evidence-based best practices; and
- approaches to co-teaching with an open mind and willingness to explore.

Further, as co-teachers, you will need equal access to (and share the use of) some essential tools and resources that support successful co-planning:

- English Language Arts, English Language Development, and core content standards
- Curriculum maps, curriculum guides, scope and sequence charts
- Content-area texts, teacher's guides, web-based supplementary materials
- Knowledge and use of technology tools for co-planning
- Co-planning framework or action plan to accomplish co-planning tasks

CURRICULUM MAPPING AND ALIGNMENT

The curriculum in a co-taught classroom must be reflective of both the grade-level content and the language-development standards. The challenge co-teachers face is to translate those goals into essential learning outcomes—what the students need to *know, understand,* and be able to *do* (KUDs; Erickson, 2006; Wiggins & McTighe, 2005, 2011)—and contain a scope and sequence of the content, the choice of resources and expected progressions (Hattie, 2012), and what formative and summative measures will indicate attainment of goals (Jung & Guskey, 2012).

Acquiring the K–12 core curriculum is a necessity for success in school and beyond. In order to develop an advocacy framework, Diane Staehr Fenner (2013a) offers a series of powerful reflection and self-evaluation questions for school and district administrators, one of which probed whether or not all ELs have "access to a challenging, high-quality and developmentally appropriate curriculum aligned to the state's standards within and across content areas" (p. 87).

The grade-appropriate curriculum serving as a road map in ELA and all content areas must be translated into meaningful instructional experiences for ELs through curricular *adaptations* and *acceleration* using the expertise of the ELD/ELL team as leverage. Adaptations may take the form of accommodations—offering access to the grade-level curriculum without altering the standards, or modifications—through fundamental changes to the grade-level expectations when the standards are not attainable by ELs due to disabilities or other factors. Rollins (2014) also notes:

> A crucial aspect of the acceleration model is putting key prior knowledge into place so that students have something to connect new information to. Rather than focus on everything students don't know about the concept, however, the core and acceleration teachers collaboratively and thoughtfully select the specific prior knowledge that will best help students grasp the upcoming standard. (pp. 6–7)

Accelerating the curriculum moves away from the notion of remediation; instead, it allows for developing relevant, thinking-oriented curricula and collaborative, low-stakes practice while also offering foundational skill-building and intentional support for students' social-emotional needs (Hern & Snell, 2013). Walqui and van Lier (2010) suggest five design factors to be included in a quality curriculum for ELs:

(1) setting long-term goals and benchmarks,

(2) using a problem-based approach that includes interrelated lessons with real-life applications,

(3) creating a spiraling progression that includes necessary preteaching and reteaching,

(4) making the subject matter relevant to the present lives and future goals of the students and their communities, and

(5) building on students' lived experiences and connecting to the students' funds of knowledge (p. 99).

Additional curriculum design decisions include (a) tiered goals, (b) culturally responsive instructional resources, (c) scaffolding the learning experiences, and (d) applying appropriate formative and summative assessment practices.

Tiered goals. Recognize ELs as a heterogeneous group of youngsters, each with their own levels of literacy, academic achievement, and English language proficiency. For this reason, supporting these students through the use of tiered goals can establish a pathway for each of them to meet academic benchmarks through intermittent steps developed for individual learners.

Culturally responsive resources. Move beyond *tokenism* that recognizes cultural holidays or includes a historical person study from select ethnic groups; instead, incorporate the lived experiences of students from the various cultural groups represented in the school. It is essential that students be able to see their lives reflected in what is being taught.

Scaffolded learning experiences. Scaffolding provides students with smaller bits of information supported by the use of graphic organizers, guiding questions, small-group activities, and so on. Through scaffolding, you can maintain the intensity and rigor of instruction yet provide smaller doses of information for students to examine, analyze, and acquire in a given time.

Appropriate formative and summative assessments. Use sound formative and summative evaluation and assessment practices to gain accurate knowledge of what students know and are able to do at various stages of their developing academic and language proficiency.

Rather than strictly defining the ELD/ELL curriculum one way or another, consider a more flexible approach. Depending on students' language proficiency levels and other individual variables depicted in Table 1.1 (Chapter 1), some ELs will need a core curriculum with foundational language and content goals (such as students with interrupted formal education), whereas newly arrived ELs with strong schooling background will benefit from a more intensive, accelerated curriculum design (Calderón, Slavin, & Sánchez, 2011). As Lynne Sacks (2014) suggests in a recent blogpost, what we must keep in mind is this:

> Administrators and teachers need to re-examine EL placement, shifting their focus from just teaching ELs English to ensuring ELs have full access to the academic curriculum. Next is a curriculum designed to foster deep engagement, creativity, and mastery taught by teachers who have been well trained to do those things. Finally, teachers must provide language support tailored to students' developing English skill levels. This means, for example, teaching relevant vocabulary explicitly and more than once, modeling writing forms for different subjects, and providing frameworks as well as time and patience for students to discuss ideas in a language they are still learning. (para. 7)

The shift to high expectations paired with high levels of support (Walqui & van Lier, 2010) allows for rigorous curriculum implementation across the grades.

The initial approach to assuring ELs are making progress toward meeting the grade-appropriate content curricular goals and their language development goals is curriculum mapping and alignment. These organizational methods are essential to assuring that ELs have access to the general academic curricula as well as appropriate English language instruction. As Valdés, Kibler, and Walqui (2014) observe,

> The curriculum must be implemented in a manner that provides the necessary content to address students' linguistic needs and facilitate their participation in inclusive, standards-based classrooms as soon as possible. The collaboration of both ESL and content-area teachers is necessary at all levels to ensure that beginning ELs have as much access to the curriculum as their English and home language proficiencies will allow, but this cooperation is particularly essential at earlier levels of proficiency. (p. 16)

When schools use a published English language development curriculum, careful examination and analysis of such resources is essential. The World-Class Instructional Design and Assessment

(WIDA) Protocol for Review of Instructional Materials for ELLs (PRIME) inventory assists in establishing to what extent key elements of any published or teacher-created curriculum, textbooks, online materials, or any other instructional resources are aligned to the WIDA English Language Proficiency (ELP) Standards. The question the tool helps answer is the degree to which the standards are represented in instructional materials for ELs, thus resulting in rigorous instruction that is based on research-informed expectations. The inventory consists of four major sections and a total of 14 criteria, including several questions associated with each criterion. See http://prime.wceruw.org for more details.

UNIT AND LESSON PLANNING FRAMEWORKS

Your school might already have a common lesson or unit planning approach, so when it comes to collaboratively planning with your co-teachers, building on existing structures is most conducive to establishing and strengthening a common language for collaboration. Some well-known lesson and unit-planning frameworks include the Understanding by Design (UbD), Gradual Release of Responsibility, Universal Design for Learning (UDL), and Sheltered Instruction Observation Protocol (SIOP). See how each of these may be adapted with co-teaching for ELs in mind.

Understanding by Design

McTighe and Wiggins (1999) introduced the UbD framework, which is also referred to as the *backward design for unit planning* since it begins with the desired outcomes in mind. It consists of three stages:

Stage 1: Co-teachers establish desired results for the entire unit and agree on the big ideas of the unit.

What long-term goals are we targeting for the students?

What will be the essential questions that the entire unit will focus on for students to explore?

How will students be able to make meaning of the big ideas in the unit?

How will students transfer the acquired knowledge and skills to new contexts?

What knowledge and skills are students expected to acquire?

Stage 2: Co-teachers agree on what type of evidence will indicate whether or not students met the goals of the unit and achieved the desired results.

What authentic student performances and products will provide evidence of meaning-making and transfer of learning?

What additional evidence will be collected using more traditional assessment practices and tools?

Stage 3: Teachers develop a learning plan.

How will students be hooked or motivated to learn?

What activities, experiences, and lessons will lead to achievement of the desired results and success at the assessments?

How will the learning sequence help students with acquiring new knowledge and skills, making meaning of big ideas, and transferring learning?

How will the unit be organized and differentiated to optimize participation and achievement for all students?

Gradual Release of Responsibility

Fisher and Frey (2008a) are best known for adapting a well-established framework (Pearson & Gallagher, 1983) for instructional delivery that fosters a step-by-step development of students to work more independently. These procedures for structured teaching are established in part on the gradual release of responsibility model as follows:

1. Focus lesson: Identify the purpose of the lesson skills; strategies or learning tasks are demonstrated or modeled.

2. Guided instruction: Students practice and apply the modeled skills or strategies together with the teacher; guided instruction may be differentiated.

3. Student collaboration: Students engage in purposeful tasks and problem solve in small groups to gain a better understanding of the lesson objective.

4. Independent practice: Students are directed to work individually to practice and review the strategies and skills they need to master.

Structuring lessons in this way allows diverse learners the various supports for practicing new strategies and skills before applying them independently.

Universal Design for Learning

Although UDL is primarily considered a curriculum design process (Novak, 2014), the principles of UDL are helpful for daily lesson planning that supports ELs. (See Chapter 8 for more information on applying the UDL principles in co-teaching.)

The three main principles of UDL are to provide multiple means of

1. Representation—the content of the lesson is presented in multiple formats to ensure that all students can access it:

   a. multiple perceptual modalities (auditory, visual, tactile, kinesthetic) infused in the lesson

   b. language-based, visual, or symbolic presentation of content

   c. variety of opportunities for comprehension.

2. Action and Expression—during the lesson, students have multiple options for expressing what they have learned and demonstrating what they can do:

   a. physical involvement and movement during the lesson

   b. choice opportunities for responding to the content of the lesson (including use of tools and multimedia)

   c. purposeful use of strategies and resources.

3. Engagement—students are motivated to participate and are engaged in the lesson in multiple ways:

   a. authentic and relevant learning experiences

   b. fostering collaboration and communication

   c. encouraging goal setting, self-assessment, and reflection about the learning process.

Sheltered Instruction Observation Protocol Model

Using the SIOP (Echevarria, Vogt, & Short, 2016) model of instruction, co-teachers focus on the following broad approaches:

- Integrate language and content instruction, ensuring that language acquisition is directly connected to grade-level content attainment.
- Make grade-level content comprehensible through the use of visuals, modeling, scaffolds, appropriate pacing of the lesson, etc.
- Provide meaningful language and literacy practice opportunities and engage all students in higher-order thinking tasks.
- Ensure that language development is promoted through frequent opportunities for student-to-student interaction.
- Activate students' prior knowledge and build background information as needed while capitalizing on students' native language skills and funds of knowledge.
- Adapt instructional materials, learning activities, and formative and summative assessments for students' varied levels of language proficiency.

We have found that co-teachers successfully use a range of other well-researched and highly regarded lesson planning frameworks such as EXC-ELL, Teachers College Readers and Writer's Workshop, Daily 5 and CAFE, and so on. Not only do these frameworks offer a common language and frame of reference to teachers who collaborate, they also contribute to curricular and instructional continuity for English learners.

UNIT AND LESSON PLANNING RESOURCES

Using an agreed-upon unit or lesson planning template (especially if the template is made into a shared Google document) enhances the effectiveness of scarce co-planning time and also supports the process of virtually completing the lesson plans by the collaborating teachers if face-to-face time does not suffice. Consider the potential of each of the following tools and experiment with the template(s) that best matches your shared teaching philosophy. Better yet, feel free to adapt any of these templates and develop a much stronger partnership by developing a shared ownership of the lesson planning template and process. You and your co-teacher might prefer a unit planning template (Figure 2.4) or one of the weekly planning tools (Figures 2.5 or 2.6), or may agree to use a daily lesson planning form (Figures 2.7 or 2.8).

A CO-PLANNING ROUTINE

To support teachers new to or challenged by the task of successfully co-planning, or when limited face-to-face time is available, we developed a three-phase co-planning framework.

Phase 1: Preplanning (completed separately)

Partners in co-planning review forthcoming curriculum, select necessary language and content to be addressed in upcoming lessons, and identify the background knowledge students will need to be successful. They begin to devise possible language or content objectives based on learning targets and standards as well as begin to determine resources, materials, and learning tasks.

Phase 2: Collaborative Planning (completed together)

Co-teachers come prepared to finalize the different aspects of their lesson(s) either in a face-to-face meeting or using an agreed-upon virtual platform for collaboration. They negotiate content and language objectives, confirm how challenging concepts and skills will be addressed and evaluated, agree on their roles and responsibilities, and discuss how the class might be configured for co-taught lessons.

Phase 3: Postplanning (completed separately)

After objectives, materials, roles, and responsibilities have been established, each teacher completes various lesson planning tasks such as scaffolding activities, differentiating materials and assessments, finding alternative resources, creating learning centers/stations, and so on.

To support this framework, co-teaching teams must first establish how they are going to communicate and how they are going to secure and organize the materials and resources needed for the co-planning process.

Let's consider two scenarios, one elementary and one secondary, illustrating how co-teachers negotiate the three phases of co-planning for a diverse group or class including ELs. First, let's see how a fourth-grade classroom teacher and her ELD/ELL co-teacher work collaboratively using the three-part framework.

Figure 2.4   Unit Planning Template

Unit Title: Grade:

Core Teacher: ELD/ELL Teacher:

Essential Questions:

Unit Goals Aligned to Standards:

Content	Language

Preassessment Strategies:

Instructional Strategies:

Teacher Modeling	Guided Practice
Productive Group Work	Independent Work

Accommodation Strategies for ELs:

Adaptations:	Modifications:

Acceleration Strategies for ELs:

Unit Assessment Plan:

Figure 2.5	Co-Planning Form for Classroom and ELD/ELL Instruction: A Week-at-a-Glance Tool

ELD/ELL Teacher: _____ Classroom Teacher: _____ Grade _____

For the Week of: _____

Weekly Overview What is the focus for the week? What content-area topics will we address?			
	Content and Language Objectives **What are we going to teach?**	**Key Instructional Strategies** **How are we going to reach all students?**	**Resources/Materials** **What materials do we need? Who is preparing what?**
Monday			
Tuesday			
Wednesday			
Thursday			
Friday			
Formative and Summative Assessment Plan:			

Adapted from Honigsfeld, A., & Dove, M. G. (2010). *Collaboration and co-teaching: Strategies for English learners*. Thousand Oaks, CA: Corwin. (p. 98)

Figure 2.6	Co-Teaching for ELs: A Weekly Planning Template

Day/ Date	Content Objective (Including Target Standard)	Co-teaching Model(s) (Identify specific teacher roles)	Materials & Learning Aids Needed	Accommodations (Adaptations and Modifications)	Formative and Summative Assessments	Post-Lesson Reflections
Mon.	Content Objective (Including Target Standard)					
	Language Objective (Including Target Standard)					
Tue.	Content Objective (Including Target Standard)					
	Language Objective (Including Target Standard)					
Wed.	Content Objective (Including Target Standard)					
	Language Objective (Including Target Standard)					
Thur.	Content Objective (Including Target Standard)					
	Language Objective (Including Target Standard)					
Fri.	Content Objective (Including Target Standard)					
	Language Objective (Including Target Standard)					

Adapted from Martinsen Holt (2004) & Long Island RBERN (2015) funded by the New York State Education Department.

Figure 2.7 Daily Lesson Planning Template

Day/Date	Content Objective (Including Target Standard)	Language Objective (Including Target Standard)	Co-teaching Model(s)

Learner Activities (Including Accommodations— Adaptations or Modifications)	Content Teacher's Role	ELD/ELL Teacher's Role

Formative Assessments (Include Accommodations for Language Proficiencies)	Notes on Individual Students

Adapted from Honigsfeld & Dove (2008) and Long Island RBERN (2015)

Figure 2.8 Daily Co-Teaching Lesson Plan for Role Definition

Subject: _____

Content Standard: _____

Content Objectives: _____

Language Objectives: _____

Key Vocabulary: _____

Preassessment: _____

Materials: _____

Lesson	Co-teaching Approach (can select more than one)	Core Content Teacher	ELD/ELL Teacher	Special Considerations
Beginning (May include: Opening; Warm Up; Review; Anticipatory Set)	☐ One Lead—One teach on purpose ☐ Two teachers (one group): same content ☐ One teach, one assess ☐ Two teachers (two groups): same content ☐ Preteach—Teach ☐ Reteach—Teach ☐ Multiple groups			
Middle: (May include: Instruction; Checking for Understanding; Independent or Group Practice)	☐ One Lead—One teach on purpose ☐ Two teachers (one group): same content ☐ One teach, one assess ☐ Two teachers (two groups): same content ☐ Preteach—Teach ☐ Reteach—Teach ☐ Multiple groups			
End: (May include: Closing, Assessments, Extension of the Lesson)	☐ One Lead—One teach on purpose ☐ Two teachers (one group): same content ☐ One teach, one assess ☐ Two teachers (two groups): same content ☐ Preteach—Teach ☐ Reteach—Teach ☐ Multiple groups			

Adapted from Murawski (2009a, 2009b)

Preplanning (completed separately)

The co-teaching partners review the forthcoming science unit on ecosystems as well as the state science and English language arts/English language development standards for fourth grade. They agree that the curriculum is rather challenging for their ELs who may have limited experience with the topic, so they begin by back mapping: The science teacher identifies what foundational skills and prior knowledge will be necessary for all students to understand the upcoming unit, whereas the ELD/ELL teacher examines the unit for key vocabulary, distinguishing between unfamiliar concepts ELs are likely to encounter for the first time in this unit (biotic and abiotic factors, producer, consumer, decomposer) and concepts they know but will need to learn the words in English (population, food chain). They each sketch out the content and language objectives for the upcoming sequence of three lessons and begin to look for appropriate supplementary materials. The ELD/ELL teacher pays special attention to finding images and video clips that depict the ELs' home countries so they can recognize familiar environments and share their expertise about them with the rest of the class.

Collaborative Planning (completed together)

Since the co-teachers have prepared ahead of time, when they meet they work on finalizing the following three aspects of their lessons:

- Lesson objectives and appropriate formative assessment measures that they will use to track student mastery of the content as well as language progressions (for example, objectives focusing on word-level, sentence-level, and text-level language skills related to the topic of biomes and ecosystems. There is a special focus on sentence frames that compares and contrasts the biomes, such as: Both _____ and _____ are _____. Whereas _____ is _____, _____ is _____ and _____. _____ and _____ are alike because. _____ is different than _____ because _____. Although _____ is _____, _____ is _____).
- The sequence of highly engaging, hands-on learning experiences (learning activities) aligned to various co-teaching models (for example, six learning stations will offer an in-depth exploration of the six biomes—tundra, desert, grassland, tropical rainforest, deciduous forest, and coniferous forest, etc.).
- Individual students who might need additional support.

They close the co-planning session by agreeing on who prepares the instructional materials and what roles and responsibilities each teacher will have during the upcoming sequence of lessons.

Postplanning (completed separately)

- After agreeing on the objectives and the lesson sequence, the major postplanning task is to prepare the instructional materials for (a) background-building lesson, (b) the six stations, and (c) the enrich/reteach lesson. One teacher will design SMART Board activities, whereas the other teacher will prepare manipulatives; tiered, partially completed graphic organizers; and scaffolded note-taking sheets and exit tickets used during each lesson.

Next, let's see how a secondary co-teaching team, a social studies teacher and an ELD/ELL teacher, might use this co-planning framework to collaboratively plan a co-taught lesson in a ninth-grade social studies class.

Preplanning (*separately*). The co-teaching partners have selected the civil rights movement as the subject for a series of co-taught lessons and begin by preplanning the first lesson on their own:

- After reviewing learning standards and the content material, the social studies teacher determines the content objective—students will be able to understand the concept of civil rights and the meaning of civil liberties, and analyze the roles of President Lyndon B. Johnson and Dr. Martin Luther King Jr. in the civil rights movement. He reviews reference materials and media on the civil rights movement, and examines selected texts for the vocabulary and phrases all students will need to understand the topic (e.g., Congress, discrimination, bona fide, affirmative action, equal protection under the law, etc.). He finds student activities used in the previous year to launch the topic, develops a list of key questions guided by Bloom's taxonomy question stems, and thinks about how students might work in teams to research different aspects of the civil rights movement.

- The ELD/ELL teacher identifies a language objective aligned with the language and literacy standards—for students to be able to analyze various accounts of a subject told in different mediums and increase their abilities to produce complex sentences in speaking and writing. She reviews the unit materials and develops questions to assist ELs to find the major points of information in different media. She also notices a pattern of two-word verbs in one of the readings—carry out, concerned about, charged with—and chooses to emphasize this element of grammar with her ELs.

Co-Planning (*together*). The social studies and the ELD/ELL teacher have uploaded their preplanning ideas on a designated template in Google Docs; they will conduct their co-planning session by phone for convenience.

- The co-teaching pair reviews the language and content objectives set in the preplanning phase. They acknowledge that certain texts might be a bit challenging for some of the ELs at lower levels of English proficiency. They decide that a one-pager—a bulleted summary of the most important concepts—should be developed for ELs. The ELD/ELL teacher volunteers to develop the one-pager for these students.

- They agree to introduce the topic using a short authentic video clip from the civil rights era. They examine the selected vocabulary, and the ELD/ELL teacher suggests how they might group students after the initial introduction to the topic to accommodate those who might need some vocabulary preteaching and grammar instruction. The social studies teacher agrees and determines that the students who do not need preteaching will examine and analyze some photographs from the 1960s to draw their own conclusions.

- They continue to plan the lesson by discussing possible learning activities, resources, and co-teaching models to employ.

- The teachers discuss their individual roles—who will set the stage for learning with a brief anecdote, who will introduce the video clip, and so forth. It is decided that the ELD/ELL teacher will open with a brief anecdote leading to a discussion about the right to privacy. The social studies teacher will preview the video clip, and as the video plays, the ELD/ELL teacher will jot down notes on a piece of chart paper. She will use these notes when the class divides into two groups for preteaching.

- They determine students should return together as a whole group for discussion and clarification of the research task. Next, students will be divided into cooperative learning groups to research different aspects of the civil rights movement. The ELD/ELL teacher will remain with a group of ELs to support their research; she will assist them to analyze various accounts of the civil rights movement told in different mediums and reinforce pertinent vocabulary and grammar. She will employ scaffolded sentence stems to enhance students' abilities to discuss the subject. In the meantime, the social studies teacher will circulate within the other groups and assist students as needed.

- For an assessment, the teaching team decides to use a 3-2-1 assessment strategy—students identify three things they learned, two things that are not completely clear, and one question they still have. This assessment can be scaffolded to be accessible for all learners to demonstrate what they know.

- Before the team ends their joint planning, they revisit their roles and responsibilities for the lesson as well as which teacher will prepare and gather materials and resources.

Postplanning (*separately*). Each teacher keeps his or her own separate plans due to preferences in organizational styles instead of sharing one completed plan as other co-teachers do.

- The social studies teacher selects places to pause the introductory video clip and develops pertinent questions. He creates student groupings for the preteach portion of the lesson as well as sets up the groups for the cooperative learning research. He develops a 3-2-1 assessment sheet.

- The ELD/ELL teacher completes a one-pager on the civil rights movement, a vocabulary sheet with words to preteach, a grammar activity that incorporates the use of two-word verbs, and a modified 3-2-1 assessment sheet.

- Both teachers finish writing their individual plans and post them in Google Docs.

Why is such an elaborate planning routine needed? "The understanding of nuances related to the language of instruction—often learned from collaboration with EL teachers—has helped classroom teachers focus their instruction and communicate to all students with increased effectiveness," said Dr. Chris Sonenblum, director of student services at the Roseville Area Schools Independent School District 623, Roseville, Minnesota, who clearly supports collaboration time for the teachers with whom she works. She also firmly believes that "joint planning among EL teachers and those providing subject matter content strengthens instruction by building confidence for each teacher; the time spent is an investment that pays big dividends in student achievement!"

The main goal of implementing an integrated service delivery for the instruction of ELs through co-teaching is to develop their academic and social language skills while building their content-area knowledge and skills as well as making sure they are fully included in the classroom instruction their peers receive. Without careful planning, coordination of instructional delivery, and intentional use of assessment measures and tools that inform collaborative instruction, co-teaching will most likely fail; one teacher will have the responsibility for planning, instruction, and assessment while the other is relegated to assistant status.

INCREASING CO-PLANNING EFFECTIVENESS

Co-planning time that is systemic and regularly available because it is built into teachers' daily schedules can be further enhanced through establishing clarity about professional expectations. We suggest creating a schoolwide professional agreement as well as individual partnership agreements, the purpose of which may be to clarify the goals and key processes of jointly planning instruction for ELs and to hold the entire school community accountable. Partnership agreements help build a strong foundation for collaboration, especially for maximizing the collaborative planning time by mapping out a shared routine or structure. See Figure 2.9 for a schoolwide professional agreement and Figure 2.10 for an individual partnership agreement.

Schoolwide agreements can be further enhanced if co-teachers enter into partnership agreements that specify how the two co-teachers engage in the entire collaborative instructional cycle (co-planning, co-teaching, co-assessing, and reflection) as well as offer some specifics on the co-planning cycle of pre-, co-, and postplanning. Note that the ELD/ELL teacher is referred to as the Language Development Coach (LCD) in Figure 2.10, which contains excerpts from the agreement between a fourth-grade teacher and the LCD. The agreement is to be revisited and adjusted every few months as needed.

Figure 2.9	Schoolwide Professional Agreement

We work in grade-level teams or professional learning communities that fully include ELD/ELL teachers and other special service providers for the year.

We choose content standards and align them with language standards for each unit of learning.

We create learning targets for content and language for each unit.

We determine the academic language and literacy demands of the standards, and design instructional materials and activities around them for each unit.

We formulate differentiated language and content objectives for lessons in the unit.

We extend differentiation of instruction into our formative and summative assessment plans.

We use assessment data to improve our teaching, to monitor student progress, and to contribute to local accountability.

Adapted from Gottlieb, 2016, p. 176

| Figure 2.10 | Partnership Agreement |

Teachers: Katie O'Neill & Mara Barry (Prairie School, Kildeer Countryside School District 96, IL)

Collaboration times: Monday at 10:30

Structure of collaboration: Meeting face-to-face

Coplanning arrangement: Roles and responsibilities

	Classroom Teacher	**Language Development Coach**
Preplanning: (before meetings)	• Preview lessons • General idea of what the week will look like • Writing	• Preview lessons • Small groups—how that will look • Begin document for the week with objectives
Collaborative Planning: (collaborative meeting)	• Talk about roles and responsibilities for the lessons • Looking at models • Staying focused	• Talk about roles and responsibilities for the lessons • Looking at models • Staying focused
Postplanning: (after the meeting, preparing for lesson)	• Reflection (written or verbal)	• Reflection (written or verbal)

Communication/Reflection Roles and Responsibilities

Communication: We agree to:

- Use face-to-face conversation whenever possible
- Texting is preferred, but e-mail is fine, too .

Reflection: We agree to:

- Try our best to reflect on our document
- Comment to one another either during lesson or afterward
- Try to add that to first 3 to 5 minutes of our coplanning time (reflection)
- Continue along the same path we are on—it is working for us

Reporting: We agree to:

- Look at student work together to plan for guided groups based on targets and/or student needs

Co-planning can also be further enhanced by using a common frame of reference such as the multidimensional support system (tools and strategies) depicted in Figure 2.11. Instructional supports refer to strategies that inform the modes of lesson delivery for ELs; linguistic supports call attention to the academic language to be addressed at the word, sentence, and text levels as well as across the four language domains of listening, speaking, reading, and writing; sensory supports help ELs rely on visual and other senses for processing new information; graphic supports help ELs access complex ideas and demonstrate their knowledge of them through visual tools rather than

Figure 2.11 Multidimensional Support Systems: Tools and Strategies

Instructional Support	• Gradual Release of Responsibility Model
	  – Explicit Teacher Modeling
	  – Guided Practice
	  – Collaborative Practice
	  – Independent Application
	• Strategy instruction

Linguistic Support	• Use of native language or home dialect • Definition of key terms within sentences • Modification of sentence patterns • Use of redundancy or rephrasing • Opportunities to interact with proficient English models • Sentence starters and paragraph frames • Language frames for oral interaction
Graphic Support	• Charts • Tables • Timelines • Number lines • Graphs • Graphic organizers • Outlines
Visual Support	• Real objects (realia) • Manipulatives • Photographs • Pictures, illustrations • Diagrams • Models • Displays • Magazines, newspapers • Videos • Multimedia, including Internet
Interactive Support	• Whole class • Large-group vs. small-group instruction • Learning Centers • Learning Stations • Pair work • Buddy system • Cooperative learning structures (See Kagan)

Adapted from Gottlieb, 2016; Honigsfeld & Dove, 2015a; WIDA, 2013.

dense text-based materials; and last but not least, through interactive support, students communicate with English-speaking peers and fellow ELs through multiple channels using English, the native language, and technology tools as well.

USE OF TECHNOLOGY FOR CO-PLANNING

One of the greatest issues facing teachers today is finding enough time to co-plan. Even when teachers are provided time during the school day to work with their colleagues, it might not be sufficient to accomplish long-term planning, problem-solving ongoing issues, or projects such as mapping the curriculum. For this reason, some teachers have discovered ways to collaborate apart from face-to-face meetings using a variety of online applications to accomplish synchronous or asynchronous collaboration.

Online tools can be an effective way to collaborate with colleagues and share information. The following are some examples of applications for collaborative work that may be used for virtual meetings, professional learning, file sharing, and consensus building as well as to co-plan instruction, develop continuing projects over time, and enhance the overall use of technology:

- Google Drive is a free online document writing and editing application which teachers use to co-develop and share instructional plans. Co-teachers can work together in real time or asynchronously to review, edit, and store documents. To use Google Drive, you need to create an account and install the application on your device.
- Dropbox is a free cloud application where co-teachers store documents, files, videos, and other media for sharing. Teaching teams can invite others to receive and contribute to files as well as access the contents of a particular Dropbox folder from any computer, tablet, or device. Like Google Drive, you must download an application and create an account to access it. However, unlike Google Drive, you may not work on documents simultaneously with another person. You can upgrade Dropbox for a fee to increase the capacity of your online storage.
- GoToMeeting is a virtual meeting tool that allows for desktop sharing and video conferencing for teachers to connect in real time via the Internet using their computers, tablets, or smartphones. Teachers can actually speak with one another or use the chat feature to type their messages. Meetings can also be recorded for those who may not be able to attend. GoToMeeting requires a paid subscription.
- TweetChat is a way to use social media for a real-time group conversation using Twitter. Tweet chats generally focus on a particular topic and are led by a moderator or host; anyone can lead a discussion. To direct the conversation to a particular group of participants, a hashtag is used. To participate, you need a free Twitter account. Tweet chats are popular among groups of teachers and administrators; it's easy to use, and it's free. It does take some time and skill to develop communicating using a limit of 140 characters.
- Chatzy is a free online chat room that requires no registration, account, subscription, installation, or hashtag to use. A lead person fills out a simple form and is able to invite others to a private chat room via e-mail. Your co-teacher or grade/content team can join instantly. There are no limits to the length of your conversations.

The above list merely touches the surface of the available online tools for teachers to use for collaboration, and many of them are free. Considering how teachers all too often are isolated from their fellow educators throughout the school day, Liane Wardlow (2013) suggests, "Meaningful, online connections help teachers collaborate, stay inspired, and feel supported. They provide teachers with increased access to best practices, new ideas, and more resources than ever before" (para. 1). Although online collaboration is not a substitute for face-to-face co-planning, it can enhance classroom practices and hone teachers' skills in using next-generation technology.

INSPIRATION FROM THE FIELD

**VIDEO 2.2:
Collaborative
Planning Tips**

http://resources.corwin
.com/CoTeachingforELs

**VIDEO 2.3:
Successes and
Challenges**

http://resources.corwin
.com/CoTeachingforELs

Read what colleagues—ELD/ELL specialists and classroom teachers as well as building and district administrators—shared with us from around the United States. We have found them inspirational and affirming. See how they reflect your own experiences or add to your understanding.

Edd Ohlsen, first-grade teacher in Patchogue Medford School, New York, had years of co-planning and co-teaching experience when he shared his perspective with us.

Co-planning asks you to change your academic and cultural perspective in order to anticipate challenges that your learners may encounter. What do they know? Where do they struggle? How does this material differ from where they have been? We are tasked with discovering what connections we can foster as a team so that everyone has a place at the learning table.

When co-planning, I've found it helpful to discuss what upcoming concepts are going to be taught in next week's lesson. We try to anticipate. My colleagues and I look for ways to introduce these concepts and new vocabulary by harnessing the power of small-group instruction. Guided Reading groups offer an easy entry point into the material. We also think about extra-help sessions that are planned before school. ELLs that may feel lost in the shuffle of a whole class lesson in a small-group instruction have an opportunity to increase their confidence and shine.

In lesson planning for ELLs, I consider the pacing. In our lessons, we purposefully create opportunities for students to increase their oral language skills through think-pair-share planned opportunities. Posted sentence frames are drafted during lesson planning. Content objectives and language objectives are crafted for each lesson. While we could come up with them as we teach the actual lesson, the sentence frames and objectives that are created off the top of our heads are never as concise or as helpful as the ones that we have thoroughly thought through.

We strive to harness the power of realia. Co-planning makes us pause and think about what ways we can pair virtual realia with a hands-on experience to support ELLs as well as all learners. Besides a picture shown on an interactive whiteboard, can we bring in an actual item? Is there someone who is an expert we can Skype or find a media clip of? Is there a virtual lab that students can use to help them?

When you co-plan, you are creating a road map to be followed with a group of people. Just like a real road trip, leave room for sightseeing, breakdowns, traffic, and being a little lost.

Next, we invite you to read about Jessica Kilbride and Melissa Loftis's (elementary co-teachers from Charlotte Mecklenburg Schools) experiences with co-teaching, and see how they have achieved specific successes and what types of co-planning routines have contributed to them.

Co-teaching is a relationship that needs to be nurtured and reflective. Not all co-teaching relationships are the same and not all work out as planned, but as long as you remain student focused, you can move students and build your relationship.

As teachers that were able to co-teach for three years together, we have seen success in many different ways. It has been extremely beneficial for our students that we have worked with, as well as ourselves as teachers. The many different strategies that we were able to implement in our classroom on a daily basis played to the strengths of our students and provided the scaffolding that they needed to grow as learners. When planning, we were able to bounce ideas off each other in order to plan lessons that were more effective, engaging, and differentiated to meet the needs of our EL students as well as all other students.

The high expectations in our classroom and the efforts put forth from both teachers pushed our students to reach beyond their levels and grow more than 1.5 years in reading and math. The students were accountable for their growth and supported each other as a community of learners. We also found success using each other's strengths to grow and develop our teaching methods and strategies to become master teachers.

Our classroom makeup:

- *Range of students and an increasing number of EL students*
- *34 out of 40 students EL*
- *Exited 50% in one year from EL services*

Co-planning practices and routines

- *Met to map out units during planning days as well as after school. The better prepared we were for the long-range goal, the easier it was to short-term plan to meet our students' needs.*
- *Plan weekly to incorporate activities and strategies to match student language levels, proficiency levels based on standardized assessments, and knowledge of content.*
- *Reflect daily in order to process student work samples and data. During these reflections, if one of us felt unsuccessful or that our group and activity struggled, the other would take this group during breakout time to reteach while the others went on with the plan.*
- *Each morning we would check in with each other to review the day and co-teaching models that would be used during each day's lessons, and also make sure that all materials were ready and in place for the day.*
- *Below is a sample lesson template we used for co-teaching and planning:*

Standard: *I can* statement:	Teacher input: Active Engagement:	Co-teaching Model and Expectations for each teacher:	Reflection/Outcome:

Next, see how Art Wong, ELD/ELL teacher at Phelps Luck Elementary, Columbia, Maryland, reflects on how a rocky beginning with a co-teacher turned around and resulted in a most successful partnership.

My first year working with Mrs. H., a third-grade teacher, didn't go very well. Our goals and schedules always seemed to be defined by conflict wherein each of us was fighting for time with the English Learners in her class. Like countries in battle over a valuable resource, our professional inter-action was a zero-sum game. The time I gained with these students was time she lost, and vice versa. We barely made eye contact when I came to pick up my students. Still, I recognized that she was an excellent teacher who cared deeply about her students. When I was assigned to third grade the follow-ing year, I decided to press into this conflict instead of running from it.

Mrs. H. and I began meeting weekly and discussed not only our plans for the week but also our beliefs about students. We shared roles, we made compromises, we gave each other the benefit of the doubt. By choosing to value our professional relationship, we grew in our understanding of each other and our effectiveness as co-teachers. Ultimately, the students benefited the most, demonstrating excel-lent progress in reading and writing as well as language development. Incredibly, this became one of the most effective co-teaching relationships of my career! Today, we promote inclusive, equitable access to rigorous instruction for every English Language Learner.

The following example comes from Thad Williams, who is a secondary ELL teacher in a cultur-ally, linguistically, and economically diverse public high school in the Pacific Northwest.

The impetus for our collaborative effort stemmed from two biology teachers and two ELL teachers identifying the need to support English language learners in biology, specifically with scaffolding the learning of the Next Generation Science Standards (NGSS) and specific science practices. As a group, we quickly realized the need to work closely together in co-planning, pre-teaching and re-teaching to create additional opportunities for ELL students to analyze and interpret data, construct explana-tions, and engage in argument from evidence.

As a district and ELL department, we had spent time learning and trying out the different co-teaching models, some with success and others with some challenges. We knew that our approach needed to be collaborative and structured around a co-planning and co-teaching model to fully sup-port our English learners with the science content and NGSS practice development, and the language development simultaneously. This collaboration quickly developed into a few established routines such as co-planning once a week for each thirty-minute biology ELL tutorial session, co-teaching the thirty-minute biology ELL tutorial and reflecting collaboratively on the biology content and science practices, and the strategies and approaches used to support the English learners in gaining access and practicing biology and academic English.

As a collaborative team, we focused on several instructional collaborative activities that increased support for our English learners and developed our own learning about teaching biology to English learners. One such instructional collaborative activity was co-planning. This took shape in two differ-ent ways. One way was preplanning where the biology teacher, Mr. Brown, shared a one-page prompt from the Biology End of Course Exam that asked students to demonstrate a science practice such as "analyzing and interpreting data" (NGSS, 2012). I then took a look at the language demands of this prompt and began to plan out specific strategies and scaffolds to use with the prompt. Collaborative planning then took place where we met for thirty minutes once a week to plan the thirty-minute Biology ELL tutorial. We talked together about what groupings and talk activities we would use during the tutorial session to get students to begin to share their thinking about the prompt. We then decided on specific parts of the prompt to read and annotate together with the class or do a read-aloud or think-aloud. Finally, we both left with a small to-do list such as create sentence frames for this part of the prompt response.

TAKEAWAYS

In this chapter, we make a compelling case for ensuring that teachers have adequate co-planning time and utilize that time effectively. Partnership building is heavily dependent upon the quality of professional time teachers spend together. Administrators must create and protect the time needed for effective collaboration, and teachers must commit to co-planning routines. We have emphasized how co-teaching partners can become better teachers as they combine their professional expertise to serve students. Through establishing and maintaining respect for the co-planning process, co-teachers can access and incorporate each other's content understandings and instructional competencies in the co-taught classroom.

QUESTIONS FOR FURTHER DISCUSSION

1. What structures and routines do you consider to be most effective to enhance teacher collaboration and co-planning?

2. What are the greatest obstacles you and your colleagues could face when it comes to co-planning? How do you overcome these challenges?

3. How do you compensate if limited face-to-face time is available for co-planning?

4. What are the most valuable resources teachers could have to successfully co-plan?

3

Model 1 — One Group

One Leads, One "Teaches on Purpose"

Image Credit: New America

AN INTRODUCTION TO THE MODEL

With this model, one teacher assumes a leading role and the other a supporting one. Similar to the above illustration, the lead teacher is positioned in front of the whole class and the supporting teacher is either situated in one particular area of the room or circulates within the entire classroom. In addition, it might be planned that the supporting teacher is seated with a particular group of students.

In this teaching configuration, the general role of the lead teacher is to introduce new information, share a PowerPoint presentation, demonstrate or model a strategy or skill, give a detailed explanation of an activity, or provide the step-by-step directions for collaborative or individual student learning. The main purpose of the supporting teacher is to check individual students' understanding, clarify information, monitor students' ability to follow instructions, and provide immediate one-on-one instruction and feedback.

For those serving in the role of "teaching on purpose," other instructional activities include the following:

> Giving short, focused mini lessons to individual students, pairs of students, or a small group of students . . . a follow-up to a previous lesson or a check and extension of what is presently being taught based on a teachable moment. Teachers who implement teaching on purpose may also keep a written log of information for each EL who needs follow-up. (Honigsfeld & Dove, 2010, p. 75)

The supporting teacher might also monitor the pacing of the lesson; from observing the class at work, he or she is best able to determine if the lesson is moving too quickly or if repetition, reteaching, adjustment in pacing, or an alternate way of presenting the material may be needed. Mutually agreed-upon nonverbal signals are often used between the two teachers for this purpose. The supporting teacher might also play devil's advocate—asking the lead teacher questions when students seem not to understand and need further explanation.

It is important to note that with this model, the classroom or content-area teacher should not always be the one who undertakes the lead teacher role. This practice will position the English language development/English language learner (ELD/ELL) teacher or other co-teaching specialist (e.g., special education, literacy, bilingual teacher, etc.) as an assistant or "helper," and the students may not view the supporting teacher equitably. Therefore, apart from other measures that are further explained in this chapter, we recommend that the lead role be shared between the two teachers to form a balance of power.

A CLOSER LOOK AT MODEL 1

As the co-taught lesson begins, both teachers should position themselves in front of the entire class—no matter how briefly—with the idea of building parity. Villa, Thousand, and Nevin (2011) identify how parity is established in that it

> occurs when co-teachers perceive their unique contributions and their presence on the team are valued . . . The outcome is that each member of the co-teaching team gives and takes direction for the co-teaching lesson so that the students can achieve the desired benefits. (p. 108)

We further recommend that students be directly told the role of each teacher for the day's lesson; explaining the function of each teacher will better inform students what to expect and from whom. In this way, students will not perceive one teacher as just "floating around'" the class. They should know that both teachers have been strategically positioned for their learning support.

Setting clear learning goals, objectives, or learning targets for students also frames this use of this model. It provides explicit expectations for the course of the lesson and also affords an anchor for both the students and their co-teachers. We have found that learning targets formulated as "I can" statements written in a student-friendly way help make teacher expectations clear and accessible.

Sample "I can" statements:

I can identify words or phrases in a text that relate to my five senses.

I can explain the difference between fiction and nonfiction texts.

I can use prefixes and suffixes to figure out word meanings.

I can determine the meaning of words and phrases based on how they are used in a story.

I can summarize the points a speaker makes.

I can use punctuation to indicate a pause or a break in my writing.

English learners (ELs) particularly benefit from a more detailed learning guide—an outline of the activities to be conducted during the lesson in addition to learning benchmarks. Written in student-friendly language with clear expectations, this type of guide can be referred to during the class period and will not only help students stay on track but the teaching partners as well. Guides might be written on the board, projected via PowerPoint slide or interactive whiteboard, or printed and placed strategically throughout the classroom. Learning guides are also beneficial to co-teaching pairs when the content of the lesson may have been planned together but the flow of the lesson has not. For an example of a basic learning guide, see Figure 3.1.

Although it may sound obvious, both teachers should speak to the *entire* class at different intervals of the instructional period. All too often, we find those who are in the teaching on purpose role maintain their perception as helper or the sole provider of instruction to English learners or other struggling students by their silence. This distance that is created between the support teacher and the rest of the class can cause ELs and other students being helped to feel singled out and segregated.

Even though it is sometimes not an easy task for support teachers to interject during the lead teacher's instruction, we strongly urge that they do so. Better yet, co-teachers should plan certain junctures of the lesson where the supportive teacher might share information with the class such as clarify vocabulary, repeat task information, comment on a spelling trick, note a point of grammar, describe an anomaly or a derivation in the English language, share an interesting anecdote, and so on. As the teaching partnership develops, this particular type of planning may no longer be necessary.

Consider the amount of instructional time that is spent using this model. Although on occasion we have observed it successfully used for an entire class period, we generally recommend that it take up no more than ten to fifteen minutes of the scheduled class time. The primary purpose of

VIDEO 3.1: Model 1—One Group: One Leads, One "Teaches on Purpose"

http://resources .corwin.com/ CoTeachingforELs

Figure 3.1 Learning Guide Sample: Social Studies, Grade 6	
Learning Guide Topic: Child Labor	**Date:** Thursday, November 13

Learning Objectives/Benchmark Performances: We will be able to:
- Identify the problems of child workers in the developing world today
- Determine the central ideas about child labor from our reading and provide an accurate summary without using our prior knowledge or opinions

Process: To achieve these objectives, we will:
- Stop and Jot—Answer the following question in writing: *Why are there so many children working in the developing world?*
- Stand up, Hand up, Pair up—share what we wrote with other students
- In triads, read selected text—after each paragraph, use stop and process routine of your choice
- Annotate or take notes to prepare for summary writing

Assessment: To share what we have learned, we will:
- Individually write summary; use graphic organizer of our choice for support if needed
- Share our summaries with teachers and peers

this model's configuration should be to set the learning stage for students. If overused or not successfully incorporated with other teaching configurations, this instructional model might reinforce a "sit and get" mode of learning. To ensure students have time to read, interpret information, think critically, write, and work collaboratively, use this model both intentionally and sparingly.

This model might also be selected when pairs of teachers are unfamiliar with co-teaching or first working together as a team. It allows time for both teachers to observe each other's teaching styles, classroom management preferences, general instructional routines, abilities to teach spontaneously, and the available resources and technology. For ELD/ELL teachers who are co-teaching in a content area where initially they may not be well versed, this model can ease them into supporting students with unfamiliar subject matter.

Teaching on purpose should never be used as the default go-to model because of lack of planning time. All too often, this practice has been the case. Without proper planning, this model equates to letting the supporting teacher render instructional Band-Aids to already academically challenged ELs; in turn, their learning will be more fragmented and their instruction less impactful.

ADVANTAGES

Like all of the co-teaching models, teaching on purpose has several advantages. For one, English learners are exposed to the same rigorous content alongside their native English-speaking peers while being well supported by two teachers—a content expert and a language-learning expert. Essential strategies—relevant for ELs and non-ELs alike—can be planned so that both the language and content being studied are accessible to all learners. The monitoring and immediate feedback offered by the supporting teacher allows ELs to better understand lessons and complete tasks.

Monitoring also gives the supporting teacher the opportunity to gather anecdotal data about individual students' progress and learning needs, providing pertinent information to better plan future lessons.

This model of instruction favors the idea of accelerated learning—a concept that rejects the notion of remediation as a key to struggling learners' academic improvement and replaces it with the strong belief in rich and stimulating environments for learning. Rollins (2014) clearly identifies the trouble with remediation as follows:

> Remediation is based on the misconception that for students to learn new information, they must go back and master everything they missed . . . The students who have the largest gaps and are thus more academically vulnerable are sent the furthest distance back . . . In addition, remedial courses typically provide a surfeit of passive, basic skills work and little real-world relevance. Boredom and futility creep in, and students often give up and shut down. (pp. 5–6)

To teach English learners, educators must embrace the idea of nonlinear learning. Students acquire skills best through discovery, problem solving, and inquiry-based tasks. These activities require a trial-and-error approach, which is not linear by nature. Carroll (2007) puts it best in his description of nonlinear learning:

> On one level, non-linear learning is the way that we naturally learned for a couple of hundred thousand years. In nature, linear learning doesn't exist. People didn't learn to swim or hunt in a linear way – through a staggered, textbook process. We learned instead by doing, through direct experience, through dealing with things as they arose, and through discovering what it was that was important at the time. But most of all, we learned through making connections between what we already knew and what we didn't. This meant we actively constructed the knowledge as we needed it. It was all very subjective and individual and not linear. (para. 12)

The different roles co-teachers assume with the well-planned use of this model can support an active learning environment and a highly effective lesson delivery—including activating and building students' background knowledge, explicit teaching of academic language, high levels of engagement with more difficult text, increased student participation and interaction, as well as many other productive and powerful learning activities. See Figure 3.2 for some additional ideas of what may be targeted by the teacher who teaches on purpose.

CHALLENGES

One of the major challenges with using this model is the perception of parity—for both teachers to feel significant and valued for their teaching practices and for all students to view them as equals. Without sufficient time for planning, it is likely that one teacher will take the lion's share of planning the lesson, while the other teacher merely walks into the room asking, "What are we doing

Figure 3.2   What to "Teach on Purpose"

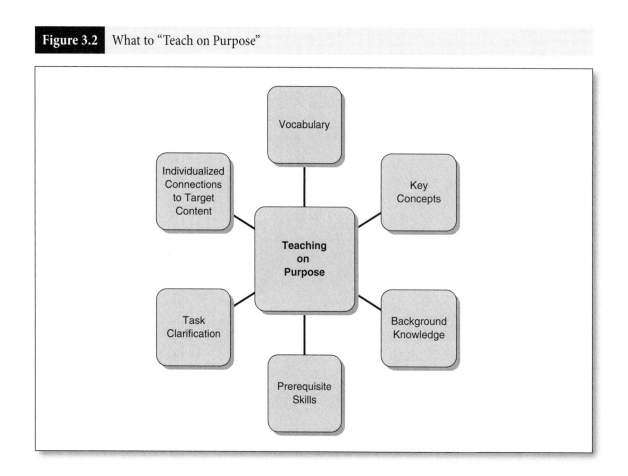

today?" This type of lesson preparation will automatically place one teacher in a position of not having ownership of the lesson and lacking basic lesson information—the content to be learned, the process chosen for student learning, and the assessment activity for identifying student knowledge and progress.

All too often we hear from ELD/ELL teachers that without sufficient planning time, they are no more effective than a teacher's aide when they "push in" to a class. Instead of developing and maintaining an equal teaching partnership, their role is reduced to that of a helper. They often move about the class, at times a bit aimlessly, looking for students who might need assistance, asking students basic questions to check their understanding, and sometimes just standing around—watching and waiting for those who may need guidance, support, or feedback.

There are times when ELD/ELL teachers take the lead, placing the classroom teacher in the supportive role. Again, a well-orchestrated plan needs to be in place to make this arrangement successful and to avoid possible pitfalls. If that is not the case, grade-level or content-area teachers on occasion will mistakenly perceive this teaching arrangement as an opportunity to mark papers, search the Internet, write lesson plans, and so on.

The least effective use of this model is to have the teacher in the supportive role monitor the behavior of all students in the class. Although this practice can be at times a great support to the lead teacher, it does little to reinforce the academic learning of ELs nor does it enhance their engagement and participation in the class. Therefore, caution should also be taken with this model to

Table 3.1	Summary of Advantages and Challenges of Model 1

Model 1: One Lead Teacher and One Teacher "Teaching on Purpose"	
Advantages	**Challenges**
Rigorous content and curriculum is accessible to all students.	If not enough planning time is given, one teacher might take all the responsibility for teaching.
All students receive equal benchmark instruction.	
Formative data may be produced via logs (for follow-up).	ESL teachers in a supportive role may be no more effective than a teacher's aide when parity has not been established between co-teachers.
The monitoring and immediate feedback offered by the supporting teacher allows ELs to better understand lessons and complete tasks.	If the ESL teacher is the one taking the lead responsibility, the classroom or content teacher might treat the co-taught time as a "break."
Constant monitoring of EL understanding is possible.	
This model of instruction favors the idea of accelerated learning.	Caution should also be taken to assure that one teacher does not become the disciplinarian.
Personal, individualized attention may be given to students in need.	As sometimes believed, this model does not afford co-teachers a reduction in their joint lesson preparation.
This model can support an active learning environment.	

Adapted from Honigsfeld, A., & Dove, M. G. (2010). *Collaboration and co-teaching: Strategies for English learners.* Thousand Oaks, CA: Corwin.

assure that one teacher does not assume the role of the disciplinarian. To establish parity, both teachers should have ownership of class management and agree upon certain routines and strategies for student behavior. What can be most productive is when one teacher takes on the role of purposefully managing the learning of certain groups of students—monitoring their time on task and overall progress in meeting learning targets.

Last but not least, do not get caught up in the myth that this model affords co-teachers a reduction in their joint lesson preparation. There are strategies that work with all instructional models that require a reduced amount of preparation but only after clear routines have been established between the co-teachers.

INSTRUCTION USING MODEL 1

Although we continue to drive home the idea that having designated planning time is essential for a well-conducted co-taught class, we recognize from our work in the field that common planning time is not always a fixed or scheduled practice in some schools. For this reason, we have identified strategies that require minimal preparation (low prep) and those preparations that are protracted (pro prep), requiring a lengthier amount of time to develop, assemble, and produce.

Low-Prep Strategies for Model 1

For low-prep strategies to be most effective, they must be readily available on an ongoing basis—either stored in the classroom and easily accessible to the teacher in the support position or as part of the routine actions that are well established between the pair of co-teachers.

Concept Webs. These organizers can offer students a clear structure for sorting lesson contents and aid in comprehension. As part of a regular routine, support teachers can have readily available generic graphic organizers for students to arrange meaningful information being introduced by the lead teacher. Simple concept webs (Figure 3.3) work well for this type of task.

Teacher as Scribe. If students are less able to discern which information is most important, the support teacher might use a portable or hand-held whiteboard to jot down pertinent content, vocabulary, and other essential knowledge being introduced by the lead teacher. In this way, as the lead teacher introduces ideas verbally, the support teacher can ensure that ELs are supported through written information. Teachers in a supporting role can also use one of the generic graphic

Figure 3.3 Concept Web

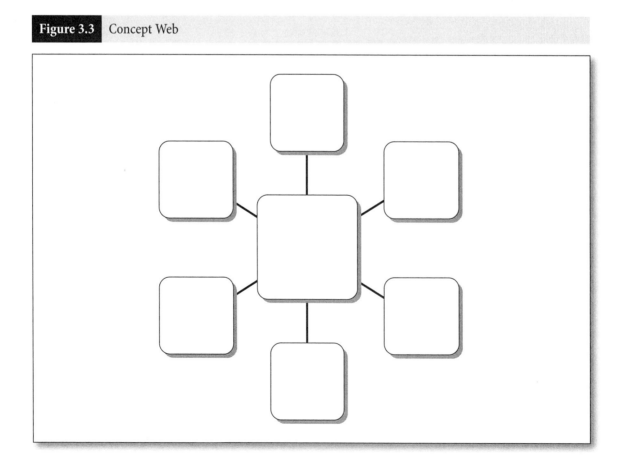

organizers identified above to partially list information and have students complete the organizer on their own or in pairs. Students can then refer to what was written and use these organized notes to better understand the topic and participate in the class lesson.

Scaffolded Speech. Teachers who teach on purpose can spontaneously break down complex sentences and vocabulary being introduced by the lead teacher. This help can be accomplished when the support teacher repeats the same information but paraphrases—reduces the complexity of the spoken words—or explains the meaning of new vocabulary in context. In this way, students are exposed to rigorous academic language, yet their understanding is well supported.

Increased Wait Time. At appropriate intervals, the support teacher might signal to the lead teacher the need for students to stop and process certain information. For this reason, either the lead or the support teacher might pose a question for students to consider and ask students to engage in a *Turn-and-Talk*—inviting students to share their ideas with a partner before a response is presented to the whole class. A variation of the strategy *Stop-and-Jot* asks students to write down their ideas, share them with a partner, and then answers are shared with the larger group of students.

Pro-Prep Strategies for Model 1

These strategies can be jointly planned or individually developed by the person teaching on purpose. However, knowledge of the lesson content to be taught and coordination between the teachers are key. The following are strategies that can help increase the comprehension of ELs and work well with this model configuration.

Partially Completed Graphic Organizers. ELs at lower levels of language proficiency are better able to organize information from content-area lessons using partially completed charts and graphic organizers. Teachers teaching on purpose use various organizers that are completed in some measure to provide ELs with a lesson's main ideas and challenge students to recall the details, or identify the details and ask students to determine the main ideas. In this way, students are engaged with the use of academic language and enhance their comprehension of the subject at hand. Figure 3.4 is an example of a Series-of-Events Chart in which some of the information is missing from the order of statements.

Realia. The use of real objects or replicas of real objects can help some students connect with lesson content. Realia is most often used in the lower-grade classes of elementary schools, but it can be just as effective in the upper grades when teaching English learners with beginner or intermediate levels of language proficiency.

Manipulatives. Especially useful during a math lesson, manipulatives can be used to clarify information that the lead teacher is introducing, modeling, or demonstrating. Working with an individual student or with small groups, the support teacher can parallel what the lead teacher is presenting but use manipulatives as an alternative strategy to enhance student understanding.

| Figure 3.4 | Partially Completed Series-of-Events Chart |

Series-of-Events Chart
Topic: The Launching of Sputnik I

Event 1
The Soviet Union launched_____, an artificial satellite, on October 4, 1957.

Event 2
Sputnik I was a technological accomplishment that captured the world's attention and marked the beginning of the_____ race between the _____ and the
_____.

Event 3
Since the Soviets had the capability to launch satellites, it was believed that they also had the technology to launch _____

_____.

Event 4
Shortly after the Soviets launched their first satellite, the United States responded by _____
_____.

Event 5
The success of the Sputnik launch also sparked the formation of the U.S. government agency known as
_____ in July 1958.

Source: http://history.nasa.gov/sputnik/

| Figure 3.5 | One-Pager: A Timeline of the Great Depression |

Date	Great Depression Event
October 1929	The American stock market collapses, marking the beginning of the Great Depression.
June 1930	Congress passes the Smoot-Hawley Tariff, sharply increasing import taxes in an effort to shield American manufacturers from foreign competitors. The tariff sends Europe into a deepening economic crisis.
December 1931	A major bank, New York's Bank of the United States, fails—the largest bank failure to date in American history—losing $200 million in deposits.
November 1932	Democrat Franklin D. Roosevelt is elected to the presidency in a landslide win against the Republican incumbent, Herbert Hoover.
December 1932	Unemployment averages 24.1% for the year.

One-Pager. This strategy offers students an overview of the main idea and details from the contents of the lesson. The information contained in a one-pager is often derived from the text that students will eventually read. As the lead teacher conducts a minilecture concerning new content information, the one-pager becomes a basic guide to whatever is being shared. The teacher in a supportive role might sit with a group of students and highlight the information on the one-pager—clarifying vocabulary and concepts—as it is being discussed by the lead teacher. Figure 3.5 is an example of a one-pager in the form of a timeline.

SAMPLE LESSONS: ONE GROUP: ONE LEAD TEACHER, ONE "TEACHING ON PURPOSE"

The following lesson segments portray co-teachers as they use the teach on purpose model to support the learning of ELs as they conduct co-taught lessons.

Teaching About Fractions in an Elementary School

In a third-grade class, Mr. Ali, the classroom teacher, and Ms. Boldova, the English to speakers of other languages (ESOL) teacher, begin a lesson on fractions with Mr. Ali leading the lesson in front of the class. After writing a problem on the board, he says, "Let's get our brains thinking about fractions; would the answer ever be four to this problem?" In the meantime, Ms. Boldova is at the board on the side of the room preparing a series of sentence frames to support students' oral responses:

Is it _____?

Yes, it is _____ because it is divided into equal parts.

No, it's not _____ because it is not divided into equal parts.

After a few students answer his initial question, Mr. Ali reads the content lesson objective and reviews its meaning. Ms. Boldova shifts to the back of the room; she clarifies a vocabulary word in the content objective just read, then proceeds to read the language objective to the class. Mr. Ali reminds students, "You are all responsible for your own learning."

Mr. Ali displays a problem on the interactive electronic board and reads it aloud. He underlines key words in the problem. Ms. Boldova focuses on one of the underlined words, *equal*, and shares some synonyms for the word with the class (same, alike). Mr. Ali demonstrates how students can solve the problem with an Understand and Plan strategy as follows:

Understand	Plan
Pedro ate 1/4 Andrew ate 1/3 Who ate more?	I will draw fraction bars to help me compare

Ms. Boldova circulates within the classroom and checks students' understanding of the strategy. She then sits with a small group of students and models how to draw fraction bars on a hand-held whiteboard:

Solve			Check
1/3	1/3	1/3	I know that _____ is greater than _____.
1/4 1/4	1/4	1/4	I know that _____ is less than _____.

The new sentence frames she provides help ELs better participate in a turn and talk with a partner in which Mr. Ali invites all students to participate to discuss and check their understanding of the Understand and Plan strategy and the Solve and Check process.

An analysis of the lesson segment. In order to establish parity, this team of teachers has set both an established teaching routine and instructional roles. In the lead teaching position, Mr. Ali is responsible for the opening review activity. He reads and explains the content objective, introduces the new content, and models and demonstrates what students need to know and do. In the teaching on purpose role, Ms. Boldova focuses a great deal on academic language and vocabulary. She supports the lead teacher's instruction with written sentence frames, reads and explains the language objective, clarifies challenging vocabulary, and circulates within the room to check students' understanding. Working with a small group, she further models the strategy introduced by the lead teacher. This lesson segment fully illustrates how a teacher in a supporting role does not just drift around the classroom but makes full use of her varied talents, teaching skills, and best practices for assisting ELs.

Exploring Elements of Plot in a Ninth-Grade English Language Arts Class

In this lesson, students explore the literary elements of plot structure by examining the events of familiar stories. The lesson commences with the ESL teacher, Ms. Delfino, asking the class to visualize a typical Monday morning in their high school and inviting students to do an independent quick-write activity on the topic, and then turn and talk with a partner to share their common experiences. Meanwhile, Ms. Echavez, the English teacher, is setting up an easel with chart paper for a quick group writing activity. Ms. Delfino elicits from the class their thoughts about what they just shared, and Ms. Echavez notes them in story form on the chart. The lesson continues with Ms. Delfino's questions shaping the story line until a short story emerges. After the writing task is complete, the ESL and English teachers change roles.

Now, Ms. Echavez leads the lesson by introducing Freytag's Pyramid, a tool for mapping plot structure, via a short PowerPoint presentation and conducts a brief discussion on the plot structure of a novel the class just read. Ms. Delfino supports students' understanding of the major elements of plot by distributing a two-column notes graphic organizer to each student and assisting them in its completion. Some of the organizers she distributes are blank, while others are partially completed (see Figure 3.6).

Ms. Echavez directs students to review the group story writing with partners and identify the different elements of plot contained in the story. Both teachers circulate within the room as

| Figure 3.6 | Partially Completed Two-Column Notes: Elements of Plot |

Two-Column Notes	
Topic: *Elements of Plot*	
Main Idea	**Definition/Details**
Exposition	
Rising Action	
Climax	
Falling Action	
Resolution	

students work to check their understanding. When time is called, Ms. Delfino selects a few student pairs to report their findings.

Subsequently, Ms. Echavez explains they will now receive multiple short synopses of story lines from popular novels and films. In pairs or quads, students are to read and discuss each story plot and determine which elements are evident using Freytag's Pyramid. For this part of the lesson, Ms. Delfino focuses on accommodating a group of English learners, whereas Ms. Echavez circulates within the entire class to assist individual students.

An analysis of the lesson segment. It is often suggested that an ESL teacher in a co-taught situation is unable to take the lead in the content-area class, particularly in secondary education because he or she often lacks certification or expertise in the subject matter. In this lesson, we find the ESL teacher taking the lead with a generic task that requires language but not content expertise. Switching between the lead and supporting roles helps this set of teachers maintain equal status in the class. This status is further established when the ESL teacher not only takes responsibility for the ELs but also facilitates the learning of all students.

MODEL VARIATIONS

From our research and work in the field, we have noted several variations on the teach on purpose model. The following are three different ways in which pairs of teachers have used the supportive role creatively and purposefully while successfully maintaining equity.

Two Lead, Two Teach on Purpose

With this adaptation, the two teachers lead the lesson in front of the whole class of students, and at strategic junctures, they both circulate within the class to facilitate students' understanding. For example, we have observed a co-teaching team in a high school algebra class working together in front of an interactive whiteboard to review word problems for content and critical language.

A short while later, they assign the class similar word problems to solve, and each teacher circulates within the room to assist students.

Tag-Team Teach on Purpose

In this variation, each teacher alternates taking the lead and supporting roles. Co-teaching partners might use this configuration when analyzing certain aspects of a text or problem solving with each teacher examining different learning points. For example, with a shared reading of a social studies text, one teacher might focus on the overall factual information while the other assists students with a structured note-taking task. Then, the teachers reverse roles. Now the teacher taking the lead is analyzing different aspects of academic language and grammar, pointing out words that signal compare and contrast, and so on, while the other teacher is circulating within the room checking on students' work, clarifying information, and offering immediate intervention or assistance.

"Tech on Purpose"

You read it correctly; it is not a typo. Tech on purpose is teach on purpose with a technology spin. This modification may be used in classrooms with one-to-one device initiatives where the entire class is working on tablets or laptops and one teacher's main focus is offering the much-needed tech support to follow along or to use the device appropriately for the task at hand. We have also seen this variation with a single iPad in the teacher's hand, who uses her device to pull up supplementary information such as illustrations, visuals, maps, and other resources available at her fingertips to enhance student understanding.

Two Lead, One Teaches on Purpose as Needed

This modification suggests both teachers begin the lesson together in front of the entire class but also affords one of the teachers the flexibility to move out of the joint lead position to a supporting role when necessary. For example, two teachers introduce a writing lesson at an interactive whiteboard to model and demonstrate the thinking behind a writing task. One teacher thinks aloud while the other one asks clarifying questions and notes conclusions on the board. When the teacher who is writing pauses to emphasize a certain thinking point, the other teacher looks for students who may not fully understand and goes directly to assist them. She then returns and continues the joint demonstration of the writing task. The teacher who is teaching on purpose moves in and out of the joint lead role as many times as needed.

MODEL COMBINATIONS

Model 1 (One Group: One Lead Teacher, One Teaching on Purpose) may be successfully combined with several other models. It is frequently utilized as a complementary approach to Model 3 (One Group: One Teaches, One Assesses). While conducting formative assessment, one teacher may offer immediate support to students who need it. Targeted intervention is necessary for many subgroups of ELs and progress monitoring is essential for all learners, so combining Models 1 and 3 allow for both of these tasks to be completed.

Model 1 may also be an effective companion to Model 5 (Two Groups: One Teacher Preteaches, One Teaches Alternative Information) or Model 6 (Two Groups: One Teacher Reteaches, One Teaches Alternative Information). Teaching on purpose is similar to the type of small-group intervention that takes place during Models 5 and 6. The biggest difference is whether teachers plan for whole-group instruction or a grouping strategy that offers immediate support for targeted students.

Once the preteaching or reteaching activity has been completed as part of Model 5 or 6, and it has been established that select students need further opportunities to practice the target skill, Model 1 (One Group: One Lead Teacher, One Teaching on Purpose) may be utilized to accomplish that goal while the other teacher leads a learning activity with the whole class.

INSPIRATION FROM THE FIELD

Read what colleagues—ELD/ELL specialists and classroom teachers as well as building and district administrators shared with us from around the United States. We have found them inspirational and affirming. See how they reflect your own experiences or add to your understanding.

See how Elena Dokshansky first experienced co-teaching in the following vignette. Please note that being an assistant or tutor is not what we advocate for in this chapter. Yet these experiences are often shared by teachers we work with. Notice how her co-teaching practice has evolved and been enhanced through technology use.

It is currently my 13th year teaching ESL. By this time, I have had an experience collaborating with different content area and ESL teachers in integrated and stand-alone settings. Even though my initial pull-out teaching experience was successful, my first year push-in experience was challenging. I was assigned to co-teach with a classroom veteran teacher who gladly shared with me her excitement of having another pair of hands in the classroom and gave me a list of "co-teaching" tasks for the day. They included catching up with a student who was absent by working with him in the back of the room, monitoring students while the classroom teacher would be giving whole-class instruction, and melting chocolate for a project. Clearly, my initial excitement and ideas of collaboration did not match the reality of the specific setting. At that moment, I thought that I could do more than assisting, tutoring, and melting chocolate.

Twelve years passed by, and my co-teaching experience has been forming and developing during that time. I realized that many teachers were interested in co-planning, co-teaching, and co-assessing, while others were not prepared or willing to be partners in a classroom. Moreover, regular common planning time, prior training in co-teaching, and constant support were not always offered. In a course of time, I learned to offer my expertise as a language instructor to collaborate with content-area teachers, seek advice from experts in the field, find creative ways for common planning time, utilize technology to facilitate communication, and use expertise of IT coaches and library media specialists to enhance collaboration. As a result, a number of collaborative efforts were successful!

As an ESL teacher, I have had the privilege of being a part of co-developing content-based, technology-infused differentiated projects with my grade-level colleagues. In addition, we have been fortunate to have a technology coach as a part of our collaborative team. As a first step, we met to outline and discuss our projects, determine co-teaching models, and set specific content and language objectives. We designated roles and decided on strategic groupings based on preassessment. As common planning time was not a part of our schedule, we had a working lunch for the first meeting. After the initial meeting, we have maintained our co-planning via technology. To facilitate our communication, we have utilized Schoology, a learning management system that allowed us to develop, post, and share resources for our students. During instruction, we observed and took notes on our respective small-group progress, and discussed activities, modifications, and regroupings as necessary. Finally, we shared small-group assessment results to determine next steps.

Clearly, my co-teaching experience has evolved over the past twelve years and shifted from melting chocolate as an assistant to being an equal partner in a co-taught classroom. Together, as a team of language and content-area experts, we can provide our students with effective co-planning, co-teaching, and co-assessing by utilizing our professional knowledge within our areas of expertise!

Kelley Cordeiro, kindergarten-first grade ESOL teacher in the Farmingdale School District, New York, reports positive outcomes with this model.

My first-grade co-teacher and I have used Model 1 with great success, particularly during math instruction, which is often embedded in lengthy word problems and challenging academic vocabulary. The general-education teacher acts as lead teacher, providing whole-group instruction on the mathematics concept being taught. Much of this instruction includes extensive visuals presented on the SMART Board. Working with a heterogeneous group of three to six students comprised of emerging and transitioning English language learners (ELLs) as well as non-ELLs, I select various points during the lesson to facilitate the equivalent of a "turn and talk." I direct the students when to "turn in," at which time their focus leaves the whole group and engages them in a smaller conversation in which we recap what was just presented. I extend the instruction by adapting some of the language used and providing expanded explanations and examples. Students are then asked to restate information in their own words and, when appropriate, demonstrate and apply the concepts using manipulatives and visual supports. The math skills of the ELLs in this group exceed their language skills, so this is a valuable opportunity for them to reinforce their own skills by providing peer support to the non-ELLs in the group, whose math skills may be weaker. This affords me several checkpoints throughout the lesson to monitor and assess students' ongoing comprehension (thus connect to Model 3), provide needed clarification and rewording, and additional instruction as needed. It also informs my conversations with the general-education teacher following the lesson, in discussing student understanding and progress, as well as planning future lessons.

Read the reflection on a recent lesson written by Mrs. Darcie LoGiudice and her co-teacher, Ms. Allyse Gulotta, elementary ESOL teacher in PS 186, Brooklyn, New York. They share how they use Model 1 in combination with several other models such as Model 2 (Two Teachers Teach the Whole Class) and Models 6 (One Teaches, One Reteaches) and 7 (Two Teachers Teach Multiple Groups).

We began our lesson using Model 6. As a co-teaching team, we believe that in order to maximize instruction, all children on all academic and language levels should experience productive struggle. Therefore, rather than starting our class with whole-group instruction, we decided to begin by splitting the class into two groups: an above-level reading group and a group for ELLs and on-level reading groups. Mrs. LoGiudice began by working in front of the classroom with the above-level reading group. Here, a minilesson was conducted focusing on the important parts of a summary. Students were then instructed to read a selected above-level text and write a summary. At the same time, Ms. Gulotta began by working in back of the classroom with the ELLs and on-level reading groups. Here, a minilesson was conducted focusing on reviewing the R.A.C.E. reading strategy in order to aid students in our later activities. An anchor chart, visuals, and question prompts were used in order to further support the academic and language needs of these children. After Mrs. LoGiudice assured that her group was on pace, she joined Ms. Gulotta's group and we continued with Model 2 (One Group: Two Teach the Same Content).

Our reading focus was using the R.A.C.E. strategy in order to ask and answer reading comprehension questions. First, both teachers reviewed the R.A.C.E. reading strategy with the ELLs and non-ELLs who needed extra support. We used various scaffolds including anchor charts, visual supports, an excerpt from the text The Goat in the Rug *(Blood & Link, 1990) a turn-and-talk visual with verbal cues, TPR, and realia. While students were involved in interactive partner discussions, both teachers aided students in asking and answering questions with their turn-and-talk partners. Students were then invited to share their partner's response by using our R.A.C.E. strategy.*

Children who needed extra support, both ELLs and non-ELLs, were invited to our meeting area. As a collaborative team, we took turns reading an excerpt from the short story The Goat in the Rug. *This story was displayed on an easel in front of our meeting area with surrounding visuals. During the reading, we used Model 1 and took turns using TPR and realia to aid students in visualizing the setting and events in our story. The realia we used included a rug, a rock, and an empty window frame. Following, Mrs. LoGiudice proposed the question, "Why does the author call this place Window Rock?" In order to aid students in visualizing "Window Rock," we placed the empty window frame around us while holding the rock beside us. Students were instructed to turn-and-talk using a verbal cue card and the realia as support. Students were reminded to use our R.A.C.E. reading strategy while responding to the question. As Mrs. LoGiudice elicited students' responses, Ms. Gulotta charted students' answers on a previously created chart, also displayed in front of our meeting area.*

Following co-teaching instruction, we shifted to Model 7 and students were broken into groups based on their academic and language levels. Mrs. LoGiudice worked with her below-level reading group on guided reading. Together, they focused on fluency and expression while answering questions using text evidence. Ms. Gulotta worked in a smaller group with the Entering, Emerging, Transitioning, and Expanding English Language Learners. Ms. Gulotta's group revisited a section of the text, The Goat in the Rug, *in order to ask and answer questions for clarification using academic vocabulary and complete sentences. Students were provided with differentiated handouts according to their language levels. Furthermore, visual supports*

Restate the question

Answer the question

Cite evidence from the text

Explain the evidence

were distributed to the Commanding English Language Learners as they worked independently. At the culmination of all group work, students were encouraged to share their responses with the class. The ELLs were provided with sentence starters and visual aids to guide them while participating in the shared discussion.

Lisa Spaulding, secondary social studies teacher from Lafayette High School, Buffalo, New York, shared with us her take on collaborating with her co-teacher Gregory Conley, certified in K–12 ESOL and 7–12 social studies, and using an adapted version of teaching on purpose.

I always have thought that two heads are better than one. I like to talk with people and discuss new ideas and then adapt them to the classroom. My co-teacher and I have a common goal of achieving success with our students. Each small and large task is informally assessed as to its success. We discuss our observations and think of ways to improve things. There are no huge egos in our class. Our teaching is like a dance where sometimes I am the lead partner or he is. We both like a highly structured classroom. I talk with my co-teacher to establish routines for the processes he will teach. We provide a visual to assist students with the procedure and we practice procedures regularly.

One routine that really works for us is mindspark. We do a mindspark every morning, which is a question about the previous day's work. I have been doing this process for a while but thought it was not engaging enough for ELs. Greg added a table with who, what, where, etc. questions that used vocabulary we had taught the day before. This new process, which has improved greatly with my co-teacher's input, allows students to formulate answers with their knowledge of new vocabulary. We both walk around the room urging students to place vocabulary into boxes and formulate answers. We follow a protocol of annotating the question, starting the answer, filling in the boxes, and then as a class formulating a complete answer.

VIDEO 3.2:

Co-Teaching
Reflections:
Amy and
Danielle

http://resources
.corwin.com/
CoTeachingforELs

TAKEAWAYS

In this chapter, we have explored a commonly used co-teaching model—along with its variations and possible extensions—in which one teacher leads instruction for the entire class while the other is offering immediate interventions or teaching on purpose based on a predetermined learning target. While we sometimes dub this model as being the most dangerous choice, it has a clear place among all the models co-teachers may select. The danger lies in one teacher taking on the role of an assistant; to avoid this pitfall, co-teachers must ensure a clear focus and purpose for the teacher who is in the supportive role and use this model interchangeably.

QUESTIONS FOR FURTHER DISCUSSION

1. What would you consider to be the most difficult challenge to overcome when using the teaching on purpose model for instructing English learners?

2. Using this model, how do you best prevent students from being singled out as the ones that always seem to be needing help?

3. What are the best ways to avoid finding yourself (or positioning your co-teacher) in the supporting role too often?

4. What are some additional strategies—both low prep and pro prep—that might be used successfully with this model?

Model 2—One Group

Two Teach the Same Content

AN INTRODUCTION TO THE MODEL

We often ask teachers what they might do if they had two teachers in front of the whole class instructing students. Imagine just one teacher modeling a dialogue, a difference in opinion, or an academic argument! The opportunity to have two teachers working elbow-to-elbow can be an enormous advantage for English learners (ELs). With this class arrangement, both teachers engage the entire class: They may remain in front of the whole class to deliver instruction or, alternately, may occupy different places in the classroom. In either context, each teacher often has different roles and responsibilities to support student learning.

Marilyn Friend (2014) has described this model of instruction as "one brain in two bodies" (p. 19), and others have referred to it as *team-teaching* (Villa, Thousand, & Nevin, 2008, 2013). To introduce a lesson, consider how one teacher might begin by sharing information about a topic while her co-teacher clarifies information by emphasizing key vocabulary through the use of various visual representations, charts, manipulatives, and other realia. One teacher might identify and demonstrate the use of a skill or strategy guided by a PowerPoint presentation while the other teacher supports students' understanding by giving them an example of how to apply the skill or strategy. One teacher may use high levels of academic language while the other scaffolds the language verbally so all students can better understand. This model of instruction works well when introducing a lesson or recapping a lesson at the end of a class period. It is also a powerful way to establish equity between co-teachers since both of them are perceived to be in a leading role.

From observing this co-teaching model in K–12 classrooms, we have noted how teachers often position themselves in full view of the class on different sides of a board or standing chart. Each teacher allows the other his or her own personal space, and as a team, they are careful to share the space and even occasionally exchange their positions in front of the class. In this way, both teachers have access to all the students.

At times, teachers who are not proficient in the class content are reluctant to co-teach using this model for instruction. This reluctance particularly seems to manifest when a novice English language development/ English language learner (ELD/ELL) teacher is asked to work alongside a veteran core content instructor at the secondary level. We agree that this task may seem daunting, yet we strongly believe that this model needs to be a part of the repertoire of any co-teaching team. As a veteran co-teacher, Wendi Pillars (2015) reminds us of the following:

> Each of you brings a lot to the table . . . I've co-taught with first year teachers and thirty-year veterans—in all subject areas and ages, from elementary through high school . . . It's critical for students to see co-teachers as collaborative partners . . . Share the lesson load, and know that even though they may not be the "teacher of record," they shoulder equal responsibility. (para. 5)

A CLOSER LOOK AT MODEL 2

In order to examine this model in detail, let us first consider what a teaching team requires to lead a lesson together. First, both teachers need to know their roles in the co-taught lesson from the onset. Although this may be true with every way a class is configured for co-taught instruction, it is particularly significant when both teachers are leading the lesson. For instance, there must be some ground rules for who will introduce students to the lesson's learning objectives, guide them to complete an opening activity, give students directions for the materials they will need, be responsible for working the interactive whiteboard, be in charge of releasing and retrieving students from a partner discussion, and so on. Often enough, the ELD/ELL teacher will concede many of these tasks to the core instructor. However, we caution about relinquishing too much responsibility to the grade-level/content teacher in that the students might perceive it as a lack of balance in power, relegating one teacher as the "helper" teacher and the other as the "real" teacher.

With this model, it is more important than ever before that both teachers leave their egos at the classroom door. In order to lead instruction together, there is no room for one person upstaging the other. Most important, students should be able to notice the mutual respect between the two teachers concerning their area of expertise, how both teachers negotiate any changes about lesson content, procedures, resources, assessments, and so on, and that both teachers are able to resolve any difficulty in a commonly beneficial way, remaining flexible, polite, and professional. We do not suggest here that each teacher relinquish his or her individuality; on the contrary, different teaching styles, abilities, humor, energy levels, personal preferences, and so on can all be valuable assets in this co-teaching arrangement.

When two teachers lead a lesson, it is akin to a well-choreographed dance. At times, it may appear as if co-teachers are involved in some form of tag-team teaching—a type of turn-taking that may occur particularly with novice instructors or if the nature of the target content requires it. Although teachers must take turns when speaking, demonstrating, and modeling instruction, the idea of rotating the lead between the two teachers is really counter to the power of this model. To capitalize on individual strengths and experiences as well as the lesson objectives, co-teachers may divide the lesson so that one teacher is responsible for a particular part of a lesson more than the other, but the key with this model is still to simultaneously deliver lessons (Villa et al., 2008).

One technique that co-teachers use to communicate with one another during a lesson is a set of hand and facial gestures. These quiet signals help keep the flow of the lesson with the least amount of interruption. Although it is perfectly fine for co-teachers to verbally negotiate in front of students any details or alterations to the lesson at hand, co-teachers have reported that their students are more apt to begin chatting and lose focus when the co-teachers practice on-the-spot collaboration during a class session.

One misconception we would like to clear up is that the content dominates the instruction in the co-taught class. In fact, content and language instruction are intertwined and inseparable: We cannot teach content without language, nor can we teach language skills without integrating them with grade-appropriate content. ELD/ELL teachers must serve as effective advocates for English learners since "they do not always possess a strong voice in their own education due to many factors that may work against them such as their developing English language skills" (Fenner, 2014, p. 1), and if co-teaching is the chosen technique for the instruction of ELs, it must follow that these students will receive the necessary language instruction they deserve while grade-appropriate content is delivered. Therefore, co-planning for effective lessons using this model is essential.

A class routine helps to build a secure foundation for the use of this model. From our research, we have often observed co-teachers beginning a class lesson with this configuration as well as ending a class lesson with the ELD/ELL teacher remaining front and center right beside her core-teacher counterpart to recap the lesson. Yet the use of this model is not always feasible to start or end every lesson. It often depends on the learning targets set as well as time factors.

Co-teachers who have reported that they spend a short period of time—35 minutes or less—in the co-taught class have identified the difficulties of using this model to begin or end a lesson. Due to the lack of time, they frequently make the most of co-taught instruction by grouping students for learning immediately when the co-teacher enters the room. This routine grouping often facilitates small-group targeted instruction and allows for greater contact time between students and teacher.

VIDEO 4.1:

Model 2—One
Group: Two
Teach the
Same Content

http://resources
.corwin.com/
CoTeachingforELs

Yet these same teachers also recognize the value of this model when teaching a topic such as opinion or argument writing in which there is a compelling need to model, demonstrate, and apply specific strategies in the writing process.

When the class remains as one group with two teachers leading, each teacher must be intentional about what they say and do in order to support all of the students, and for this reason, they should each have the opportunity to share their abilities, knowledge, and skills. Because of this, we are frequently asked what this co-teaching model resembles in action. Table 4.1 illustrates the ways in which two teachers may teach the same content to the whole class and well support the language acquisition and literacy development of ELs. Remember to add your own strategies and see this summary chart as a beginning, and not the end, of possibilities.

ADVANTAGES

When an ELD/ELL and core content teacher stand side by side to deliver instruction to a whole class, there are greater opportunities for modeling and/or demonstration of new strategies, skills, and ways to apply new information. For example, we have observed in a high school math class

Table 4.1 Roles and Responsibilities of Both Teachers Leading a Whole Class

When one teacher . . .	The other teacher . . .
Explains the lesson objective or reviews the learning targets	Models or demonstrates what students need to know and do
Introduces new information on an interactive whiteboard	Scaffolds the information verbally and creates a written outline on chart paper
Describes a strategy or skill (e.g., how to annotate a text)	Gives students examples via a document camera
Focuses on sharing content vocabulary	Notes the vocabulary, provides synonyms, and uses visuals to clarify
Reads aloud	Thinks aloud
Models spoken language by initiating an academic conversation with co-teacher	Responds to co-teacher and engages in a dialogue
Asks students questions	Invites students to turn and talk to a partner
Presents one perspective on the topic	Presents another perspective on the topic
Models a strategy or task by showing what students are supposed to be doing	Explains or verbally annotates the modeling done by the other teacher
Presents an argument	Presents a counterargument while modeling how to examine a complex issue
Elicits student input	Jots down student ideas on chart paper

how one teacher demonstrated one solution to a two-step algebraic equation using the class interactive whiteboard while the other teacher explained and illustrated a set of alternative steps in the solution process using chart paper. Sharing alternative thinking processes can appeal to the different learning needs of students as well as build their confidence and allow older students increased autonomy in deciding how to problem solve.

This class configuration also can provide students with immediate reinforcement and remediation by having both teachers intermittently check for understanding. Ferlazzo (2012) suggests,

> When teachers regularly check for understanding in the classroom, students become increasingly aware of monitoring their own understanding, which serves as a model of good study skills. It also helps ensure that students are learning, thinking, understanding, comprehending, and processing at high levels. (para. 11)

With two teachers in front of a group of students, there are ample circumstances to check the knowledge and perceptions of ELs as the lesson progresses as well as leverage opportunities to clarify information. According to John Hattie (2009), teacher clarity—one's ability to explain information in an organized way, offer students exemplary models, and guide students in practice and application of their learning—is one of the top ten influences affecting student achievement. In line with Hattie's work, the power of co-teaching is most often how the co-taught learning environment provides for the implementation of the most effective, research-informed teaching practices.

This model also allows for collegial observation, a way for teaching teams to explore their individual as well as joint teaching practices. These observations incorporate before-and-after conversations about planning, implementation, and evaluation of student learning as well as how a specific language focus is targeted in the core content in order to reshape practice (Gray, 2012). However, in the co-taught situation where both teachers are addressing the whole class, an equitable playing field is established for both teachers to observe one another, and the takeaways that can transform practice are guided by the perceptions of the teaching team—how the teachers worked together and incorporated their individual roles and responsibilities within the co-taught lesson.

When well planned and executed, this model is a most effective means of co-delivering instruction to an entire class. It establishes both equity and parity for teachers as well as students. This model sets the stage for co-teaching pairs to share the power and authority in the co-taught class. Having both teachers front and center delivering instruction together, well establishes an equitable partnership making each of them integral to favorable academic outcomes. With the necessary supports and resources to be successful, co-taught classes for the sake of ELs using this class configuration can provide access to the core curriculum while developing students' English language skills

CHALLENGES

Recognizing that the success of this model is dependent on the frequency and commitment of teaching teams to find time to collaborate, we must contend that lack of time is probably the greatest challenge for the successful implementation of this model for instruction. Yet Fullan (2007)

recognizes that "significant educational change consists of changes in beliefs, teaching style, and materials, which can come *only* through a process of personal development in a social context" (pp. 138–139). In other words, without the time to plan together and develop a shared understanding of this class configuration, co-teachers may not be fully able to engage a whole class for co-taught instruction in this manner.

Much organization and orchestration with this co-teaching model needs to occur. Who says and does what? Where will each teacher stand? Who controls the interactive whiteboard or the progression of the presentation slides? Who is responsible for calling on students when their hands are raised? Who will set the pacing for the lesson? Who will monitor student participation and assess student output? Ideally, both teachers will become comfortable with taking turns where they stand, sharing the control of the classroom technology, answering students' questions, and so on. As educators become more aware and trusting of the talents their partners possess, the commitment to this practice over time will unfold the positive aspects of this teaching model.

There is no getting around the need for time to fully develop the effortless flow that teaching teams require to achieve continuity with this model of instruction. We have observed teaching teams who seamlessly incorporate this model of instruction into their co-teaching repertoire, and the following is what we have observed:

- Core teachers are not territorial about their classroom space.
- When one is speaking, the other waits for opportunities to clarify information and further support what has just been presented.
- Teaching teams freely share their own materials and resources, or
- During the lesson, they frequently and quietly check with one another to make sure the lesson is heading in the appropriate direction.
- Both teachers are flexible as each allows his or her partner to run with an idea devised on the spot if a teachable moment arises.
- Both teaching partners are comfortable teaching both the content as well as the language aspects of the lesson, although they may not be "experts" in the field.

For a growing number of co-teaching teams for ELs, it may be challenging to consider how an ELD/ELL teacher might fare in a core content class such as secondary geometry, biology, or American history when they have not had the training to teach such subjects. Even in today's elementary school classes, where literacy and mathematics education is so vastly different from yesteryear, the content might be perceived as a considerable obstacle for some. However, the ELD/ELL teacher need not be the content expert in the class: the core teacher already is. The ELD/ELL teacher will demonstrate his or her expertise by helping ELs acquire discipline-specific language and literacy skills, breaking down complex content by applying multidimensional mediation strategies (see Chapter 2).

And then there is magic: It occurs in a co-teaching partnership over time when each teacher acquires the other's content and pedagogical skills. Co-teaching may well be one of the most effective ongoing, job-embedded professional learning opportunities in which both teachers expand their expertise beyond what they had prior to their partnership.

But what are the ELD/ELL and core teacher to do when not much time has passed and they really do not know each other's content? One key piece of advice we can offer is to start reading, sharing, and participating in the lesson. First, the ELD/ELL teacher may need to review core subject material by staying one chapter ahead of the students in the text. In turn, the core teacher will develop an understanding of language acquisition and the necessary "tools of the trade" to assist ELs in developing language proficiency and literacy skills in English. Second, in class, the ELD/ELL teacher might play the role of devil's advocate—asking the core teacher questions to clarify the content, and vice versa, with the core teacher asking questions to the ELD/ELL teacher about different aspects of the language involved. Asking questions is one of the best ways to have material repeated for your English learners, and both teachers receive further explanation of the language and content aspects of the lesson.

The conditions needed for teaching using this model do not always work for all teams. The amount of compromise as well as the ability to give up a certain amount of control may not be feasible for all co-teachers. This model requires team partners to strike a delicate balance between teaching both language and content, and strong personalities may not always see eye-to-eye on what needs to be accomplished when teaching English learners in the co-taught class. Table 4.2 outlines both the advantages and challenges of Model 2.

Table 4.2 Summary of Advantages and Challenges of Model 2

Model 2: Two Teachers Teach the Same Content	
Advantages	**Challenges**
There are greater opportunities for modeling and/or demonstration of new strategies, skills, and ways to apply new information.	The lack of time is probably the greatest challenge for the successful implementation of this model.
Sharing alternative thinking processes can appeal to the different learning needs of students.	Much organization and orchestration need to occur with this model.
This class configuration also can provide students with immediate reinforcement and remediation.	Teaching teams must fully plan to develop the effortless flow that teaching teams require to achieve continuity of instruction.
There are ample opportunities to check the knowledge and perceptions of ELs.	An ELD/ELL teacher might be overwhelmed when co-teaching in a core content area where they lack expertise.
It allows for collegial observation, a way for teaching teams to explore their individual as well as joint teaching practices.	Without a shared understanding of this class configuration, co-teachers may not be fully able to engage a whole class for co-taught instruction in this manner.
It establishes both equity and parity for teachers as well as students.	The conditions needed for teaching using this model do not always work for all teams.

Adapted from Honigsfeld, A., & Dove, M. G. (2010). *Collaboration and co-teaching: Strategies for English learners.* Thousand Oaks, CA: Corwin.

INSTRUCTION USING MODEL 2

The goals for this co-teaching model are to design instructional activities that meet the needs of all students, even when they remain as one group, and ensure access to the core curriculum for ELs. Villa et al. (2008) liken this model to a dance, "similar to a tango; it is complex, sophisticated, and intimate" (p. 64). We also equate this model to a dance; however, we note how novice partners might be taking very different steps and moves than the more experienced dance artists.

With those teams who are just beginning their co-teaching journey together, their dance—their roles and responsibilities—is carefully delineated and observable; they often take turns during the lesson to ensure equity for the partnership and at times may be a bit unsure of the steps they take. However, the experienced co-teaching team is seamless, smooth, and ostensibly effortless in its use of this model; their dance resembles partners who have nearly perfect rhythm. Whether teams are experienced or novice, each set of partners can select the appropriate strategies to enhance the use of this model for the instruction of all students.

Low-Prep Strategies for Model 2

Strategies that take little or no preparation work well when this model is used as part of a co-teaching routine. Stephanie Harvey and Anne Goudvis (2013) have reminded us that

> as teachers, we can flood the room with engaging texts, we can share interesting ideas, we can model our own curiosity, we can foster thoughtful conversations. Only they can turn what they hear, see, read, and talk about into knowledge by thinking deeply and expansively. (p. 433)

We would also expand on Harvey and Goudvis's (2013) observation and remind you to have students engage in deep thinking as well as speaking and writing about the topic. The following strategies take advantage of having two teachers in front of the class to model the use of academic language, critical thinking skills, academic curiosity and thoughtful conversations, and writing techniques as well as to clarify information.

Think Aloud is a technique co-teaching partners use to demonstrate critical thinking skills about a text using a shared reading. It can help students to determine unfamiliar words, better understand core concepts, review sentence structures, and learn specific reading strategies to aid comprehension. The following describes the steps in the think-loud process with co-teachers:

- Select a short piece of text to be read aloud; if possible, project the text on a screen using projection camera or interactive whiteboard.
- Have one teacher read the text; pause at intervals to explore particular aspects of the text—vocabulary, core content, sentence structure, and so forth.
- With each pause, the other teacher models his or her thinking about the meaning of targeted words, various text connections, pertinent predictions, the unusual way words are strung together to express ideas, and so on.
- Play off of one another by modeling a conversation about the different possibilities being explored so that the teacher reading the text can offer his or her own ideas as well.
- Examine further evidence in the text by pointing out diagrams, drawings, and photographs as well as talking aloud about possible clues to the meaning.

After modeling the activity, engage students in a guided practice using a different text. Have students work in pairs or small groups with both teachers circulating within the room assisting students with the task and directing students step-by-step to consider different text aspects, meanings, and features. When both teachers explicitly share their individual thinking processes, it gives students the opportunity to explore and apply multiple strategies. Working in pairs or small groups also allows them to share their ideas with their peers.

Think-alouds are also a great complement to read-alouds. What Richard Anderson, Elfrieda Hiebert, Judith Scott, and Ian Wilkinson (1985) noted over three decades ago—"the single most important activity for building the knowledge required for eventual success in reading is reading aloud to children" (p. 23)—continues to be shared by many educators. Jennifer Renner Del Nero (2013) reminds us, "In whole-class instruction, we need to use grade-level text to be sure that students are exposed to and guided through complex materials" (p. xii). If one teacher reads aloud to the class, the other teacher reveals the thought process that goes into comprehending the text by making text-to-self, text-to-text, and text-to-world connections. Through think-alouds, students are allowed to gain insight into the teacher's meaning-making process and how accomplished readers use a range of strategies such as predicting, clarifying, summarizing, and making connections (Zwiers, 2014).

Scaffolded Opinion Chart is a way to assist students to not only state their opinion but to support their opinion with reasons and evidence. Co-teachers can model different opinions using the chart demonstrating how to connect explanations of opinions with cited evidence. Co-teachers can take opposing opinions to illustrate how multiple opinions are not only acceptable but they can also be justified by evidence. Co-teachers may also engage students in a guided practice to complete the chart in order to help students better understand how to organize their ideas about a stated topic or text. This chart can be part of an established class routine when students are asked to state their opinions either verbally or in writing (see Figure 4.1).

Use of Nonlinguistic Cues is a basic strategy to support the understanding of ELs, and though it is often observed in lower elementary grades or stand-alone classes for English learners, it is one that is sometimes overlooked in core content classes. In upper grades, teacher talk is invariably increased, which often makes content less accessible for ELs. We recommend using sketches, diagrams, gestures, voice intonation, and other nonverbal cues to make both language and content more accessible to students. When one teacher speaks, the other teacher can clarify information by using nonverbal cues. In this way, the rigor of the lesson can be maintained, yet the comprehension of ELs can be better supported.

Pro-Prep Strategies for Model 2

When presented with new material and complex information, ELs need strategies to aid in their comprehension, to organize ideas, and to develop their own thoughts in a way that they can express themselves successfully. The following approaches need to be preplanned and prepared, yet they work well with this co-teaching model.

Visual Cues help clarify the rigorous curriculum content co-teachers convey. Students' knowledge can be built using a variety of images related to the content. In the tech-savvy classroom, images are just a click away using interactive whiteboard technology or a digital projector. One teacher can share information with students using photographs, maps, charts, timelines, drawings,

Figure 4.1 Scaffolded Opinion Chart

Opinion	What do you think? _____ _____
Reasons	Why do you think so? _____ _____
Evidence	How do you know it? _____ _____

Adapted from Dove & Honigsfeld (2013)

Figure 4.2 Two-Column Notes

Title: Ancient Civilizations: Mesopotamia	
Main Idea	**Details**
It was the first civilization	A civilization is _____ _____.
Location: Modern-day Iraq	Part of the _____ near the Persian Gulf. Near the modern-day countries of _____. _____.
Government: Ruled by kings	Each king ruled only _____. An assembly of the people who could _____ _____.
Religion: Polytheistic (belief in many gods and goddesses)	Each city had _____ guarding the people and its king. Mesopotamians also believed in demons created by _____.

Information adapted from: http://www.ancient.eu/Mesopotamia/

and other prepared graphic representations via a PowerPoint presentation, in print form, or on a hand-held electronic tablet.

Two-Column Notes help students organize the main idea and details presented using this class configuration. One teacher might convey information verbally or engage students in a shared reading while the other teacher models how to chart information using the two-column notes. This organizer can strengthen students' abilities to recognize the difference between core concepts and superfluous information. They can also enhance students' understanding of new vocabulary. Figure 4.2 is an example of a partially completed two-column note organizer.

Write Aloud is similar to the think-alouds in that both teachers take on roles to model for students, yet the purpose of this strategy is to guide them in the process of writing. Both teachers demonstrate the procedures for developing written work—planning for writing, transferring thoughts to written words, handling missteps, revising, editing, and so on. Moreover, co-teachers share their thought processes to help students develop their metacognitive awareness. In this way, all students can better understand the steps experienced writers take to fully develop a piece of writing.

In the co-taught class, one teacher might model his or her thinking while the other teacher takes notes. Then, they reverse roles, and the teacher who conducted the note taking becomes the one who shares thoughts and ideas for the written piece while the other teacher jots down information. Another method is for both teachers to demonstrate different ways a piece of writing might be accomplished, each writing their own ideas on separate boards while having a conversation with one another about their thinking processes. This technique gives students the opportunity to experience writing in diverse ways, with one maybe appealing to some students' learning styles more than the other. We strongly recommend using this strategy in core content classes where writing is often assigned but not taught.

Scaffolded Comprehend Alouds. According to Jeff Zwiers (2014), think-alouds support the development of a range of reading strategies, whereas comprehend alouds make thinking visible about processing and analyzing the language of complex readings at the word, sentence, and text levels. Review Table 4.3 for sentence starters you can use to model think-alouds and comprehend alouds with just about any text. Depending on the grade level and content area, adaptations to these scaffolds will have to be made.

Table 4. 3 Sentence Starters for Think-Alouds and Comprehend Alouds

Think-aloud sentence stems	Comprehend-aloud sentence stems
Predicting • When I read the title of the book, I thought of . . . • I predict . . . • In the next chapter, the author will . . . Clarifying • I have to go back to page . . . • I became confused when I read . . . • I had to think back to what I learned about . . . Summarizing • I think this section is mainly about . . . • The most important point the author is making . . . • So I think the purpose of this article is . . .	Word- and phrase-level • I am not sure what this word means here. I think I will have to reread this section . . . • I noticed that the same word appears here . . . • I have seen this word but never used it myself. Let me see if I can figure out the meaning by . . . • I have never seen this word before. Let me see if I can figure out the meaning by reading ahead/looking for some examples/finding an illustration • The author uses several idioms that I have to stop and think out • I noticed that this sentence with the phrase . . .

(Continued)

Table 4. 3 (Continued)	

Think-aloud sentence stems	Comprehend-aloud sentence stems
Making Connections • This part reminds me of . . . • The paragraph I just read is similar to . . . • When I read this part, I thought of . . . • I think the author wants me to . . .	Sentence- and text-level • In this section, I noticed that the sentences are short and have a similar pattern • The author uses a very long sentence in this paragraph. I think if I can break it down into shorter sections, I can understand it better . . . • I noticed this section has a lot of dialogues and quotes. I wonder . . .

Adapted from Honigsfeld & Dodge, 2015

SAMPLE LESSONS: ONE GROUP: TWO TEACH THE SAME CONTENT

The following lesson segments portray co-teachers as they both lead a lesson to a whole group of students to support the learning of ELs as they conduct co-taught lessons.

Critical Thinking About the Arrival of Columbus in Grade Five

In this co-taught introductory lesson segment, students must discern from various sources whether or not Christopher Columbus should be viewed as a champion or a criminal. The lesson begins with Ms. Rios, the fifth-grade teacher, and Mr. Scott, the ELD/ELL teacher, positioned in front of the class. After they greet the students together, Mr. Scott begins to read the lesson objective posted on the board while Ms. Rios pulls up a piece of text on the interactive whiteboard for this lesson.

There are 26 students in the class; 10 students are English learners. All students are seated strategically in the room. Since they have no regularly assigned seats, the teachers divide the students into groups according to the lesson demands. For this lesson, the lower proficiency ELs are seated directly in front of where Mr. Scott is standing. As Ms. Rios begins a verbal review of some basic facts most school children know about Columbus, Mr. Scott offers their ELs some nonverbal cues. He jots down information on the board and completes some quick sketches to illustrate vocabulary (e.g., Columbus's ships, a map of the ships' route, etc.).

After the brief introduction, Ms. Rios moves in front of the interactive whiteboard where they will conduct a shared reading of some excerpts from *Lies My Teacher Told Me* by James W. Loewen (2007). It is a challenging text, so after each sentence is read (teachers take turns), they pause to explain some vocabulary and comment on some of the sentence structure. Additionally, they engage in a joint think aloud about the text by sharing their realizations, opinions, judgments, questions, and conclusions with the class. They use the following list of questions from Reading Rockets (n.d.) to guide them:

- What do I know about this topic?
- What do I think I will learn about this topic?
- Do I understand what I just read?
- Do I have a clear picture in my head about this information?
- What more can I do to understand this?
- What were the most important points in this reading?
- What new information did I learn?
- How does it fit in with what I already know? (para. 3)

During the shared reading, students are guided to use the think-aloud strategy with a partner. Next, they are given texts to read about Christopher Columbus that are closer to their independent reading abilities. Their task is to develop opinions—whether or not they believe the information to be accurate accounts of Columbus's voyage using their assigned text. They must give their reasons and cite evidence from the text. During this reading, students may work alone, in pairs, or in small groups. At this time, Mr. Scott sits with the group of lower-proficiency ELs to guide them through the task using a scaffolded opinion chart (see sample in Figure 4.3). Meanwhile, Ms. Rios circulates within the room and offers assistance as needed.

Analysis of the lesson segment. In this lesson, both teachers take full advantage of the class configuration—one group: two teach the same content—by engaging in dialogue about the shared reading using the think-aloud strategy. Although both teachers are teaching the whole class, Mr. Scott is able to pay added attention to the lower-level ELs due to where they are seated. He also uses nonverbal cues—writing and illustrating on the board—to aid in their comprehension. When students are given a task to complete, they are then divided into multiple groups but also have the option to work independently. Here we see Model 7—multiple groups: teachers monitor/teach—being combined with Model 2 to support students best in their task completion.

Figure 4.3	Opinion Chart: Christopher Columbus

Give Your Opinion: Was Christopher Columbus a hero?	I think Christopher Columbus was not a hero.
Give Your Reasons: Why do you think that?	Columbus was not a hero because he tried to take away things and control the people that lived in America.
State Your Evidence: What does the author state?	The author states, "Columbus treated the native people he encountered cruelly. He took land and natural resources and began a long chapter of European abuse."

Discovering the Perception-Brain Connection in Eighth Grade

The following eighth grade co-taught science topic on perception and the brain was inspired by Science & Health Education Partnership Lessons (http://seplessons.ucsf.edu/print/1721). For the purpose of this lesson description, the class consists of intermediate- and advanced-level English learners who are studying alongside their fluent English-speaking peers in the same class. We will call the science teacher Ms. Lourdes and the ELD/ELL teacher Mr. Unger.

The objective of this science lesson is for eighth graders to be able to explain the concept of perception, how perception is physically perceived, and how the brain interprets sensory signals. Use of comparative forms of adjectives will be emphasized. Students will observe how the brain adapts to changes in a person's perception. The prerequisite skills for students to be able to make scientific observations and collect data were reviewed during small-group instruction in a previous lesson. To introduce this lesson, Ms. Lourdes and Mr. Unger have decided to keep the class together as one group to facilitate student learning.

To open a discussion on perception, Ms. Lourdes projects a series of optical illusions on the interactive whiteboard while Mr. Unger explains the meaning of an optical illusion and writes the Spanish language cognate, *ilusión óptica*, on the erasable board. To demonstrate language use, Ms. Lourdes asks Mr. Unger to compare the size of the objects in two of the optical illusions, and Mr. Unger models the comparative forms of adjectives—for example, "This line appears to be shorter than that line" and "This car seems to be larger than that one." Mr. Unger then elicits students' reactions to various illusions, asking them to compare the size or color of the images they see by turning and talking with a partner. He reveals some sentence frames on a piece of chart paper to guide students to verbally compare and contrast the images in various optical illusions with one another. Each teacher circulates within the room to "listen in" on students' conversations and give on-the-spot feedback for language support.

Next, Ms. Lourdes presents one of the slides of the PowerPoint presentation that she and Mr. Unger jointly prepared (see Figure 4.4). She asks the students to read the text quietly, select the most import phrase in the paragraph, and jot it down on a sticky note. Mr. Unger explains that

Figure 4.4   PowerPoint Slide: Senses and Perception

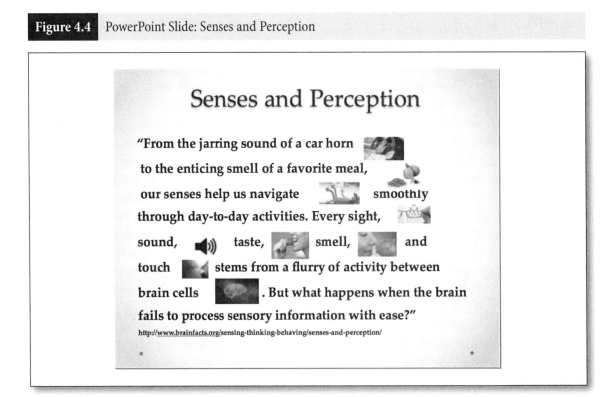

the most important phrase is a group of words that gives a person power to talk about the topic. He further suggests that students jot down any of the words they are not sure about.

Mr. Unger directs the students to turn and talk in pairs or triads to share their power phrase and explain to each other why it was selected. They also are asked to figure out the meaning of any unknown words they jotted down collaboratively. The key for this activity to work is to pair students who are less proficient in English with students who are more proficient. After a few minutes, students are directed to return to the group as a whole, and both teachers report what they heard from student conversations. Mr. Unger asks the students if there are any words that need further clarification. In addition to any students' questions, he chooses to focus on the verb "jarring" and how it can be confusing because of its similarity to the noun "jar."

Mr. Unger and Ms. Lourdes present the additional slides from the PowerPoint in similar fashion, giving students opportunities to process the information as well as ask clarifying questions. After the introduction, which takes approximately 12 minutes of class time, Ms. Lourdes leads students in a review of the steps in a process in order to conduct an experiment on perception. Mr. Unger invites a small group of English learners to a side table to directly explain the steps of the experiment and clarify any language that is on the lab form students need to complete. After the review, students are divided into heterogeneous groups to complete the experiment.

Analysis of the lesson segment. In this lesson, both teachers share information equally with students, although they take on distinct roles. In the beginning of the lesson, Ms. Lourdes's focus is squarely on the content, whereas Mr. Unger directs students' attention to the vocabulary and supports their understanding by using their home language. He also incorporates the comparative forms of adjectives infusing grammar instruction with the content. Later in the lesson, when students are grouped for collaborative inquiry and practice, he is able to work with his English learners to further strengthen their understanding and use of adjectives. Yet during this lesson segment, both teachers take on the role of teaching the language and the content as they circulate with students working in groups to offer them feedback.

MODEL VARIATIONS

There are few model variations with this configuration; co-teachers generally lead together when both are in front of the whole class. However, we have observed some modifications as to where teachers position themselves in the classroom with this model.

Two Teach the Same Content, One Front, One Back

With this reworking of the model, we have observed one teacher remaining in front of the room while the other teacher positions himself or herself away from the front, either in the middle or the back of the room, even though they are both equally leading the lesson. This difference in stance has several advantages. First, the teacher who is positioned away from the front has a more favorable vantage point to determine if all students are able to follow along during step-by-step instructions or a guided practice. Second, the variation in positioning can support classroom management to promote and monitor students' acquisition of skills, time on task, and expected behavior. We have noted that this variation sometimes occurs when a class is difficult to manage; the more veteran or experienced teacher often takes the position of leading from the middle of the whole group of students to check time-on-task behavior and assure lesson continuity.

Two Teach the Same Content, One by the Board, One by the Computer

With this variation, one teacher remains standing in front of the class, usually positioned by an interactive whiteboard or screen, while the other teacher operates the technology generally seated at a computer. This alteration in positioning is purely practical and often has to do with teacher preference or established roles in the co-taught class. Sometimes, teachers reverse positions so that each gets an opportunity to navigate the technology. The challenge here is not to position one teacher regularly at the side of the class to operate the hardware. He or she may then be perceived as a helper and not jointly leading the lesson.

Two Teach the Same Content, Both "Between the Desks"

"Teaching between the desks" (Ermeling & Graff-Ermeling, 2014) is an instructional strategy borrowed and adapted for co-taught classes from the Japanese practice called *kikan-shidō*. Japanese educators use this approach in classes taught by a single teacher with the intention of engaging their students in deeper learning around challenging problems and tasks. The deeper thinking emerges from the interaction that the teacher has with individual students. It is these between-the-desks conversations that are deliberately not carried out in a hushed, whispering voice; on the contrary, teachers talk to students in a way that those sitting around the target student may also benefit from the explanation. When adapted to the co-taught classroom, two teachers cover even more territory as they position themselves between and among desks to offer short-targeted interventions and opportunities to make sense of the content and to practice the academic language that is connected to it.

MODEL COMBINATIONS

Model 2 (One Group: Two Teach the Same Content) serves well as an introduction, minilesson, warm up, or lesson opening routine to any of the other models. Model 2 already requires both teachers to work with the entire group, so Model 1 and Model 3 are viable options for being combined with Model 2. If teachers decide that one of them will need to offer intervention to targeted students before moving on or to collect assessment data on how students are understanding the lesson, shifting to these two models may be performed seamlessly.

Model 2 also allows for introducing a minilesson that will be followed by any of the following grouping configurations. Based on the lesson target, teachers may decide to transition to

- Model 4, in which each teacher works on the same content or skills by forming either two heterogeneous groups of students where ELs and non-ELs are together or two homogeneous groups of students where all ELs are together for more language-based differentiation;

- Model 5, in which one teacher will focus on some essential concepts and skills that present as gaps in prior knowledge and experience for some students while the other takes the opportunity to go deeper into the topic and offer enrichment;
- Model 6, in which one teacher revisits previously introduced lesson content while the other takes the opportunity to go deeper into the topic and offer enrichment; or
- Model 7, in which learning stations or centers are utilized or productive group work is expected.

Model 2 (One Group: Two Teach the Same Content) is a natural opportunity to explain to students what to expect as the entire class moves into groups. It is essential that both teachers actively participate in giving directions (or at least one carefully listening and also monitoring student comprehension) so as to make sure they are both on the same page when the shift to groups has been completed.

INSPIRATION FROM THE FIELD

Read what colleagues—ELD/ELL specialists and classroom teachers as well as building and district administrators—shared with us from around the United States. We have found them inspirational and affirming. See how they reflect your own experiences or add to your understanding.

Janeen A. Kelly, director of the Department of English Language Learner and World Languages, Washoe County School District, Nevada, shares her district initiative with co-teaching and teachers' and students' experiences with Model 2.

In our district, we were asked to develop a plan that included English Learners in a more inclusive model of instruction. In an effort to provide equitable access for ELs in a general-education setting, we selected to combine Model 2 and Model 4 during a 45 to 60-minute block of instruction. During this instructional time, an EL teacher and a grade-level general-education teacher collaborated to plan and deliver the instruction that was based on the Nevada Academic Content Standards (CCSS) and English Language Development (ELD) Standards.

The teachers planned their unit by starting with the language proficiency levels of their students and focused on the language needs of those students in developing opportunities for the students to practice using the language. During the whole-group lesson, all students were taught by both teachers. The general-education teacher and the EL teacher were both in the front of the classroom delivering the information simultaneously. The general-education teacher focused on the content and the EL teacher used strategies such as rephrasing the information, using gestures, visuals etc., to scaffold the information for the students. When observing the teaching, it was difficult to determine who the general-education teacher was and who the EL teacher was, as they each began supporting each other in delivering the instruction with a language focus. One student commented, "I love having two teachers to help me. I no longer have to wait in line for my EL teacher, both teachers know how to help me say or do it."

Prior to instruction, students were strategically paired with a partner so that when the teachers asked them to interact, using the academic language that was needed, no instructional time was lost. A student that was at a level 1 may be paired with a student at a level 3, a student at a level 2 paired with a student at a level 3 or 4, and a level 3 or 4 could also be paired with a student at a level 5 or 6. Usually, this strategic placement of partners occurred during the teacher collaborative planning time, and partners remained constant for at least one month. This strategic placement of partners enabled student interaction to occur and teachers to observe and monitor interaction. A protocol of "no hands raised" was in effect to assist students in being held accountable for their learning. During the whole-group lesson, both teachers modeled the language and modeled the learning expectations and outcomes. They specifically referred to the language and content targets of the unit, as well as the language and content objectives of the day or week. When students left the whole-group instruction, they understood what was expected of them in small-group instruction. One student commented, "My teacher is no longer just talking at me about what I am going to learn and do, but showing me."

When students move into Model 4, they are flexibly and strategically placed in a small group based on their language or content needs. Each teacher is teaching the same content, but the EL teacher may be scaffolding the activity more and the general-education teacher may be providing enrichment for students. All students are expected to show their learning in a variety of ways. For example, both teachers are using the same graphic organizer to assist students in preparing to write on the topic studied. The EL teacher may be writing on her graphic organizer the students' ideas, and then students write those ideas on their graphic organizer. The general-education teacher may be prompting with questions to have students individually write their ideas on the graphic organizer and then share with whole group. One student commented, "I am finally doing what everyone else in the class is doing."

At the end of small-group instruction, students gather together to reflect on their learning and teachers have an opportunity to clarify any misunderstandings or monitor if reteaching or further practice is needed. One teacher commented, "This time for closure is very important, and I did not realize that it truly gave my students an opportunity to explain their learning or ask important questions. We never take enough time to reflect, and bringing all the students back together in a whole group allows for them to think about their thinking and learning."

Kieren Barnes, an elementary English as a New Language (ENL) teacher who teaches at Tecler Arts in Education Magnet School in the Greater Amsterdam School District, New York, shares her approach to using Model 2 and combining it with Model 1:

My co-teachers and I mostly use two models during our instruction. We alternate using Model 1 and Model 2. When we first introduce new content, we will use Model 2. We create the lesson with the goal that we both introduce the new content. We simultaneously present the content, but we each focus on different aspects. As the ENL teacher, I will focus my portion of the presentation on explicit instruction (e.g., teaching key vocabulary or showing pictures to enhance understanding). After the initial presentation, my co-teachers and I transition to use Model 1. We transition to this model because at this point the students are being asked to use the new skill in their work. If we switch to this model, I am able to more closely work with the students and directly assist them and assess their understanding. I can give them very quick feedback and assistance.

Andrew Dawson, ELD/ELL teacher, and Lynn Hennessy, first-grade classroom teacher from Mesnier Primary School, Affton School District, Missouri, found Model 2, which they refer to as team-teaching, highly effective.

For the Reading Workshop model, we decided team teaching was the best approach when delivering minilessons. One of us would take the lead on the lesson, with the other interjecting thoughts and ideas. One great success was the implementation of language objectives in Reading Workshop for a first-grade classroom. I started first by modeling how to write objectives with my co-teacher. Then, to help in the transfer of ownership where the classroom teacher would start to write objectives on her own, we took the time to write them together during our plan time. After awhile, we realized the need and importance of including sentence frames during written response and partner shares. I would catch students stopping and looking to the objectives for support. My co-teacher, Lynn Hennessy, believes "students were able to share with visiting administrators, as well as their parents, what they were learning and how they were doing it." We stressed when we conferred with students, "What are you doing today?" and then "Can you show me how?" Mrs. Hennessy then had the brilliant idea to add a think bubble to our objectives. For example, when practicing fluency, students would ask, "Am I reading too slow?" or "Am I reading too fast?" This pushed students to take a metacognitive approach to their learning. By including a think bubble and sentence frame to the objectives, students had specific ways to deepen their learning.

The huge benefit with having two teachers in the room is that we could meet with twice as many students for conferring and small groups. All the students were OUR students, and not just the ELLs. A conferring schedule was also posted as a visual, so students could count on being seen by one of us. We used two binders, dividing the students in half, so students knew they would be seen on a weekly basis. The binders included conferring notes on strengths, weaknesses, and next steps. These notes were essential for communication between myself, the co-teacher, and students.

Finally, see how Stephanie P. Vogel, secondary ESOL teacher in Patchogue-Medford High School, Medford, New York, reflects on her co-teaching journey with specific attention to teaching the same content together to the entire class.

Admittedly, I've been a skeptic of co-teaching, not because I think it's a bad idea but because prior to this year, I hadn't been placed in optimal situations to truly see how amazing co-teaching can be. This year, my co-teacher, Geeta Vir, and I were together teaching Algebra A for two periods and Algebra B for two periods to exclusively teach ELs. In addition, we had a co-planning period together and we were on the phone talking or texting, writing in shared documents, or FaceTime calling each other several times a week. Our co-teaching worked beautifully! One of the things that we did—which we hadn't planned but just became part of our routine—was to work side by side at the board showing students how to solve problems in different ways. We had done this with combining like terms, solving two-step equations, and graphing, so when it came time to teach solving systems of equations, the students were quite used to seeing the two of us at the board. The simultaneous solving that we did became a friendly competition, and the kids would cheer us on challenging me, the ELL teacher, to beat Ms. Vir, the content math teacher, to the final result. It was fun and everyone was engaged. One student, who wasn't the strongest math student, was particularly fond of when we'd do this, and when he saw us take two different methods and wind up getting the same result, he exclaimed, "Que Brujería!" (Spanish for "It's Witchcraft!") So, for the rest of the year when we were teaching a new topic, the students would ask us to do 'brujería' and show them different methods for solving equations, systems work, reading and setting up word problems, and factoring. Doing this not only made the class fun, but we'd challenge students to then pick their favorite method and solve their own problems. Giving the students choices was great, and they took ownership of their learning. This year, we were very proud to find out that 80% of the students in our classes who took the Algebra regents passed!

TAKEAWAYS

In this chapter, we explore the ways in which two teachers can jointly lead a lesson, or part of it, and engage the whole class in learning through Model 2 (One Group: Two Teach the Same Content) in a co-taught class. While this may present itself to be among the most challenging models of co-teaching to become fully comfortable and successful with, we urge you to practice this every day to ensure that both teachers are fully engaged with the entire class, are recognized as experts, and support content and language development in tandem (Honigsfeld & Dove, 2015b).

QUESTIONS FOR FURTHER DISCUSSION

1. Consider the importance of parity in this model. How would you negotiate roles and responsibilities that capitalize on both teachers' areas of expertise?

2. We made some suggestions in this chapter on getting started with this model. What creative opportunities can this model offer to more experienced co-teachers?

3. What do you consider the greatest benefits and pitfalls of using this model with a large heterogeneous group of students?

4. In what ways may this model serve as an effective tool for mentoring or peer coaching? What are the inherent dangers of using it as such, and how would you ensure that co-teachers remain equal partners?

5

Model 3 – One Group

One Teaches, One Assesses

Image credit: New America

AN INTRODUCTION TO THE MODEL

The importance of this instructional model rests in part in the change in assessment practices over a decade ago. Since the inception of No Child Left Behind (NCLB) legislation in 2002, students' academic progress has been an all-encompassing goal in school districts across the nation, and the mainstay for determining such progress has been standardized assessments. Yet the U.S. Department of Education (2015b) has recognized that "over time, NCLB's prescriptive requirements became increasingly unworkable for schools and educators" (para. 4). In short, NCLB's goals for having all students reach or exceed grade-level academic benchmarks within 12 years of its enactment have never been realized.

More recently, the passage of the Every Student Succeeds Act in 2015 triggered numerous reforms to NCLB; however, this new legislation still calls for rigorous accountability, which translates again into heavy reliance on standardized assessment practices. Although some may disagree, this continual cycle of measurement of academic achievement through standardized tests often lacks value for instructional improvement. It has done little to enhance actual instruction (Kohn, 2004), and the data received from standard assessments not normed on language-diverse pupils offers little, if any, significant evidence of the progress of English learners (ELs).

In fact, the overuse of testing has prompted considerable amounts of time spent on test preparation, narrowing the curriculum significantly and resulting in even less time for teaching subjects such as art, history, and music (Van Roekel, 2011) as well as needed English-language instruction. In contrast, this co-teaching model, dedicated to gathering authentic assessment data without halting class lessons, has the potential to truly impact and improve the quality of instruction.

Among many others, Conley (2014) criticizes the overdependency educators have placed on standardized testing and argues for assessment reforms. He suggests that educators rely more fully on a broader range of assessment tools to determine students' levels of skill. We concur with Conley, and therefore highlight the benefits of this co-teaching model to do just that—provide on-the-spot, formative, and summative assessment data to support the learning of students in various ways.

The critical aspects of this co-teaching model stem from how challenging it is for *one teacher* to collect specific and relevant data on students' progress during a class period. Much of what can be regularly gathered is general information about student learning, such as whether or not most students understand the basic tenets of a lesson. A lesson reteach and review is often sparked when it becomes overwhelmingly obvious that several students are struggling with a concept or skill. However, some students, particularly ELs who often are restrained and remain silent even when they are confused about the lesson content, may be overlooked. On the other hand, with *two teachers* in the room, one can concentrate on the specifics of the lesson while the other is engaged in collecting meaningful, formative assessment data. As Alvarez, Ananda, Walqui, Sato, and Rabinowitz (2014) note,

> In order to use formative assessment effectively with this student population, teachers must attend simultaneously to the students' needs both in learning content and skills and in developing the English required to express their learning. (p. 1)

There are also variations of this co-teaching model, discussed later in the chapter, in which both teachers can be involved in the instruction and assessment of students, and additional types of data may be collected as well.

A CLOSER LOOK AT MODEL 3

In the classic configuration of this model, one teacher leads the instruction for the entire group of students while the other teacher collects formative assessment data by circulating around the class, observing students to evaluate their skills and abilities, most often according to some criteria that have been set. The teacher conducting the lesson may introduce a new topic, take students step-by-step through a new skill or strategy, or conduct a shared reading in which students are asked to pause, process information, and perform some task, or engage students in a review of content materials. During this time, the focus may be on assessing prior knowledge and readiness (at the onset of a new unit or lesson), monitoring student progress (during each unit or lesson), or evaluating how close students are to mastery (when approaching the end of a unit or lesson).

Formative assessment data may provide critical evidence, and as such, it may be used for a range of purposes, on which co-teachers need to agree prior to the lesson:

- To immediately adjust instructional practices during the same lesson or in subsequent lessons
- To address individual students' needs specific to the lesson
- To maximize learning for all students by adapting teaching methods
- To gauge individual students' areas of strengths and needs
- To differentiate instruction based on teacher-collected data rather than student label
- To determine student grouping
- To offer immediate intervention or plan targeted, longer-term interventions

(In Chapter 10, we revisit the role of formative assessments in terms of how two teachers may most effectively collect, organize, analyze, document, use, and report formative assessment data.)

The teacher conducting the formative assessment may be taking broad-based anecdotal notes on various groups of students or might be concentrating on just one or two students in the class (Figure 5.1 is an example of one set of general measures for observing ELs in the co-taught class). At other times, a simple checklist (see Figure 5.3 on p. 103) may be used to assess all students' progress or mastery, or a more complex scoring rubric (see Figures 5.2 and 5.7) might be employed to gather more specific data on students' learning a particular concept, building a specific skill, familiarity with a subject topic, or working toward meeting a language objective.

Generally, the teacher in the assessment role will carry around a clipboard to log data or use an electronic tablet to document anecdotal information. The benefit of the latter is that evidence gathered using a computerized method could be more readily stored and shared. At times, it may appear as if the teacher leading the lesson is undertaking the majority of the work; however, the teacher in the assessment role is gathering meaningful data that can guide future joint instruction.

We have observed this model used for an entire class period for more extensive data collection or for short periods of time for specific purposes. For example, sometimes a brief assessment at the beginning of a class period using this model can render immediate information about which students lack the required background knowledge on a particular subject or which students need reteaching to reinforce understanding of information previously taught. These immediate data in turn help co-teachers to group students for additional instruction accordingly.

Setting learning targets for ELs and then following up to evaluate these targets is another way this model can be used productively. For instance, performance-based assessments, formulated from the instruction students receive and the tasks they are given to complete, can be used to both assess students' progress in the content area as well as determine improvement in English language proficiency. These types of assessments can examine the way students are able to perform a task such as the ability to gather appropriate data, analyze and annotate text, use academic oral language

Figure 5.1 General Observation of Learning Progress for ELs

Co-Teachers:		Grade/Subject:	
Lesson Objective(s):			
Target Student(s)	**Criteria**		**Observations/Comments**
	How appropriate are the lesson objectives for the student(s)?		
	To what extent do student(s) understand the basic concepts of the lesson? Advanced concepts?		
	Can the student(s) produce grade-level work: • In content? • In language?		
	What lesson supports are used most often? What additional supports are needed?		
	Additional criteria: • _____ • _____		

to collaborate with fellow students, and so on, as well as complete a task like writing and revising a piece of writing.

Although this model may be sometimes implemented at short notice using teacher-developed forms and established instructional routines, adequate co-planning and follow-up analysis and application of the collected data are critical for this model's successful employment. Anecdotal data and information gathered through performance-based assessments are based primarily on teacher judgment, and they must be shared, analyzed, and discussed to determine the language and academic progress of your ELs as well as how the data will inform instructional practice.

VIDEO 5.1:
Model 3—One
Group: One
Teaches, One
Assesses

http://resources
.corwin.com/
CoTeachingforELs

ADVANTAGES

The ability to gather assessment data through observation of students at work can help teachers to better understand what students know and are able to do within a particular context. It allows teachers to focus on certain aspects of student learning, often to determine how students' English language proficiency levels can aid or hinder their comprehension and application of new information, and adjust instruction accordingly. This co-teaching model can facilitate the routine documentation of students' academic growth and language development so that student progress can be monitored, instruction adjusted, and additional support can be provided if warranted.

This model can be useful for collecting assessment data in which the process of students reading various texts or writing for authentic purposes is observed and noted by one partner in the co-teaching pair. Students may be observed in an authentic context discussing certain aspects of a text in small groups, creating a graphic organizer to summarize information, writing their reflections in log books or journals, reworking a piece of writing, and so forth. Anecdotal notes,

| Figure 5.2 | Rubric for Student Engagement in Cooperative Learning Groups |

	Active Engagement	Engagement	Active Compliance	Passive Compliance	Resistance	No evidence
Initiates conversation						
Leads group activities						
Asks questions						
Seeks answers						
Works collaboratively with peers						
Stays on task w/o teacher intervention						

Inspired by Silver, H. F., & Perini, M. J. (2010). The eight Cs of engagement: How learning styles and instructional design increase student commitment to learning. In R. J. Marzano (Ed.), *On excellence in teaching* (pp. 319–344). Bloomington, IN: Solution Tree.

checklists, rubrics, or other set criteria can be used to collect data on an ongoing basis. In time, systematically collected data can be ascertained to monitor student progress and pinpoint topics/skills for follow-up minilessons to enhance the learning of ELs. This type of authentic data is crucial for the co-taught class. It can support a tailor-made curriculum for developing the English language proficiency of ELs.

Gathering this type of data can determine whether or not minilessons developed for student learning have been effective. It can detect whether or not students can successfully apply their knowledge by focusing on specific sets of subskills students have been previously taught. After all, it is one thing for students to demonstrate their understanding of new information, an added skill, or strategy through a quick assessment conducted during a minilesson but quite another score when students are able to apply their learning during a broader-based task.

A further advantage of this co-teaching model is that it can promote the use of authentic, engaging activities in the class in which students apply new information or practice using a skill or strategy. At times, small-group activities such as sharing opinions, developing arguments, or debating various concepts presented in a text cannot be readily assessed unless data concerning students' abilities to acquire, analyze, and apply information as well as use their language skills are gathered through observational note taking on the part of the teacher. However, the accuracy and detail required for this type of assessment is rarely accomplished easily when classes are not being co-taught.

Last but not least, this model can be an opportunity to offer teacher-to-teacher feedback. When assessment data are being gathered, the teacher in the position of observing the class may also note the effectiveness of the lesson being taught and offer peer support to his or her partner. Students' level of engagement and success with the use of particular strategies may be noted as part of the data-gathering process. In turn, feedback might be offered and plans reviewed accordingly.

CHALLENGES

The accuracy of data obtained through observation sometimes falls under scrutiny. It can be said that observational annotations are often more subjective than objective in that the evidence noted may be dependent on the design of the observation task, the accuracy of the observation tool, and the skills of the observer. There are remedies for such concerns, such as having a set criteria for each observation, setting an understanding for the behavior to be observed prior to the lesson, and having co-teachers reverse roles on occasion to observe and assess. In addition, we strongly suggest that co-teachers never rely on one type of assessment data to make decisions about student progress; instead, design a variety of assessment tasks (what the students will do) and use a variety of assessment measures (how students will be evaluated).

Apart from general concerns about collecting data, co-teachers have other reservations about using this model for instruction. To begin with, one teacher has the sole responsibility for teaching the lesson or at least part of the lesson if the model is not used for an entire class period. Instruction can be challenging when there are several groups of ELs at various levels of English language proficiency that need diversified instruction. Data collected via whole-class instruction might be very different from data collected through small-group instruction.

Co-teachers must be flexible and able to shift into other co-teaching models as needed when using this configuration. Teachers must recognize the limitations of planned lessons and be willing to make adjustments to take advantage of teachable moments with ELs. Although teachers in the role as observers are charged with the important task of gathering assessment data, they must recognize that there are times in which they must immediately support learning if a student is struggling or off task.

When multiple students exhibit off-task behaviors or are disruptive, they may trigger the co-teacher conducting the assessment to be the disciplinarian. As a consequence, the teacher's time is spent controlling student behavior instead of collecting data. To avoid this scenario, routines for common classroom management practices should be in place; if inappropriate behavior continues, it might need further examination and remedies both inside and outside of the class.

With this model, students may not perceive the teacher who is conducting the assessment as an equal co-teaching partner as compared with the teacher delivering the instruction. This situation is similar to what may occur with Model 1 (One Leads, One "Teaches On Purpose") in which one teacher may be perceived as the "real" teacher and the other teacher as the "helper." To avoid this issue, equity and parity should be established between the teachers who are co-teaching before the employment of this model.

Finally, this model cannot be effective unless it is used purposefully. The purpose of this model is to collect ongoing valuable data to be used to plan future instruction for ELs to acquire both language and content skills. It should not be used haphazardly or as a default model when there is no time to plan. And last but not least, it should not be used to curtail or police student behavior during lessons.

Table 5.1	Summary of Advantages and Challenges of Model 3

Model 3: One Group: One Teaches, One Assesses	
Advantages	**Challenges**
Co-teachers can focus on certain aspects of learning to determine how language proficiency levels aid or hinder student progress.	The accuracy of data obtained through observation sometimes falls under scrutiny.
Anecdotal notes, checklists, rubrics, or other set criteria can be used to collect data on an ongoing basis.	One teacher has the sole responsibility for teaching the lesson or specially designated portion of it.
A great amount of data can be ascertained to monitor student progress and pinpoint topics for follow-up minilessons to enhance the learning of ELs.	Co-teachers must be willing to make adjustments to take advantage of teachable moments.
It can detect whether or not students can successfully apply their knowledge by focusing on specific sets of subskills students have been previously taught.	The co-teacher conducting the assessment should not be the disciplinarian.
It can promote the use of authentic, engaging activities in the class in which students apply new information or practice using a skill or strategy.	Students may not perceive both teachers as equal partners.
It can be an opportunity to offer teacher-to-teacher feedback.	This model must be used purposefully for it to make an impact on student learning.

INSTRUCTION USING MODEL 3

When it comes to educational excellence, Reeves (2006) notes that "monitoring, evaluation, values, beliefs, and implementation" (p. ix) work better than intricate planning. Although we believe that planning is essential for a well-run co-taught class, we also find monitoring students' progress and incorporating regular assessment practices with this co-taught model are fundamental to building instruction that is productive for all students. John Hattie (2009) also suggests that

> the major part of this story relates to the power of directed teaching, enhancing what happens next (through feedback and monitoring) to inform the teacher about the success or failure of their teaching, and to provide a method to evaluate the relative efficacy of different influences that teachers use. (p. 6)

In considering the strategies used to gather assessment data with this model, we have identified tools that teachers use to collect data as well as what students use to report what they know.

Low-Prep Strategies for Model 3

This model's strength lies in its capturing assessment data that might not be accomplished through other means to determine students' progress. Observations of students involved in completing various tasks either alone, in pairs, or cooperative teams can render information that is invaluable. Using low-prep strategies, one teacher can ask questions, make statements, or display a problem for students to consider while the other teacher notes whether or not students were successful. Here, we offer some assessment strategies that take little time to prepare, and therefore can be easily incorporated into any co-teaching routine.

Student-assessment low-prep strategies. There are many methods teachers use to create opportunities for an immediate determination of student abilities and needs. The following methods and tools can be used as quick assessment opportunities for students to demonstrate their knowledge and skills.

Hand-held, erasable whiteboards. Personal, portable dry-erase boards offer a simple solution for students to display what they know using a write-on and wipe-off surface. As they hold up their individual boards, their answers can be assessed.

Yes/No and True/False cards. These double-sided cards can be used to assess students' prior knowledge or for a quick fact check to establish their acquisition of language, knowledge, and skills. Responses are noted as students hold their selected answers in front of them.

One Hand/Two Hands. Students are given a series of statements to which they wave one hand if they believe the statement is true or two hands if they believe the statement is false. They may also raise both hands palms facing up and shrug their shoulders if they do not have enough evidence to guess whether or not a statement is true or false. A variation of this approach is *Right Hand/Left Hand* in which students raise their right hands if they believe a statement is true or their left hands if the statement is false.

Sentence summary. Using a blank sheet of paper, students are asked to summarize a topic, concept, story plot, and so on, using one complete sentence. Sentences can be assessed for both content and language. A variation of this strategy is to ask students to paraphrase information that is shared, such as definitions or concepts, using their own words.

Teacher-assessment low-prep tools. In order for co-teaching partners to commit to ongoing assessment practices, we offer these low-prep strategies and routines to gather student assessment data.

Generic checklists. Generic checklists can be ready to use for various content assessment purposes. They can be completed with a simple checkmark or can note numeric as well as other pertinent information. Checklists may be combined with student low-prep techniques identified in the previous section as well as used to assess other student tasks. See Figure 5.3 for a sample generic checklist.

Anecdotal notes. Observations of student progress can be documented by writing brief remarks in some systematic way using note-taking templates and routines. Specific or more general aspects of

Figure 5.3	Sample Generic Checklist

Co-teachers: *Ms. Franklin & Mr. Perez*			**Grade:** *2* **Content:** *Science*		
Date	*2/1/16*	*2/8/16*	*2/22/16*	*2/29/16*	
Names	*Drawing of a plant*	*Label parts of plant*	*What plants need*	*Steps for planting seeds*	
Anna A.	√	6	4	√	
Isaac T.	√	6	4	√	
Barry C.	√	6	4	√	
Jayson M.	√	4	3	-	
Raul G.	√	5	3	√	
Fatima C.	√	3	3	-	
Desiree K.	√	abs.	4	√	
Jacek L.	√	5	4	√	
Aisha J.	√	6	3	√	
Hector N.	√	6	3	√	
Enrique D.	√	6	3	√	
Paloma R.	√	6	4	√	
Min L.	√	6	4	√	
Mariposa G.	√	5	4	-	
Elena S.	√	6	4	√	
Assessment Focus and Comments:	*All students able to reproduce drawing*	*Voc: roots seeds stem leaves flower fruit*	*Voc: water air sunlight nutrients*	*Some students had steps out of order*	

content and language learning may be noted for individual students. Some teachers create an anecdotal notebook for record keeping that may be tabbed to divide pages for recording information on each student's progress. In this way, all assessment data are kept in one place and readily available for review and analysis.

Monday–Friday note-taking routine. One routine that works well in documenting student progress is a systematic way to gather anecdotal notes for each student in a class. Groups of students are assigned to different days of the week for observation, and their progress will be observed and noted only during their specified day. For example, five students are assigned to the "Monday" group, and only those five students' progress will be documented during Mondays. In this way, co-teachers will have the opportunity to gather data on all students at least once per week. See Figure 5.4 for a partially completed sample template for taking anecdotal notes with this routine.

Figure 5.4   Monday–Friday Anecdotal Notes

Student's Name: *Eun Ryu*		Proficiency: *3/Developing*	Day: *Tuesday*
Class: *3-205* **Co-teachers:** *Ms. Martin & Mr. Lewis*			

	Dates	Notes
SPEAKING	*11/23*	*Can communicate facts and ideas in some detail; continues to drop definite articles.*
WRITING	*11/16*	*Can write simple sentences easily; difficulty with more complex grammar (tense, noun phrases) and punctuation.* *Enjoys adding elaborate illustrations even when not required.*
READING	*11/16* *11/23*	*Reads with some fluency; difficulty with texts that are less predictable.* *Grammatically complex texts remain difficult to understand.*
LISTENING	*11/16*	*Understands multistep routine or familiar directions in context without repetition.*

Sticky notes. Some teachers use an individual manila folder for each student and use sticky notes to jot observed academic behaviors as they circulate within the room. At the end of the class, they place these notes in the appropriate student's folder.

Pro-Prep Strategies for Model 3

Hattie (2015a) is a proponent of the use of assessment to offer feedback to students about their academic progress. Yet he further explains,

> It is more critical to use this information to inform teachers about their impact on students. Using assessments as feedback for teachers is powerful. And this power is truly maximized when the assessments are timely, informative, and related to what teachers are actually teaching. (p. 23)

What better way to gather such assessment information than to have immediate information on student improvement or challenges using this co-taught model to collect data? Here we offer strategies that may take a little more time to prepare, yet they can often reveal very particular and detailed data sets about students' knowledge and skills.

Student-assessment pro-prep strategies. Formative assessment should be at the heart of co-teachers' instructional routines. However, what is frequently neglected is the assessment of the speaking and listening abilities of students. Creating opportunities to assess students' spoken language in the co-taught class is essential for targeting skills to build language proficiency. The following are some examples of assessment tasks that need some preparation, yet they can reveal students' competencies to use particular language functions when interacting with one another.

Tabletop summary tents. With this strategy, students are guided to use a series of sentence starters that are printed on card stock folded in half (see Figure 5.5) to create a "table tent" to share summarized information with peers either in pairs or small groups. These sentence frames support students to practice various language functions such as describing a particular character, comparing and contrasting information, offering an explanation of a problem and its solution, and so on. Co-teachers can focus on individual students' oral language performance as well as content knowledge and note their ability to achieve each spoken task.

Socratic seminar. Writing highly strategic questions for this activity can take a great deal of preparation time in addition to selecting a suitable topic, texts, and providing students opportunities to practice the rules for engaging in the activity. Yet the effort put forth to develop a thought-provoking, open-ended activity for students can be the impetus for initiating rich conversations about a given topic. In turn, students develop the ability to ask their own questions to delve even deeper into the topic. To assess students using Socratic seminar, one teacher would lead the activity while the other teacher makes notations of students' contributions to the discussion, with specific focus on grammatical, pragmatic, and discourse competence.

Four quadrants. For this activity, teachers prepare enough spinners divided into four sections for teams of students that are marked for one of the following language functions: explain, predict, summarize, and evaluate. During a shared reading, the teacher leading the reading will pause at certain intervals and prompt students to consider certain aspects of the text. The other teacher invites students to take turns spinning the spinner in their group in order to respond to the prompt in one of the four ways indicated on the spinner. One or both teachers might circulate within the room during this activity to collect anecdotal information on various students. This strategy might also be combined with tabletop summary tents in order to provide students with sentence starters that support students' explanations, predictions, and so on.

Teacher-assessment pro-prep tools. Some assessment approaches offer more detailed information about students' progress in language and content development. As indicated in a recent World-Class Instructional Design and Assessment (WIDA, 2014) position paper,

Figure 5.5 Tabletop Tent

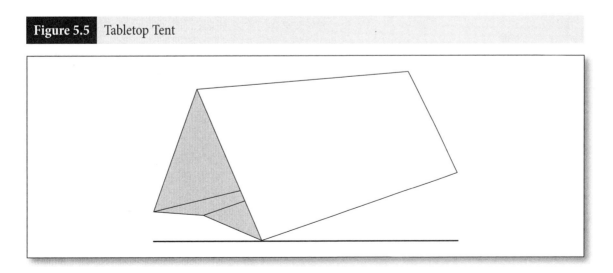

there is now general agreement that all students are learning to manage new sociocultural and language routines in classrooms and schools and that in each content area, students make use of specialized vocabulary, grammar, language functions and related discourse structures, and text types. (para. 1)

Here are some examples of tools co-teachers can prepare to gather formative data concurrently with instruction or summative assessment data at the completion of each unit of study.

Content-specific checklists. In contrast to generic checklists, these assessments focus on specific content, concepts, and language skills. They include a range of competencies—from a set of developmental milestones expected of students in preschool and kindergarten to distinctive literacy, mathematics, or other core content curricula learning targets. These checklists can be written to match specific benchmarks or learning goals as identified in particular units of study. In addition, they can focus on explicit language development skills. See Figure 5.6 for an English language arts (ELA)-specific checklist that narrows the focus of assessment to target literacy subskills such as key ideas and details (KID), integrating knowledge integration (IKI), and craft and structure (C&S; ReadyGEN, see www.pearsonschool.com/ReadyGen). Based on the data collected during a lesson, teachers determine what differentiated resources students will receive and/or which groups they will join.

Rubrics. Rubrics are prepared scoring guides that evaluate students on a scale according to certain criteria. According to Moskal (2000), "scoring rubrics are typically employed when a judgment of quality is required and may be used to evaluate a broad range of subjects and activities" (para. 2). Common uses for rubrics are to assess writing skills, particularly on standardized tests. Many teachers have adopted this practice when scoring essays and other class projects. Co-teachers for English learners also use rubrics to determine students' performance in their abilities to comprehend spoken language, participate in academic conversations, speak with fluency and facility, and so forth. With rubrics such

---

Figure 5.6 ELA-Specific Checklist Based on the ReadyGEN Curriculum

Name	GIST	Vocabulary	Reading/ Language Analysis	KID	IKI	C&S

Adapted with permission from the work of Ruth Goldstein-Hernandez and Katherine Lameras of PS 200, Brooklyn, NY.

as those in Figure 5.7, one or both co-teachers might observe students working in groups and use a highlighter to indicate where individual students performed.

Online assessments. Technology and game-based applications can play a role in assessing students in the co-taught class. Two such applications are Kahoot! and Plickers. According to its website, Kahoot! "is a free game-based learning platform that makes it fun to learn—any subject, in any language, on any device, for all ages" (getkahoot.com). It is easily played as a whole class, but there is a need for an interactive whiteboard or computer with a digital projector as well as students having their own devices—smartphones or tablets—to play. Students answer multiple-choice questions projected on a screen using their own personal devices, and their answers are later revealed to show how many students achieved the correct answer. Plickers is somewhat similar; however, with this application, an interactive whiteboard or computer with a digital projector is required, but students do not need individual devices. They use prepared cards to answer questions, which are scanned with a device (smartphone or tablet) by one of the teachers to project their answers on the screen. Both applications are fun, fast paced, and crowd pleasers. They do take time to prepare, and assessment data are limited to whole-class assessment and not that of individual students.

Figure 5.7 Sample Rubrics for Oral Language Assessment
Oral Language Performance Rubrics
Score 5
Actively participates in class/group discussions
Asks appropriate questions using academic language
Responds to questions with evidence from text, multimedia, or previous statements
Uses appropriate vocabulary and grammatical structures with no errors
Responds with appropriate detail
Speaks with fluency and facility; native-like intonation and pronunciation
Score 4
Takes a somewhat active role in class/group discussions
Asks appropriate questions
Usually demonstrates understanding with response to questions
Uses appropriate vocabulary and grammatical structures with few errors
Responds with sufficient detail
Speaks with some gaps in fluency; acceptable intonation and pronunciation
Score 3
Takes a limited role in class/group discussions
Asks simple questions
May not understand information as evidenced by responses
Uses limited vocabulary and grammatical structures with several errors
Responds with limited detail
Speaks with hesitation, with errors in intonation and pronunciation

(Continued)

Figure 5.7	(Continued)

Oral Language Performance Rubrics
Score 2
Interacts minimally or uses home language in class/group discussions
Attempts to formulate questions with support
Can respond to questions with support
Demonstrates little knowledge of vocabulary and grammatical structures
Responds with detail with support
Excessive hesitation to speak; errors in intonation and pronunciation impede ability to be understood
Score 1
Unable to interact without the use of home language
Has difficulty or is unable to ask questions with support
Has difficulty or is unable to use vocabulary and grammatical structures in English
Has difficulty or is unable to respond with detail with support
Has difficulty or is unable to speak; frequent errors in intonation, pronunciation, and reliance on home language impede ability to be understood

Adapted from Rubrics for Foreign Language: Model Assessment Project, Ohio Department of Education. Retrieved from https://education.ohio.gov/getattachment/Topics/Academic-Content-Standards/Foreign-Language/Ohio-Foreign-Language-Model-Assessment-Project/Appendix_1.pdf.aspx

SAMPLE LESSON SEGMENTS: ONE GROUP: ONE TEACH, ONE ASSESS

The following lesson segments portray co-teachers as they incorporate teaching and assessment practices into their co-taught lessons to gather formative assessment data.

Lesson 1—Kindergarteners Act Out Vocabulary

In this lesson segment, kindergarteners are assessed on their retention of vocabulary—action words—presented during a unit of study on fairy tales. In preparation for the unit, the co-teaching team selected a set of verbs from the stories to be shared and engaged students to act out parts of the different stories. As part of the unit, the team planned to have students sequence the actions of characters from each fairy tale kinesthetically. In this way, students would be able to connect their actions with the targeted words as well as demonstrate their understanding of new vocabulary.

After several stories from the unit were completed, the teaching team assessed students' knowledge of targeted vocabulary. Keeping students together in one group, students were invited to demonstrate their understanding of each word by acting it out. For example, students were asked, "Show me how you can twirl." And students were expected to twirl in place.

As one teacher asked students to act out each word, the other teacher noted on a checklist which students were unable to match their action with the words spoken. After students were asked to demonstrate about 12 words, the team quickly reviewed the checklist, and students were then divided into two groups—those children who needed reinforcement of the vocabulary and those youngsters who would begin a writing assignment as an alternative lesson. In this way, the students who needed additional support received it, while the other students engaged in enrichment activities without going ahead in the unit.

An analysis of the lesson segment. In this lesson, co-teachers planned to assess their students midway through a unit of study on fairy tales to determine how students were retaining information about new vocabulary concepts—in this case, action words. They used an appropriate format for kindergarteners, a kinesthetic activity, to gauge student learning. This assessment gave co-teachers information about student progress that was specific to and targeted on a certain aspect of their linguistic development. This type of brief, formative assessment gives co-teachers the opportunity to reteach and reinforce the learning of ELs through immediate intervention and small-group learning strategies. It is a simple yet effective practice that can be incorporated into the periodic routine of the co-taught class.

Lesson 2—Developing Oral Language Proficiency in a Seventh-Grade Science Class

In this lesson, there were multiple opportunities for the co-teaching team to collect student data during the different phases of the lesson. It began with the science and English language development/English language learner teachers in front of the room explaining to their seventh graders the instructional objective—to develop a critical position on an environmental issue and develop an oral argument for their selected position. One teacher read the objective while the other teacher paraphrased points in the objective or asked students questions such as: What is a critical position? Students were then asked to think of environmental issues that were important to them.

Next, each teacher shared an issue that she was passionate about— loss of biodiversity and animal conservation—as examples. Students then completed a Think-Pair-Share activity in which they discussed possible issues with a partner or in a triad. During this time, each teacher circulated around the room to observe students' oral-language skills and take anecdotal notes on a select number of students. Teachers also asked students questions to stimulate their thoughts and conversation.

Subsequently, the class generated a list of environmental concerns—climate change, air pollution, flooding, drought, and so on. Students were asked to volunteer to report out what their partners had expressed to them. During this part of the lesson, one teacher jotted down the information students shared on the board while the other teacher noted which students chose to contribute to create the common list of environmental concerns. The input of each co-teacher extended the list of additional topics to explore.

In teams, students were asked to select one of the topics on the list to explore in greater detail. Using tablets connected to the Internet, students were asked to research the topic to gain more background knowledge. Both teachers once again circulated within the room and jotted down anecdotal notes to assess students' abilities to access, evaluate, and integrate the information they found. They worked with small groups of students in a rotating fashion to assist them in their search on the Internet as well as to encourage students to begin to form a critical position about the topic as they shared information with one another.

The class ended with the students together as one group with individual or teams of students sharing what they had discovered about certain issues and the critical positions they were developing about their topic. One of the teachers led the discussion while the other teacher completed some anecdotal notes on the session. Before the bell rang, the science teacher briefly explained that during tomorrow's lesson, students would be developing an oral argument based on their findings.

An analysis of the lesson segment. Oral language and literacy skills may be overlooked in secondary science or social studies co-taught classes, which often contain dense and challenging curricula that must be addressed in a timely manner. In this lesson, the co-teachers pay careful attention to the language development of their students by their focus on the oral discourse and literacy abilities their students need in order to express their ideas and research science concepts. During this lesson, the co-teaching team takes multiple opportunities to assess student learning. At times, both teachers assessed students' abilities, while at others, one teacher led instruction while the other teacher gathered data. These data might be shared on the spot to enhance instruction immediately, or they might be part of the overall data that are gathered on this multiday lesson and reviewed for further instructional planning. The co-teachers might also use the data to reflect on their co-teaching practices.

MODEL VARIATIONS

Both Teach, Both Assess

Co-teachers may establish a unique flow or routine in their classroom in which both teachers engage the entire class in a learning experience that also serves the purpose of yielding formative assessment data. Total physical response (TPR) is a good example: both teachers model and encourage students to participate in a kinesthetic activity such as attaching motions to a song, rhyme, or chant that may serve as a mnemonic device. Then, each teacher observes the entire class and takes notes on which students are participating and which are not, as well as document target language performances. Having both teachers assess students lends a different point of view, particularly to anecdotal assessment data. In turn, co-teachers can compare their notes and come to a more detailed understanding of student abilities.

One Assesses, One Monitors/Teaches

The main goal of this variation is classwide assessment data collection that takes center stage; thus, the role of the assessor is to move from student to student to collect specific data, such as the use of specific vocabulary or phrases in oral or written work. The lesson is designed to allow for one teacher to observe students in authentic contexts, for example, during pair work or other small group interactions, including paired reading, triads, or project-based learning. In the meantime, the other teacher's role is to circulate within the room to assist students with the task they need to complete.

Two Monitor/Teach, Students Self-Assess

This model variation can be used to assist students to develop their own self-assessment techniques. The co-teachers model the development and/or application of a self-assessment tool by thinking aloud and allowing students insight into their metacognitive and reflective processes. After modeling self-assessment in this collaborative manner, students are invited to complete their own self-assessment tool (see Chapter 10 for self-assessment).

Rotate and Assess
(One Teaches, One Assesses, or Two Assess)

This model variation is similar to Model 7 (see Chapter 9). While co-teachers set up multiple stations or centers, one (or two) of those stations is designed with the sole focus of progress monitoring, data collection, and assessment. As students rotate through the stations, they are all monitored by one teacher; the other teacher remains seated with and focuses on the group that rotates to his or her station to be able to conduct a targeted, small-group assessment. Alternately, two stations are designed as assessment sites, while the rest of the stations or learning centers are designed for independent work.

MODEL COMBINATIONS

One Teaches, One Assesses/Teaches
On Purpose (Models 1 and 3 combined)

Model 3 is not just for assessment; it can be combined with teaching on purpose to support students as needed. For example, if one teacher is collecting data, and he or she observes a student having difficulty with a concept or a task, this model lends an opportunity for that teacher to offer on-the-spot instruction for such students by teaching on purpose.

One Teaches, One Assesses/Two groups:
One Reteaches, One Teaches Alternative Information (Model 6)

By virtue of collecting formative assessment data that inform instruction, co-teachers can seamlessly combine Model 3 with Model 6. The data collected may be used during the same class period or during subsequent lessons to determine which students need additional opportunities to learn new information or practice new skills, while the rest of the class may benefit from enrichment or extension activities.

One Teaches, One Assesses/
Multiple Groups: Two Teachers Teach (Model 7)

The information about student progress gleaned from formative assessment data may also lead to co-teachers setting up multiple groups with tiered instruction. If more than a small group of students need reteaching, or if students have performed on multiple levels according to the assessment collected during the previous lesson, a more comprehensive approach to intervention may be used via Model 7:

Group 1: Foundational skill building (Teacher 1)

Group 2: Reteach target concept or skill (Teacher 2 divided between Groups 2 and 3)

Group 3: Practice target concept or skill (Teacher 2 divided between Groups 2 and 3)

Group 4: Student-led enrichment group work on or above target

Group 5: Independent enrichment work above target level

INSPIRATION FROM THE FIELD

Read what colleagues—ELD/ELL and classroom teachers as well as building and district administrators—shared with us from around the United States and see how they reflect or add to your own experiences.

Laura Shimkus, Michelle Mannino, and Christina Ruggiero collaboratively serve ELs in a Brooklyn middle school, where Laura and Christina are English as a New Language (ENL) teachers and Michelle is an ELA teacher. In their unique arrangement, the ELA teacher joins the ENL teachers in their classrooms rather than the other way around. They use a variety of models, but Model 3 seems to be a critical way to enhance their impact on student learning. See how they reflected on the use of Model 3 when combined with Model 6.

We use Model 3 when we feel that students may struggle with grasping a concept and we know we will need feedback to determine student understanding. For example, in one lesson, the focus was on essay writing. After the ELA teacher taught the parts of an essay, the ENL teacher taught the language of counterclaim. During the ENL teacher's minilesson, the ELA teacher circulated around the room to assess if the writing that the students were completing in their graphic organizers was correct and reflected an understanding of the lesson. Model 3 allowed us to assess our students and alter our lessons accordingly. Then, we followed up with Model 6 (Two groups: One Reteaches, One Teaches Alternative Information). After assessing our students' grasp of the topic of counterclaim, the ELA teacher came to the conclusion that some students needed extra support with writing a counterclaim. The next period, the ELA teacher pulled these students into a group and retaught counterclaim using additional scaffolding while the ENL teachers continued with the writing workshop with the rest of the students.

Violeta R. Gamez, an EL resource teacher in Woodridge School District 68, IL, shared with us how she and her colleague use Model 3 routinely and how they combine it with Model 1.

Every lesson follows the same routine, making it easier for us to transition into our roles. For example, while I (Ms. Gamez) am presenting to the whole group, Mrs. Hall is walking around the room ensuring students are on task, as well as assessing their work. This allows her to provide immediate feedback to students. Once my role to lead the lesson is completed, we switch roles, and Mrs. Hall teaches a whole-group lesson while I serve as the assessor. By walking around and observing students, we are able to determine which students have caught onto the lesson and which students are still struggling and require additional support in a specific area. This additional support may consist of reviewing a concept, drawing a picture to explain word meaning (i.e., gag, twine, wrench), and so on. If we notice that students don't understand or cannot remember the multistep directions, the assessor will write instructions on the board with picture cues or examples. To guide speaking and writing, one teacher will write sentence frames on the board as the other teacher is modeling the specific language to be used and how it should be used (i.e., I agree/disagree because; the author says/the text says, and so on).

Jamie Bottcher, formerly a K–5 ENL teacher in Brentwood, New York, has also established various routines according to which she and her colleagues purposefully weave together models for co-taught instruction:

Using the different types of co-teaching models has had an extremely positive impact on our learning environment. The ability to transfer between different models throughout lessons has increased the academic success of our students as well as my success as a co-teacher with multiple partners. I have found it extremely productive to use Model 3: One Teaches, One Assesses. This model allows one teacher to demonstrate and practice a skill with all students, and creates an environment in which the co-teaching partner can observe, conference with, and record anecdotal notes on students (formative assessment). This class configuration is particularly helpful in that we may then form additional, and occasionally immediate, academic groups for reteaching or enrichment exercises. Although we have gotten comfortable enough to switch between models easily, having the background and understanding of our roles in each model keeps us on target and focused as teaching partners.

TAKEAWAYS

In this chapter, we discuss how Model 3 (One Teaches, One Assesses) could be effectively integrated into your co-teaching repertoire. In light of the importance of incorporating formative assessment in your daily practice, the use of this model has the potential to further enhance the co-teaching experience for you and your partner as well as language and literacy development and content attainment for all students in the co-taught classroom.

QUESTIONS FOR FURTHER DISCUSSION

1. What distinguishes Model 3 (One Teaches, One Assesses) from Model 1 (One Teaches, One Teaches on Purpose)? On the other hand, why is it essential to connect these two models of co-instruction, and how can you best do it?

2. What are the challenges of conducting formative assessment practices in Model 3 with a dual focus on content and language learning? What are some possible solutions?

3. How would you establish an assessment and progress monitoring routine using Model 3?

4. In what ways can you continue to maintain parity for the two co-teachers taking on different roles while implementing this model?

6

Model 4—Two Groups

Two Teach Same Content

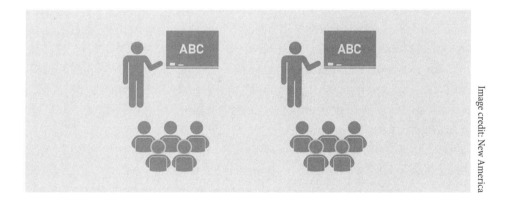

AN INTRODUCTION TO THE MODEL

In this chapter, we begin to discuss one of the ways students are divided into two groups for co-taught instruction, a common practice in integrated programs for English learners (ELs). Teachers who incorporate this model into their repertoire of approaches to co-teaching find that it can yield many benefits for ELs. To configure this model, students are set into two groups for instruction that are fairly equal in size. However, the main objective for each co-teaching team is to maintain high expectations and develop rigorous lessons for all students as instruction is planned for two separate groups.

One of the main functions of this particular model is that it reduces the student-teacher ratio. The reason why decreasing group size is effective stems from the various opportunities teachers may have to adjust instruction for selected students as well as foster their efforts, initiatives, engagement, and time on task (Schanzenbach, 2014) in the smaller group. From a very practical standpoint, having fewer students to teach allows more student-teacher contact time and increases the teacher's ability to offer immediate feedback, build student-teacher relationships, and offer on-the-spot remediation. All of these practices, according to Hattie and Yates (2013), have large effect sizes; in other words, by virtue of the instructional practices that generally take place with smaller groups of students, the impact on their learning is greatly increased.

This model of co-teaching also has been identified as *parallel teaching* in the research and literature about inclusion for students with disabilities (Friend & Bursuck, 2014; Murawski, 2010; Villa, Thousand, & Nevin, 2013). It is well regarded as an approach to teaching in the area of special education and used regularly by co-teachers who teach in inclusive education programs. Yet when describing the use of this model, Wendy Murawski (2010) offers the following advice:

> [This model] sometimes enables teachers to feel that they can adopt a "separate but equal" approach . . . Teachers should not plan and teach on their own "island." As with all approaches, teachers should discuss what they'll be doing with their individual groups and collaborate on the best approaches. (p. 200)

We also strongly suggest caution when employing this model in the English language development/English language learneres (ELD/ELL) context and guard against creating situations in which in-class segregation of ELs occurs. The decision-making process behind separating students for instruction should be one that is flexible and dependent on their immediate needs in contrast to using broad-based labels to group them. Dividing the class for instruction—one group ELs and one group non-ELs, for example—can place a stigma on students, foster low expectations, advance stereotypes, and create situations in which students' competences and strengths are overlooked and underutilized. If this type of rigid division of students is maintained, inadvertently, de facto separation and an in-class pull-out program are created (Triplett, 2013).

Like all co-teaching approaches, this model works best when it is purposefully selected and applied for the instruction of English learners as well as the rest of the students in the class. Lesson goals and objectives for both content and language learning must be considered along with class dynamics, material resources, class space, and the ability to reconfigure its contents—desks, chairs, technology, and so on—and each co-teacher's comfort with the subject matter to be taught.

A CLOSER LOOK AT MODEL 4

Most characteristic of this model is the division of the class into two separate groups of students, with each group working directly with one of the co-teachers in select areas of the room. A very typical setup would have one group of students working with a teacher in front of the room while the second group is being taught by another teacher in the back. To reduce the volume of sound and possible distractions, co-teachers face each other while the two groups face away from one another. Alternately, the groups may be set up to be at an angle opposite each other, with one group significantly out of sight of the other. This configuration also allows co-teachers to communicate with one another nonverbally as to the pacing of the lesson.

A different way to configure the class for instruction in smaller spaces is to keep students seated in rows in their same seats and divide the class in half, having students turn to face one teacher or the other (see Figure 6.1). Also, consider having half the class maintain their seating facing front, giving their attention to one teacher, and have the other half turn to face the back of the room to focus on the additional teacher. We have also observed students seated in a u-shaped formation with one teacher guiding a portion of the students and the other teacher focused on the remaining students on the opposite side.

In certain class settings, we have noted one teacher working with students using an interactive whiteboard while a second group of students is seated in a carpeted area with one of the co-teachers using different learning tools such as manipulatives. After a designated amount of time, the groups switch teachers so that the students who were previously using the manipulatives are now working with the teacher at the interactive whiteboard and vice versa. In this way, both groups of students have an opportunity to work with the same sets of resources as well as both teachers, even if the lesson content, depth, and instructional strategies used may be planned and executed somewhat differently. Specifically, each group's lesson is devised to meet the needs of those particular students, so frequently co-teachers prepare two separate lessons to match the strengths and abilities of each group. We must stress here that the configuration of the class for instruction is always dependent on what is being taught, what formative assessment data tell teachers about their students' needs for grouping, and how meaningful the group placement will be to meet the specific needs of the students identified prior to the lesson.

This model is frequently used for explicit teaching, modeling, demonstration, and/or guided practice. To accomplish these tasks, the prerequisite material resources (books, notebooks, notepads, tablets, etc.) must be in place for lessons to be effective. Each teacher needs to have at his or her disposal adequate space, a comfortable seating area for students, and a surface to write on if the task so requires. Since students may also need something to support their writing, such as the use of notebooks, clipboards, or erasable whiteboards, organizing instructional resources prior to implementing this model is highly recommended.

Deliberate, systematic attention to this model will yield positive results from its use. Teachers who use this approach to instruction routinely have their students well prepared by carefully demonstrating, modeling, and practicing how to move from whole class to group work. In this way,

Figure 6.1 Model 4: One Configuration

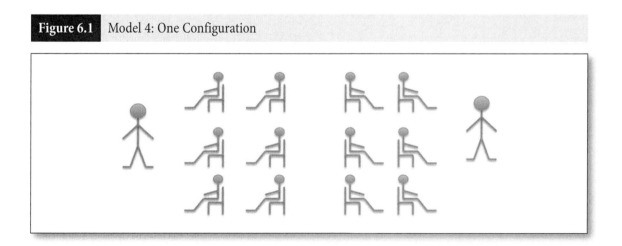

co-teaching procedures become predictable patterns for students—they allow for smoother transitions and take up less instructional time. Displaying each student's assignment within one group or the other before the class begins likewise facilitates where students should go and what they need to do as well as eases the application of flexible student groupings.

In our observations of this model, students are sometimes divided into EL and non-EL groups. This type of grouping must be relevant and advantageous for all ELs as determined by the lesson objectives and the language proficiency of the students. However, it has been our experience with few exceptions that English learners' instructional needs within one class are varied; therefore, their learning may not be best supported by being automatically placed in homogenous groups. Additionally, ELs should not be separated from the native English-speaking peers for the entire class period on a daily basis. We understand that direct contact time with the ELD/ELL specialist is vital for certain programs for ELs to be in compliance with state and local mandates. However, from an instructional vantage point, segregating students as a general practice is not advisable (U.S. Department of Justice & U.S. Department of Education, 2015).

A frequently asked question concerns the use of an alternative space to teach separate student groups. In other words, might one teacher bring his or her group of students to the library, computer lab, a gymnasium, outdoors on the playground, or to another classroom to render instruction? Our answer is always the same—yes and no! Student groups may be placed in an alternative setting if it is essential, meaningful, and enhances students' overall learning experiences. Take a group of students to the library if they need to learn research skills; set up the computer lab for a group if students need to build technology skills; use open spaces like the gym, school yard, or the playground for kinesthetic activities that help build background knowledge; or any available space if taking a group of students there purposefully supports learning critical skills. However, if students are removed from the classroom frequently, it is just a manipulation of co-taught instruction and akin to stand-alone teaching for ELs.

Generally speaking, this model is best employed when it is coupled with other class configurations. Co-teaching teams often avoid using it to open a lesson unless it is an extension of instruction begun the previous day. However, some co-teachers, due to time constraints or consistent lesson objectives focused on a particular type of instruction (e.g., guided reading), begin class by dividing the students from the onset. This practice, coupled with segregating groups of students, can create a class atmosphere in which English learners are contradistinguished—viewed as less-capable learners. In addition, students may not consider the ELD/ELL specialist as a *real* teacher. Conscious consideration for the use of this model is integral for productive co-taught practices.

VIDEO 6.1:
Model 4—
Two Groups:
Two Teach
Same
Content

http://resources
.corwin.com/
CoTeachingforELs

ADVANTAGES

As mentioned in the introduction to this model, one of the greatest advantages of this approach is the reduction of the student-teacher ratio. Some studies have shown the positive effects on student achievement when placed in smaller classes (Chingos & Whitehurst, 2011). From a content and language learning point of view, English learners have more opportunities to ask questions, clarify information, and take risks to practice their language skills in a smaller and often safer environment. To wit, small-group instruction, when used purposefully, can boost the content and language learning of ELs.

By the nature of the size of the group, there is naturally an increase in opportunities for student interaction—student to teacher, teacher to student, and student to student. As Quaglia and Corso (2014) also point out, "While efforts to close the achievement gap are noble, we must question how much farther we will get without first closing the participation gap" (p. 87). When students are better engaged in learning, they are better able to stay focused, retain information, develop their speaking and listening skills, and build their confidence. It only stands to reason that teachers would be better able to engage students and encourage their participation in a smaller group.

Considering that all students do not need the same interventions and support for their learning, attention might be more easily paid to differentiation of instruction when fewer students are being taught. For this reason, dividing students into two groups will benefit those students who need additional support while allowing those students who are able to work more independently to do so. For example, one teacher might monitor a group in completing a task while the other group is given more direct instruction or additional modeling and demonstration in order to apply a new skill or strategy.

Careful attention can be paid to students' learning style preferences with this approach to co-taught instruction. In addition to an awareness and concern for the way in which students prefer to learn (e.g., auditory, visual, tactual, kinesthetic, sound, light, mobility, etc.), recognition of the aspects of cultural diversity in learning is a particular concern when teaching English learners. Guild (2001) cautions that the homogeneity of instruction does not serve culturally and linguistically diverse students:

> The emphasis on uniformity is a serious disadvantage for students whose culture has taught them behaviors and beliefs that are different from the norms of the majority culture most often emphasized in schools. Students whose families value collaboration are told to be independent. Students whose culture values spontaneity are told to exercise self-control. Students who are rewarded in their families for being social are told to work quietly and alone. (para. 13)

In other words, well-planned lessons using carefully selected student groups can help meet the perceptual, environmental, psychological, and cultural needs of all students.

Planning time may be somewhat different for co-teachers who have selected this model for instruction. Once the content and language objectives have been set and the learning targets identified and carefully aligned, co-teaching partners' planning for their group lessons might be completed independent of each other. Therefore, this approach to co-teaching might facilitate a reduction in face-to-face co-planning time.

Teachers can more readily conduct informal assessments using this co-teaching approach. Student observations; recording anecdotal notes; completing checklists concerning students' knowledge, ability, and skills; noting students' acquisition of vocabulary and grammar; and so on are some of the ways teachers can obtain information and make judgments about student learning. The smaller group size gives teachers a better opportunity to complete data gathering.

Positive student-teacher relationships may develop due to the reduction of group size. Students need to feel valued, and establishing good relationships with students helps to foster a learning climate in which students are more motivated and willing to take risks. During small-group instruction, teachers are better able to share their high expectations, give students individualized intervention and positive feedback, and support them to believe in their own abilities.

CHALLENGES

Explicit teaching is most challenging for teachers who may not be proficient in the content being addressed. ELD/ELL teachers have shared with us their reluctance to take a leading role in teaching students in content areas in which they are neither trained nor experienced. For this reason, planning for lessons using this model with teachers who are unfamiliar with the content must carefully consider what the group lessons will address. In these situations, lessons in the small group might focus on additional practice, follow-up activities, or disciplinary literacy—learning the language of the content in order to think critically as well as speak and write fluently about the subject matter.

Sound levels encountered in the co-taught class may be distracting for both students and teachers. Secondhand sound in the form of multiple conversations taking place between various groups of students sometimes creates a negative effect on how some youngsters learn. Some students may be unable to understand or follow directions, pick up cues for learning, or just feel overwhelmed. However, high levels of student engagement including the promotion of academic-rich conversations are among the highest-ranking practices that influence student achievement (Hattie & Yates, 2013). In our co-teaching research, we have yet to observe students who are distracted or confounded by high sound levels when they are actively engaged in group conversations or hands-on learning. More often, it is the teachers who have the difficulty with classroom noise. For this reason, co-teachers who opt to use this model need to negotiate the amount of sound they can tolerate and balance activities so that the classroom environment has periods of both mild clamor and quiet.

A concern some teachers have with dividing the class into separate groups for instruction is the maintaining of instructional rigor and accountability for high-quality instruction by both teachers. Although the same or similar learning goals and objectives are set for each student group, some teachers are uneasy about how lessons will be executed in the separate groups. As countermeasure to alleviate such concerns, ample coordinated planning needs to be in place. Furthermore, co-teachers should have the opportunity to offer input into each other's final lesson plans so that further discussions can take place if needed to assure lessons are on target for both language and content learning.

Caution should be used when identifying student groups or initiating grouping strategies that may create student segregation and characterize certain students as less able. This type of marginalization might occur if students are assigned to only one group and/or one of the co-teachers all the time. Consider grouping students according to their learning preferences, interests, or achievement in the content instead of just by language proficiency. Do not assume that English learners will need different types of support than their native English-speaking peers. Consider conducting some preassessment of students before grouping them for instruction.

Creating flexible groupings for delivering instruction can be a bit confounding when working with ELs, but consider first the purpose of the grouping, what students will be able to accomplish when they are separated for learning, and resist the temptation to simply group students according to their EL status. In addition, examine how students can be temporarily arranged for instruction to enhance achievement outcomes as well as meet their social and emotional needs. This type of grouping requires a great deal of consideration and discussion among co-teachers, making the use of flexible groupings quite time consuming. Use of preassessment strategies, reviews of current achievement data, knowledge of students' strengths, identification of special needs, and considerations for adequate peer support, in addition to language proficiency levels, are some of the many factors to consider when forming flexible groups.

Teachers' positioning in the classroom also can play a part in the balance of power between co-teachers, and this model of instruction might be problematic if one teacher is perceived as having and maintaining a more spacious, comfortable, or resource-accessible part of the classroom as compared with the other. For example, having one teacher always in front of the room with access to an interactive whiteboard, document camera, material resources, student desks, and so on, while the other teacher is in back of the room with no technology seated on the floor with students puts one teacher at a great advantage over the other. To guard against this happening, both teachers should equally share spaces in the classroom as well as material resources.

We have observed this model frequently being used in elementary classes and less often in secondary grades. For the most part, we have concluded that it comes down to logistics—the ability to organize, plan, and manage a lesson according to the actual space, furniture, and time frame available using this configuration. In elementary schools, classroom space tends to be more fluid and adjustable with areas for small-group instruction, carpeted floor spaces, and a class library, and children tend to be smaller in size, taking up less space than those students in middle or high school. In contrast, student desks take up most middle and high school classrooms. Time frames for classes also differ between elementary and secondary schools. Middle and high school classes average between 40 and 45 minutes, whereas elementary classes have considerably more time to organize students, shift furniture, and create classroom spaces that are conducive for this model to work.

INSTRUCTION USING MODEL 4

Identified here are strategies that go beyond the traditional scaffolding and use of graphic organizers for English learners and others who need additional support, although these approaches to teaching during small-group instruction are very appropriate, meaningful, and effective. Instead, we include here some ideas that will assist teachers in focusing on language development as well as content application.

Low-Prep Strategies for Model 4

This model's main purpose is to reduce the student-teacher ratio so that teachers are better able to directly support, guide, ensure differentiated instruction, offer feedback, and monitor

Table 6.1	Summary of Advantages and Challenges of Model 4

Model 4: Two Groups: Two Teach Same Content	
Advantages	**Challenges**
A reduction in the student-teacher ratio can boost the content and language learning of ELs.	ELD/ELL teachers may be reluctant to take a leading role in teaching students in content areas.
An increase in opportunities for student interaction and engagement in a smaller group.	Sound levels in the co-taught class may be distracting for both students and teachers.
Attention might be more easily paid to differentiate instruction.	Dividing the class into two groups for instruction may reduce the instructional rigor of one group compared with the other.
Learning style preferences and aspects of cultural diversity for learning can be better met.	Some grouping strategies might segregate students or characterize them as less able.
This approach to co-teaching might facilitate a reduction in face-to-face co-planning time.	Creating flexible groupings for instruction can be confounding and time consuming for co-teachers.
The smaller group size gives teachers a better opportunity to gather data by conducting informal assessments.	Co-teachers do not always have equal access to classroom spaces or material resources with this model.
Positive student-teacher relationships may develop more readily.	Implementation of this model is a challenge in middle and high schools due to logistics.

students' progress. Implementing low-prep strategies for small-group instruction can help teachers offer critical support for diverse learners to apply content information and skills through the use of oral and written language. The following strategies can be readily incorporated into co-teachers' instructional routines with this model of instruction.

Grouping strategies. The question of how to group students in integrated classes for instruction can be a bit of a quandary for co-teachers. The following strategies for grouping students focus on the purpose for using a particular approach for dividing students for instruction as well as maintaining a steadfast mindfulness about the benefits of student integration, peer models and support, and having high expectations for all students. It is important to remember that all types of student groups have their place in the integrated ELD/ELL class.

Homogeneous. When students are grouped according to similar factors such as achievement in the content area or English language proficiency, students who have comparable learning needs can be targeted more specifically. This grouping can benefit ELs to develop their vocabulary, build their background knowledge, or clarify grammar points, which can be addressed during small-group instruction.

Heterogeneous. With this type of grouping, students are purposefully mixed to include and balance the number of students at different levels of content ability, achievement, and English language proficiency to be placed and work together. Small groups are designed in this manner so that students benefit from targeted peer support, the diverse ideas and perspectives from a variety of learners, and a combination of native and nonnative English speakers.

Flexible. Diverse learners sometimes have similar learning issues, and flexible grouping strategies allow for students to be combined for a particular learning purpose for a short period of time to address their immediate needs. This type of grouping is similar to homogeneous groupings, yet labeling the group as *flexible* emphasizes that it is a one-time-only grouping that is unpredictable in its inclusion of students and purposeful for a specific immediate intervention.

Random. Creating random groups allows for a greater combination of students to interact with and learn from one another. There are various methods for randomly grouping students. Technology can help to create random groups through the use of applications such as *Team Shakes* or *Group Sort*. In this way, your tablet or smartphone can assign your students to groups. Low-tech ways to group students can be accomplished by using playing cards to select students according to a card's suit or color.

Conversational strategies. It is essential for ELs to have opportunities for and take part in academic conversations. They need to develop the ability to ask and answer questions, share their decisions, explain their choices, and defend their ideas. The following low-prep approaches to enhancing students' speaking and listening skills are ideal for this model of instruction.

Inside-Outside Circle. This strategy can be used with any grade level for developing both oral and written language in content-area classes. In the small group, students are first asked to individually complete a short written task on an index card or small piece of paper. It might be a response to a question, prompt, math problem, or completion of a fill-in-the-blank sentence. The small group is then divided into two equal parts with half of the group forming one circle of students facing outward, and the other half completes another circle surrounding the initial circle facing inward. Students are then partnered up—one from the inside circle with one from the outside circle—and share their answers to the written task. Students can share with multiple partners by having the outside circle shift one or two students to the right.

Line Up and Fold. Another way for students to be involved in conversation and discussion is to have students line up according to a preset determining factor—alphabetically, according to their birthdays, by selecting numbered cards randomly, and so on. Once the students are lined up, the idea is to *fold* the line in order to pair students for conversation. To accomplish this pairing, the student at the top of the line walks down to face the student at the opposite end of the line. Students follow the line leader until the line is virtually folded in half. Similar to the Inside-Outside Circle, students begin by having a prepared short written task to share when partnered with another student through this strategy. Students can be partnered with different students by shifting one of the lines.

Pro-Prep Strategies for Model 4

The power of small-group instruction often lies in the plans for the instructional approaches that will be employed to enhance student learning and make lessons meaningful. The following approaches take students' understanding to the next level by allowing for more in-depth interaction with complex academic language.

Figure 6.2 Line Up and Fold

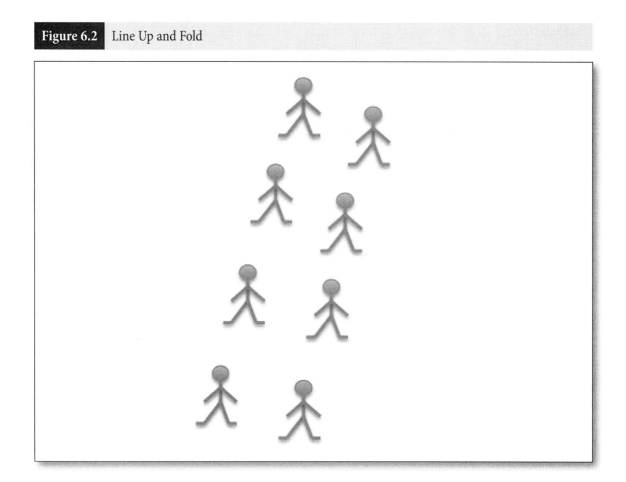

Building Academic Language—Sentence Dissection. In addition to the concepts presented in content area study, diverse learners need to develop a better understanding for the unique ways language is used to identify, examine, and explain concepts and ideas. Small-group instruction can complement students' building their academic language through a strategy known as Sentence Dissection (Dove & Honigsfeld, 2013; Honigsfeld & Dove, 2013), which offers both elementary and secondary ELs and their English-speaking peers opportunities to explore strategically selected complex sentences from a text already being used in class. By examining the structure of individual sentences, students are better able to understand the complex use of vocabulary and grammar structures. Try the following steps, but allow for individual variances as needed:

1. Select a sentence from the target textbook, trade book, or other assigned readings.

2. Present the sentence on chart paper, whiteboard, traditional blackboard, document camera, or SMART Board.

3. Facilitate an in-depth discussion of what the sentence means and how the author expressed his or her idea, inviting student input into meaning making first.

4. Ask probing questions—about the deep structure and meaning or the *who, what, when,* and *where* of the sentence.

5. Pinpoint one or more unique linguistic features of the sentence to call students' attention to select language complexities.

6. Use color coding or other visually engaging methods to chunk the sentence into smaller units, such as clauses or phrases.

7. Employ think-alouds as they called attention to grammatical or stylistic choices in some (but not *all*) of the language chunks to keep the activity brief and engaging.

8. Invite students to use the sentence as mentor text and to create similar sentences of their own to be able to internalize the language complexity, which is a key follow-up activity.

Readers' Theater. This strategy is intended to develop students' fluency and reading confidence by creating favorable circumstances for them to read aloud from a script either commercially prepared or developed from a text, either fiction or nonfiction, being used in the class. It is a great approach for small groups because a great deal of repetition is involved in the process—echo reading, choral reading, and rereading assigned parts of a script—along with text that is altered to meet students' various reading abilities and language proficiency levels.

Shared Reading and Writing. Supporting students to plan their writing based on text is a critical step for success. Incorporating visual frameworks for targeting and noting information from text offers students the assistance they need to complete writing tasks. Following a shared reading in the small group, students can complete a number of activities, such as:

- Fact Strips—a way for students to organize information from a nonfiction text by identifying key facts in a series of prepared boxes;
- Fact cards—index cards in which students record important facts (one per card), read to one another in pairs, and write summaries using both sets of students' cards;
- Timelines—a means of graphically representing the order of events in a text, students have the opportunity to summarize key events and details by noting when they occurred; and
- Summary charts—an organizer that categorizes key ideas related to the topic to assist diverse learners in logging information via a chain-of-events chart (event by event), problem-solution chart, or story pyramid (see Figure 6.3).

Text-Analysis. Select a target text and work through it to complete the four-quadrant graphic organizer adapted from Margo Gottlieb (2011) in Figure 6.4. Start by identifying the overall purpose of the text, then move on to highlighting the key words and phrases that give the main idea of the selection and/or are essential for understanding the authors' message. Focus on a few sentence-level grammatical features such as verb tense usage, and finally, examine the overall characteristics of the text with special attention to transitional words or other linguistic markers that help identify the text type or genre.

Figure 6.3   Story Pyramid

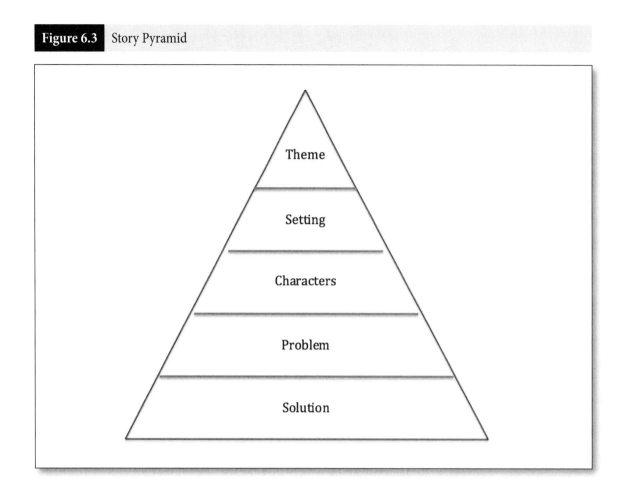

Figure 6.4   Text Analysis Grid

The Overall Purpose	Key Words and Phrases
Grammatical Forms	Genre or Text Type

SAMPLE LESSONS: TWO GROUPS: TWO TEACH SAME CONTENT

The following lesson segments portray co-teachers as they separate students into two fairly equal groups for co-taught instruction.

Persuasive Writing in a Fourth-Grade Class

This lesson was adapted from a unit plan written by Vanessa Estevez and Mary Kate Vaughan, both in-service teachers pursuing their master's degree in teaching English to speakers of other languages.

This lesson segment focuses on writing an opinion piece in a fourth-grade class, which contains both beginning- and advanced-level English learners integrated with fluent English speakers. It is part of a greater unit of study on persuasive writing. In this session, students will be guided to write a persuasive letter to the state governor on the topic of homework assignments. For the purpose of this narrative, we will call the fourth-grade teacher Ms. Vincent and the ESOL teacher Ms. Hyland.

The lesson opens with both teachers in front of the whole class (Model 2, see Chapter 4). Ms. Vincent reads to the class a letter from a ten-year-old girl who is trying to persuade her mother to buy her a cell phone. Ms. Hyland projects the written letter on the whiteboard using a document camera. She guides students to follow along while the letter is being read. At intervals, Ms. Vincent pauses and Ms. Hyland explains part of the text, clarifies vocabulary via verbal scaffolding and/or visuals, or asks students questions. Her questions help to build comprehension for those children who need additional language support. Ms. Vincent also asks questions but devises them for all students to dig deeper and think critically about the text. Both teachers encourage students to seek out and share the information used by the writer to persuade the reader.

Next, the teachers divide the class into two equally sized groups to organize their writing. Here is where Model 4—Two Groups: Two Teach the Same Content—comes into play. For this part of the lesson, they have decided to divide students according to their facility with letter writing. They place the beginning-level ELs, students who are struggling readers, and reluctant writers in one group. They place most of the advanced-level ELs and the rest of the students in the other.

Ms. Vincent takes the group with the majority of advanced-level ELs and distributes the written directions for the writing task. At first, she asks students to read the directions silently; then, she reviews the directions with them together, clarifies the task for students with questions, and presents them with the graphic organizer. She asks them to either work alone or in pairs to complete the organizer to plan their letter writing. In contrast, Ms. Hyland reads the directions aloud as her students follow along with copies of the text. She pauses frequently to paraphrase the directions, review vocabulary, use visuals and realia to support students' understanding of the task, and model what students will need to do with the graphic organizer, which is scaffolded with partially completed sentences to support students' writing (see Figure 6.5).

All students complete their graphic organizers in their respective groups. Once the organizer is complete, the students in Ms. Vincent's group are directed to write their persuasive letters to the state governor independently. They return to their own desks, and Ms. Vincent circulates and monitors their progress. At the same time, Ms. Hyland keeps her students together in the group. She walks them through step-by-step on how students can transfer their ideas from the graphic organizer to a written letter.

An analysis of the lesson segment. The teaching team begins by keeping the class together, which helps to establish the lesson objectives and sets high expectations for all learners. The teachers decide that flexible grouping—combining students with similar learning needs—is the best choice for lesson delivery, so they divide the students into two groups accordingly. Although the content (forming and writing an opinion) and the product (composing a persuasive letter) remain constant objectives for all students, the use of this model facilitates the differentiation of the process for learning, allowing students who need additional guidance and support with understanding the content and ultimately producing a written letter to receive such attention. In this way, all students have access to the same English language arts curriculum and rigorous instruction can be maintained.

Figure 6.5   Scaffolded Graphic Organizer for Persuasive Writing

Persuasive Letter Writing
Name: _____   Date: _____.
My Point of View/Opinion: <u>In my opinion, there should be more homework/less homework assigned in my class</u> _____.
Reason #1: <u>The first reason why there should be more/less homework is</u> _____.
Supporting evidence #1: <u>It is important to realize that</u> _____.
Supporting evidence #2: <u>Another key point is</u> _____.
Reason #2: <u>Another equally important reason why there should be more/less homework is</u> _____.
Supporting evidence #1: <u>It must be remembered that</u> _____.
Supporting evidence #2: <u>The most compelling evidence is</u> _____.
Conclusion: <u>From the reasons and evidence presented, I hope that I have been able to convince you that</u> _____.

Lesson 2—Identifying Five Types of Angles in Sixth Grade

In this mathematics co-taught lesson, students were asked to identify five different types of angles and pertinent mathematics vocabulary through various instructional methods used by their co-teachers including total physical response, interactive whiteboard technology, tablets, document cameras, Popsicle sticks, and pencil and paper activities.

The lesson began with both teachers in front of the entire class. The ELD teacher read the objective, and the mathematics teacher explained some of the tasks students would be completing. Next, the class was divided into two fairly equal groups of students according to their ability in mathematics and their learning-style preferences. One group of sixth graders sat in the front of the interactive whiteboard with the mathematics teacher, and the other group went to the opposite corner of the room and arranged their desks to face the ELD teacher.

The mathematics teacher displayed definitions of the different angles on the interactive whiteboard—acute, right, obtuse, and so on. Students were given a sheet that illustrated various angles, but they were unlabeled. The students had to read the definitions and collaboratively determine which illustration matched each definition. Next, they were asked to draw their own design, which was to include as many types of angles as they could in the allotted time. Using different colored markers, they traced all of the same angles with one color and labeled them. They shared their angle designs with the rest of the group via a document camera that projected them on the board.

At the same time, the ELD teacher introduced the characteristics of a right angle, and using her arms, she demonstrated what the angle looked like. She invited students to create the angle with their arms as well. She guided students to carefully examine the definition of a right angle—*a 90° angle, found in the corners of a square or at the junction of two perpendicular lines*—written on chart paper. She displayed a steel square and explained it was a *tool* for carpenters to use. She invited students to find 90° angles in the class, photograph them with their tablets, and share them with the group. The ELD teacher continued to review the definition of each angle in the same way, emphasizing vocabulary such as *perpendicular, parallel, intersecting, obtuse, acute*, and so on. Next, she invited students to create their own individual angles with Popsicle sticks to match the definitions that were displayed on the chart.

Near the end of the period, students were brought back together to play a concentration game in teams on the interactive whiteboard, matching pictures to their corresponding definitions. The ELD teacher led the assessment at the board while the mathematics teacher jotted down anecdotal data concerning students' performance.

An analysis of the lesson segment. In this lesson, all students had the same objective—to identify different types of angles and related vocabulary. The selection of Model 4 for instruction during the lesson was critical. Each group of students was introduced to the same material, just not in the same way. For one group, each angle was reviewed separately—step-by-step—while the other students were exposed to the material all at once. In addition, each group completed different tasks. Ultimately, both sets of students had met the benchmark goals that were set. By differentiating the tasks for each group, students who had prior knowledge or better facility with the mathematics concepts were able to move at a quicker pace. Yet within the same timeframe, students who needed more detailed support to develop the concepts and language use were able to receive it without holding any students back.

MODEL VARIATIONS

The hallmark of this model is that the class is divided into two basically even groups; each group is taught by one of the co-teachers, shares the same classroom space, and is taught the same fundamental content. In contrast, the following configurations are modifications of the model devised to accommodate different teaching goals and students' needs.

Two Groups/Two Teachers Teach Different Content or Skills

With this adaptation, the class is divided somewhat equally with a focus on homogeneous or flexible grouping. Students would be assigned to a group according to the particular lesson objective for each group. This type of variation has been successfully implemented with English learners and other diverse students who may need to build certain aspects of their language skills—speaking, writing, reading, and listening—with one teacher while a second group of students digs deeper into the content topic or the target skill with the other teacher.

Two Groups/Two Teachers Teach Different Content (Jigsaw)

Similar to the previous variation, each group is working with a teacher on a clearly defined target. Unlike the previous example, in this variation the teachers form heterogeneous groups and explore a different dimension of the curriculum, thus each group will become an expert in a different content target: two main characters from a novel, two competing sides of a historical event, two geographical regions, two countries, two explorers, and so on.

Alternative Spaces: One Group Inside and One Group Outside

At times, co-teachers may have the option to plan for one of the groups to be instructed at a location other than the regular classroom. The use of alternative spaces might be due to plans for some type of kinesthetic activity (see Inside-Outside Circle and Line Up and Fold strategies earlier in this chapter), or it is anticipated that the volume of sound might be too high when one or both groups complete a task in the same room. Taking one group out of the room on occasion for all or part of a class does not suggest in any way that the class is not being co-taught. However, if this model becomes the norm, co-teachers should reassess their goals for co-instruction.

One Teacher Instructs/One Teacher Monitors Independent Work

This model provides a great amount of flexibility as to what occurs in the separate groups. With this variation, each teacher can provide a group of students with varied levels of teaching and support. For example, one teacher might conduct a lesson via direct instruction while the other teacher is monitoring a group of students who remain at their own desks to complete a writing task. This amount of adjustability makes this model of co-instruction a welcomed choice for many co-teaching pairs.

MODEL COMBINATIONS

Model 4 (Two Groups: Two Teach Same Content) may be naturally sandwiched between implementing Model 2 (One Group: Two Teach Same Content) twice: first and last in the sequence of models. Start out the lesson with both teachers introducing the lesson and presenting a minilesson. To reduce teacher-student ratio and to allow for more differentiation, break the class into two subgroups and continue with a more focused guided lesson. Before the lesson ends, bring the entire class back together for closure.

The joined portion of the lesson may include Model 3 (One Group: One Teaches, One Assesses), which yields meaningful assessment data that help group students for leveled or tiered instruction via Model 4. While the content-based learning target may be aligned for the two groups, language and literacy targets and the corresponding instructional materials may be quite different.

Begin the lesson with one teacher leading and the other teacher providing support for student learning through Model 1. Divide the students into two basically even groups with one teacher taking one group and the other the rest of the students (Model 4). End the lesson with the class returning to one group for recap or assessment.

INSPIRATION FROM THE FIELD

Read what colleagues—ELD/ELL and classroom teachers as well as building and district administrators—shared with us from around the United States and see how they reflect or add to your own experiences.

Cynthia D. Close, ELD team lead from Douglas County School District, Colorado, has identified this model to be her most favored one. She refers to the model by its alternate name, *parallel teaching*, indicating that two teachers each take their own group and align their instructional goals and objectives.

The most enjoyable and successful co-teaching experience of my career occurred when I co-taught middle-school literacy using the parallel co-teaching model. There are so many plusses! The advantages were students saw both of us as equal teachers. Students benefited from two different styles of teaching or ways of acquiring the same skill. Due to the smaller numbers of students with each teacher, students were allowed to use more academic conversation between partners or cooperative groups. In forming the class, we included ELs who were 4.0 or higher overall (composite) on ACCESS but still needed to boost their reading and writing levels. From there, we planned to divide and conquer. We split the class in half, not based upon ability but mostly to form two groups that would work well together. Another perk of heterogeneous grouping was that the ELs' English improved by listening to the English-only speakers' vocabulary, sentence structure, syntax, and inferential skills. Additionally, all students were more engaged with the lesson because of the smaller number of participants. We each taught the same lesson twice, once to group A and once to group B. Each co-teacher focused on the same skill but with different material, modeling, and scaffolding. Essentially, we were preteaching and reteaching key concepts or skills using different examples and strategies. The reading and writing data we collected demonstrated that our parallel co-teaching class increased student achievement for both ELs and English-only students significantly more than the other literacy classes that had one teacher.

Irina Roughley, Lillian Chen, and Tammy Castellanos have a unique take on this model in a first-grade class at PS 69, Brooklyn, New York. Since there is a large concentration of ELs in Irina's class, their principal, Mrs. Jaynemarie Capetanakis, assigned two English as a New Language (ENL) teachers (Lillian and Tammy) to work together with Irina, which allowed for creative interpretations of the co-teaching models.

We have used Model 4, slightly modified where we have three groups instead of two, because it addresses the makeup of the class and the needs of the students. We definitely see Model 4 as the most advantageous for us since it offers:

- *Alternative ways to learn same content*
- *Automatic differentiation*
- *There is more interaction due to a lower student–teacher ratio*
- *There is consistency with particular groups*

The way we negotiate our triad model is by first attending the grade-planning sessions. Once a unit outline is created and reading/writing lessons are plugged in, the ENL teachers can begin to gather the materials that will be necessary to ensure that the ELs will receive the same content information as the non-ELs. The ENL teachers can also brainstorm strategies and appropriate scaffolding based on the students' levels and needs.

In a recent lesson, our three groups had differentiated content as well as language objectives. The students remained with their assigned teacher for the majority of the lesson to accomplish these goals, and then we ended the lesson by having students report to the whole class what they had accomplished. Here are the objectives for the three groups:

Mrs. Roughley's group:	Non-ELs
Lesson Objective:	*Write the procedure section of our procedural writing*
Language Objective Challenge:	*Use conjunctions*
Ms. Chen's group:	*(Mid- to high-proficiency)*
Lesson Objective:	*Write the steps for our "How to Make Fruit Salad" books using transition words*
Language Objective:	*Explain verbally and in writing the steps we need to make fruit salad using verbs*
Mrs. Castellanos's group:	*(Low proficiency)*
Lesson Objective:	*List the steps for the procedural writing books using transition words*
Language Objective:	*Explain verbally and in writing the steps needed to make apple pizza using verbs in all tenses*

The ENL teachers are always in communication with classroom teachers. We frequently discuss past and upcoming lessons during lunch, common preps, and any other time we feel that we need to clarify something. We bounce ideas back and forth and share materials with each other and the classroom teachers, which is especially beneficial since the ENL teachers work with different English language proficiency levels in different classrooms.

Susanne Marcus, Great Neck, New York, high school ENL teacher, also participates in a three-way collaborative model. Described here is also the entire initiative in a nutshell as well as how Model 4 served a very specific purpose in the program.

The Humanities Course is an interdisciplinary two-year program for high school ESL/ENL students. It is taught by an ESL teacher, an English teacher, and a social studies teacher. The course is scheduled for two consecutive periods, which allows for more project-based learning as each period is only 43 minutes in duration. The class is designed to explore themes that can be approached through a cross-curriculum lens, with a focus on making connections to students' lives.

After all the planning we had done the summer before the class began, we found that the EL students were not overall at the level of proficiency we had planned for. By definition, this population is unpredictable and varied, so we found that our planning, as broad as we'd thought it was, was not broad enough.

After the middle to end of the first quarter, we were able to assess which students would gain the most by remaining in the Humanities program and which ones were actually ready to go into an ESL-supported content area English or ninth-grade social studies class.

We realized that we had a number of proficiency levels in the remaining Humanities group, and in order to meet all their needs, we divided the group into two smaller groups of about six students each. Using the same topic of instruction, the ENL teacher worked with the true beginners, and the English and social studies teacher worked with those higher beginners who had stronger literacy skills in English.

Different models were tried out, from two circles in the same average-sized classroom to separating the two groups and using an adjacent classroom. The true beginners felt more comfortable being separated from the more proficient students at first. After another quarter passed and the beginners developed new language skills, we concluded that they needed to be in an interactive environment with students who were more proficient than they were. Additionally, we wanted to have more diversity of student backgrounds. So the two groups were merged back into one.

The ebb and flow of the dialogue between the ENL and the English teachers as well as the ENL and the social studies teachers developed into a predictable pattern. Students quickly realized that each teacher held equal desire for them to succeed, and the fostering of ELs to succeed is the most powerful factor of all in teachers collaborating. We modeled mutual respect while recognizing that each one of us held our own specialty. Additionally, we respect one another's specialty and specific strengths.

TAKEAWAYS

In this chapter, we explore the ways in which two teachers can jointly lead a lesson, or part of it, and engage the whole class in learning through Model 4 (Two Groups: Two Teach Same Content) in a co-taught class. We emphasize the importance of the way students were grouped for this model

**VIDEO 6.2:
Co-Teaching
Reflections:
Joel and Lia**

http://resources
.corwin.com/
CoTeachingforELs

as well as the various learning strategies that can be integrated. Last but not least, co-teachers share their stories about how they made sense of this particular model within their own classroom and program contexts.

QUESTIONS FOR FURTHER DISCUSSION

1. How do you ensure that Model 4 does not lead to a further well-sanctioned segregation of ELs?

2. How do you negotiate the planning and pacing of lessons that include two teachers working independent of each other with their own groups?

3. What is the role of assessment when using Model 4 prior, during, and after the lesson is completed?

4. What are all the ways you can differentiate instruction using Model 4?

7

Model 5—Two Groups

One Preteaches, One Teaches
Alternative Information

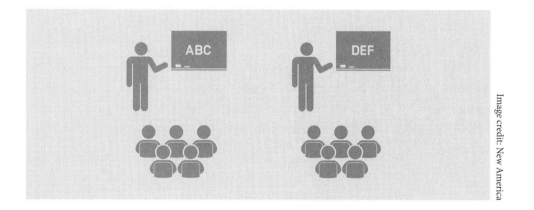

AN INTRODUCTION TO THE MODEL

In this chapter, we continue to explore ways to group English learners (ELs) as well as other students with diverse learning needs for instruction in the co-taught class. With this model, preteaching is at the forefront of configuring classes for learning. ELs often encounter challenges in content-area classes because they have yet to acquire the needed level of English language fluency and academic language to understand the subject matter. The language demands are distinct from

135

class to class, with each requiring a different set of literacy skills. For this reason, preteaching strategies, frontloading information, and building background knowledge are all an important part of the co-taught class with ELs.

Preteaching strategies include ways to assist students to tap into their prior knowledge, activate their schema related to the new topic, as well as expose students to new information prior to the target lesson. These strategies include discussions about subject matter, text previews, ways to critically think about text or concept, uncovering new vocabulary, and so on. Based on the availability of native language resources and the co-teachers' language proficiency in their students' home language, preteaching may also be conducted in languages other than English.

Frontloading information refers to guiding students to discover new information using various teaching strategies. Realia, videos, field trips, text bites, and shared reading are all part of frontloading information. The task is to build students' background knowledge, which involves the marriage between what students already know and what new information students need even before they acquire rigorous content information and skills that are planned for a particular lesson. To accomplish this task, preteaching needs to be an essential part of the co-taught class, particularly when there are ELs who are developing their basic language skills in English.

According to Marzano (2004), "What students already know about the content is one of the strongest indicators of how well they will learn new information relative to the content" (p. 1). Yet English learners may not have the same content knowledge as their English-speaking peers. ELs generally come from diverse cultural and educational backgrounds, and likewise, their school experiences are equally diverse. Those students who have had a high degree of rigorous academic instruction may come from schools that have far different curricula than those schools found in the United States. Some students may have had inconsistent schooling, or they may have been born in the United States yet have had different cultural experiences with and perspectives about topics being presented in class. Therefore, students' background knowledge related to a particular content area could vary considerably.

It is imperative that students have a firm grasp of the background knowledge needed to understand, synthesize, and apply lesson content. Without it, students will not only lose their focus on, interest in, and persistence to learn, but their comprehension will also suffer. Campbell and Campbell (2008) have identified the importance of planning and executing class time for activating prior knowledge as follows:

> When preparing for instruction, most of us focus tremendous effort on the content we teach. Often, less planning and instructional time is dedicated to accessing preexisting knowledge. This oversight can have significant implications. If preconceptions are not engaged, children may fail to grasp new concepts or give up on a subject altogether . . . Further, if students' preexisting knowledge conflicts with the new content, the presented material information risks being distorted. (p. 8)

English learners have an even greater challenge than their English-speaking peers to read grade-level text with little or no background information on the subject. Their often limited knowledge of certain vocabulary and their encounters with unfamiliar syntactical patterns in the text are sufficient in and of themselves to hinder their comprehension. However, an absence of adequate background knowledge further impedes ELs' facility with making predictions, inferencing, comparing and contrasting information, and so on, which puts a greater strain on their overall understanding and ultimately learning the subject matter.

In *Building Background Knowledge for Academic Achievement*, Marzano (2004) notes that one critical way to build background knowledge is to provide students authentic learning experiences, such as academically and linguistically enriching hands-on learning opportunities. Marzano refers to the *direct* approach to building background that may take place through out-of-school field trips to local places of interest such as museums, art galleries, and other sites within the community, and it also connects to multiple disciplines, life experiences, and literacy development.

Model 5, organizing students for *preteaching,* and Model 6, grouping students for *reteaching,* are very similar in their class configurations. Yet we feel very strongly in the writing of this book on co-teaching for English learners to address preteaching and reteaching in separate chapters. This allows us to further emphasize preteaching as an essential instructional practice when working with this population of youngsters in the co-taught classroom as well as underscore the need for multiple meaningful learning opportunities for ELs through reteaching and practice.

A CLOSER LOOK AT MODEL 5

The principle feature of this co-taught model is how students are organized into groups, the dominant pattern being two groups that are uneven in number. One group is frequently smaller than the other to support students' learning needs. The purpose of this class configuration is to allow one group of students to engage in a minilesson with one teacher to gain the essential knowledge, strategies, or skills for successful completion of the set objectives for the scheduled lesson. In turn, the other group of students is exposed to alternative information, which might also include previewing the topic with the second teacher using various materials not part of the main lesson to explore the subject matter. Consequently, this instructional model allows students who need the time to build their background knowledge before the lesson takes place to do so, and it also provides the other students with ways to make connections to the topic by activating their prior knowledge.

You may have noticed that we did not specify English learners as a designated group for preteaching. In reality, there are countless variables in selecting students who would benefit from pretaught minilessons, and the criteria vary from subject to subject. In an English language arts (ELA) class, a student's reading level might be the guiding factor for organizing a class for a vocabulary lesson if Tier 1 words (common words in everyday speech) or Tier 2 words (high-frequency, cross disciplinary words for academic learning) need to be addressed via preteaching. However, if underlying math skills about fractions are at issue, then the focus for student selection might be based on their ability to add or subtract fractions. Preteaching key concepts and introducing background information may also be accomplished in the students' home languages when appropriate resources are available.

One of the most important points to remember is that implementation of this model requires careful assessment of students' understandings, abilities, and skills to determine who would benefit from preteaching. Most often, we find that the group in need of preteaching is a diverse mix of English learners, struggling readers, students with disabilities, students who come from poverty backgrounds, students with gaps in their academic knowledge, and other underperforming pupils. At the same time, some ELs might have adequate background knowledge on select topics based on their prior education or out-of-school experiences. In fact, it is critical that teachers recognize and capitalize on students' knowledge base. According to Ntelioglou, Fannin, Montanera, and Cummins (2014),

> classroom practices that draw on students' funds of knowledge and linguistic and cultural capital help students to develop a positive sense of who they are and how they relate to their teachers, classmates and to the outside world. (p. 4)

Such practices also allow students to connect to the curriculum and instruction with heightened levels of success. For these reasons, co-teachers should avoid automatically dividing their students solely by their ELs' status.

Assessment practices are key to the successful implementation of this co-teaching model, the reason being that the more accurate your assessment data, the more likely you will be able to determine the individual learning needs of your students and how to best group them for instruction. Gathering accurate data can be time consuming, and teachers who may be in schools that have high-stakes, test-driven cultures might want to avoid additional testing to be imposed on ELs. However, what we want to emphasize here is the great importance of assessment routines developed alongside instructional practices so that both co-teachers can engage in

> collecting data from multiple measures or sources over time, analyzing and interpreting that information in light of its specific purpose, and using the accumulated information or evidence to improve teaching and learning. (Gottlieb, 2016, p. 158)

With sufficient data, co-teachers can confidently make decisions about how to best group their students for instruction.

If you do not have sufficient preassessment data regarding an upcoming topic of instruction, might you end up dividing students into EL and non-EL groups? Absolutely! Although this idea may seem counter to what we have just suggested, if the instructional planning for preteaching is providing lessons that are specifically geared for English learners to develop language proficiency skills, and the prior data revealed that ELs in the class would benefit from such instruction, then by all means group students in this way.

Although most times we have observed a group of five to seven students designated for preteaching, on some occasions with this model we have found a greater number of students—up to two-thirds of a class—assigned to the pretaught group. This reversal in group size has been noted in classes where there are large populations of English learners as well as other students who need such support. We have also visited classes where there may have only been one or two students designated as English learners. In this situation, we have noticed that teachers face an added challenge for grouping students in a way that ELs may receive the needed background information, the vocabulary building, the computation skills, the writing strategies, and so on; with this model of instruction, ELs, too, may be successful with the set lesson objective.

Teachers tend to be more reluctant to plan pretaught instruction when fewer students require support. They may be concerned that preteaching would take valuable time that could have been devoted to other types of instruction. However, we urge you and your co-teacher to reconsider the importance and the value of pretaught skills and activated prior knowledge. Fisher and Frey (2012) conclude the following about preteaching, which they also refer to as *frontloadings*:

> Although there are times when preteaching would not be appropriate, there are times when it *is* appropriate. In essence, the difference has to do with the background knowledge of the students combined with the purpose of the lesson. If a lack of background knowledge will prevent students from accomplishing the purpose of the lesson, frontloading may be necessary, but that need must be balanced with the time allocated for learning the specific content and the skills that students need to develop. (p. 84)

If you and your co-teacher agree to incorporate preteaching into your lesson plan, how much time should be designated for it to occur? It all depends on the background knowledge students require for a particular lesson. We frequently have noted that teachers' plans for co-taught instruction with this model focus on the preteaching of vocabulary for English learners. Although this type of frontloading is very valuable, co-teachers must also consider the other information, skills, strategies, and concepts that should be addressed. In addition, co-teachers should also consider the time it will take to accomplish the primary goal of the lesson. One rule of thumb could be that no more than ten minutes should be devoted to preteaching activities during an average period of instruction to allow for a whole group, shared minilesson, additional grouping configurations, and review and assessment. However, if students need more time to develop more proficiency with background information, consider designating a longer period of time to preteaching while the rest of the class receives enrichment or extension activities. You might find that Model 7 may well serve the purpose of additional preteaching through rotation stations, in which students are set in multiple groups to accomplish different learning tasks to prepare them for the new lesson (see Chapter 9).

Along with the question of how much time should be spent preteaching is where these skill-building activities should take place. Areas of the class used for preteaching should be equipped with the necessary tools and be comfortable for all learners. We have witnessed small-group instruction in classes where students were asked to sit on the floor in a bare corner of the room to receive direct instruction by one teacher while the other students sat comfortably at tables or desks and had the full advantage of classroom technology. If this model is to be used successfully, strategies for arranging the classroom for such instruction needs to be addressed. If space in the classroom is an issue, consider alternative spaces for preteaching—a hallway, an adjacent classroom, an outdoor space, and so on. While a caution of taking students out of the classroom is in order, if it is purposeful, and targeted to specific skills, alternate learning environments are critical (library for researching skills, computer room for keyboarding skills, empty classroom next door or down the hall to engage in a hands-on or kinesthetic activity or to preview a video clip related to the topic).

VIDEO 7.1: Model 5—Two Groups: One Preteaches, One Teaches Alternative Information

http://resources .corwin.com/ CoTeachingforELs

ADVANTAGES

For English learners, their knowledge and understandings about particular subject matter will vary depending upon their prior schooling, the complexity of the content, their exposure and access to technology, their interests, and their general experiences with the world. Therefore, one of the many advantages of this model is the ability for co-teachers to focus attention on the students' unique needs. Using student data gathered through various preassessment activities, co-teachers can plan distinct lesson segments for preteaching in order for all students to master challenging content in core subjects such as English, mathematics, science, and social studies.

In order for students to speak, read, and write about detailed concepts, they not only need prior knowledge and schema, they must also have the necessary language and literacy skills to do so. For this reason, targeted instruction in vocabulary, reading comprehension, oral language skills, and other literacy skills needed for success combined with content information are often the focus of pretaught sessions. Teaching small groups of students allows for instruction using literature and informational texts at a reading level that makes content more accessible. In addition, pieces of complex text can also be introduced—breaking them down into manageable bits of information and analyzing them for their language and content.

Through a guided or shared reading, small-group discussions can build students' background knowledge with select information and literacy-building strategies. For example, consider beginning-level ELs developing their English-language skills in a tenth-grade social studies class exploring the topic of the Holocaust and the concept of prejudice. In order to develop basic understandings for ELs and other students who need support, one of the co-teachers shares the picture book *Terrible Things: An Allegory of the Holocaust* by Eve Bunting (1989) with a small group of students during a preteaching session. The enduring understandings of this book, the vocabulary that is introduced, and the conversations that ensue in the small group are a springboard for later discussions during the main lesson that involve historical data and the meaning of injustice (see Sample Lessons in this chapter).

So far, we have established that content-area background knowledge and the development of English language competency are key to favorable learning outcomes for English learners. This model provides ample opportunity for students to engage in pretaught minilessons that involve the back-mapping of the curriculum—identifying the concepts, strategies, and skills students need to acquire before grade-level benchmarks can be met. In other words, small-group instruction can begin at the level students are performing academically, and plans for building the essential intermediary skills students need creates the trajectory for meeting grade-level expectations.

Another fundamental technique for working with English learners is differentiated instruction—varying the way the content, process, and product of a lesson is planned to meet the various English language proficiency levels of students. Small-group instruction prior to the main lesson can provide ELs with a broad-based overview of the lesson's topic, the time to introduce and have students "prepractice" a strategy or skill, and the appropriate setting to demonstrate or review a modified model of a lesson's culminating task, particularly for entering and emerging students.

Last but not least, small-group instruction creates a welcoming environment for ELs to ask for and receive specific instructional support. It allows students the opportunity to participate in some experiential learning tasks (sort and categorize different objects or images related to the upcoming topic), receive multiple meaningful exposures to the upcoming content (watch a short video simulation of a science concept), or ask questions that they may be unwilling to address during the main lesson. In addition, the information shared and the skills introduced and practiced during preteaching can build students' confidence for upcoming instruction.

CHALLENGES

There are a few challenges to incorporating this model into the co-taught class, the first being the danger of segregating students for instruction. If the pretaught group always and only contains English learners, then these students will feel singled out and may not reap the benefits of the pretaught lesson. We recommend that co-teachers do not assume what English learners may or may not know. The danger of the deficit approach could not be more apparent here; instead, we invite you to rely on assessment data to determine what students *can do* and what they *need to know* to move to whole-group instruction or the next phase of the lesson. We further suggest that teaching teams consider the needs of all students in the class and use preassessment strategies that identify the knowledge and facility that both ELs and non-ELs have with the prior knowledge necessary to meet the lesson objective.

What English learners are taught during this session should be key to supporting their learning during the lesson. In other words, this model should not be used to teach students isolated grammar points, spelling rules, lists of common words, and so on, from ready-made worksheets or prepackaged programs. Its specific purpose is to help students gain background knowledge of the content and the needed language to learn the subject matter presented to all students in the upcoming lesson.

As with all grouping strategies, the level of sound in the classroom may reach an uncomfortable volume for some students to learn, particularly when one group is much larger than the other and engaged in a lively discussion. We advise careful coordination for the planning of activities during this model as well as careful consideration and wise use of classroom space or an alternative space if available for this part of the lesson to be completed. As suggested above, alternative space might include use of an adjacent classroom, a hallway, or an outdoor setting if appropriate.

The required time for preteaching may exceed the allotted time needed to serve certain groups of English learners. Students who are just beginning to acquire English or have little background knowledge of the subject matter being addressed may need more extensive time to build the required skills. For this reason, co-teachers need to have alternative instructional plans to accommodate the needs of these learners. For example, if the initial plan was to use this model to begin the lesson and then shift to use a model in which all students are together as one group for instruction, an alternative plan might be for all students to explore the initial topic in multiple small groups (see Model 7 in Chapter 9), yet not all students would be using the same material or learning the exact same information. In this way, students who need to continue to build their language skills while learning the basic background and content can be accommodated.

Frequent use of this model may result in ELs having a less rigorous curriculum. If the pretaught session is always conducted with simplified materials, less demanding work, or if it eliminates opportunities to speak and write, English learners may not have adequate exposure to subject matter and needed academic language to be successful. The end result might lead to lower expectations for achievement by both the teachers and the students themselves.

Table 7.1 Summary of Advantages and Challenges of Model 5

Model 5: Two Groups: One Preteaches, One Teaches Alternative Information	
Advantages	**Challenges**
Co-teachers have the ability to focus attention on students' unique needs by planning pretaught lesson segments for ELs to master challenging content.	If the pretaught group always and only contains English learners, these students will feel singled out and may not reap the benefits of the pretaught lesson.
Targeted instruction makes content more accessible—breaking down the needed language into manageable formats such as using graphic organizers with visual support.	Publisher-prepared worksheets or English to speakers of other languages (ESOL) prepackaged programs should not be used to teach students isolated grammar points, spelling rules, lists of common words, and so on, during preteaching.
Small-group discussions and inquiry-based learning can build students' background knowledge with select information and literacy-building strategies.	The level of sound in the classroom may reach an uncomfortable volume for some students to learn, particularly when one group is much larger than the other.
Preteaching can provide minilessons that involve the back-mapping of the curriculum—identifying needed instruction before grade-level benchmarks can be met.	The required time for preteaching may exceed the allotted time needed to serve certain groups of English learners.
Small-group instruction allows for varying the way the content, process, and product of a lesson can meet the various English language proficiency levels of students.	Frequent use of this model may result in ELs having a less rigorous curriculum.
Small-group instruction creates a welcoming environment for ELs to ask for and receive specific instructional support.	

INSTRUCTION USING MODEL 5

Strategies for preteaching students will vary greatly depending on the content area involved, the background knowledge to be developed, and the grade level and proficiency level of the students. Therefore, we chose to identify here crosscutting strategies that can be incorporated into the use of this model no matter what subject is being targeted or the facility students have with English.

Low-Prep Strategies for Model 5

This model emphasizes the specific importance of frontloading information and presenting and practicing essential skills for English learners. It can be achieved by reviewing pertinent information, building background knowledge, previewing vocabulary, introducing prereading skills, and so on. In order to determine which students can benefit most from preteaching sessions, we suggest the following preassessment strategies to consider using before grouping students. In addition, we have provided instructional strategies to use during a pretaught segment.

Preassessment Strategies

To determine the selection of students for preteaching as well as the direction for instruction, we suggest creating routine opportunities for assessing your students' current background knowledge and skills. Selection of preassessment strategies often depends on what students will need to learn. Co-teachers need to consider the best possible ways of having students reveal what they know and are able to do, and if individual or group assessment strategies would work the best. For this reason, we suggest implementing a variety of strategies such as the following to quickly assess students with little or no preparation. For additional formative assessment ideas, see Chapters 5 and 10.

A–Z Lists. The purpose of this strategy is for students to be able to identify relevant vocabulary related to a given topic. Students are either given a prepared paper with the letters A through Z written down the side, or they may be asked to write the alphabet themselves on a blank piece of paper or in a notebook. Working alone or in pairs, students must write as many words or phrases as they can related to the topic within a given time frame. Students may then be asked to compare their lists in teams to create one combined list without duplication of words. Another variation is the use of separate boxes instead of lists (see Figure 7.1). These lists can be reproduced and ready for distribution when the need to assess students arises. This assessment strategy can also be used during and after a lesson to determine acquisition of language and concepts.

Figure 7.1 A–Z List			
A	B	C	D
E	F	G	H
I	J	K	L
M	N	O	P
Q	R	S	T
U	V	W	XYZ

Take a Stand. Determine the depth of knowledge of individual and groups of students about a particular topic by asking them to take a stand on certain aspects of an issue. Begin by making a broad statement about the topic such as, "Good always triumphs over evil." Write or project that statement on the board or offer students a short list of open-ended prompts that can have various perspectives. Ask students to jot down on an index card whether or not they *agree, disagree, strongly agree,* or *strongly disagree* with each statement and briefly write their reasons why. Limit the prompts to three or four. Next, name the four corners of the classroom—Agree, Disagree,

Strongly Agree, and Strongly Disagree. Invite students to stand in the corner of the room that corresponds to their ideas concerning each prompt. In each corner, have groups of students share their own reasoning with one another and listen to their classmates' ideas. As they interact with their classmates, they should select a spokesperson that will report to the whole class a summary of what had been shared in the group. Figure 7.2 gives an example of possible prompts about nuclear energy.

Figure 7.2	Take a Stand: Prompts About Nuclear Energy

Nuclear power produces inexpensive electricity.

Nuclear energy is environmentally friendly.

A nuclear power plant can operate without disruption in any weather or environmental condition.

Nuclear power plants need a great deal of security to operate safely.

K-W-L Charts (Ogle, 1986). Often used as a prereading activity, a K-W-L chart, which identifies what students **K**now, **W**ant to know, and **L**earned about a topic, is a tried-and-true strategy that can be used to determine students' prior knowledge of subject matter, set a purpose for the lesson, and guide students in their comprehension. It is also used to survey students' interests and document their actual learning about the content. K-W-L charts can be used to quickly gather data about what students know in order to group them for preteaching. Variations on this strategy include K-W-H-L—with the same meaning the letters K-W-L had on the original chart with the addition of H standing for *how* students find the information they need—and K-W-H-L-A-Q— again, same letters as before yet adding A to represent the *actions* students will take and Q signifying the new *questions* students will have as a result of the inquiry. Each stage of these charts can offer co-teachers rich assessment information for grouping students for preteaching or for possible intervention through reteaching (see Chapter 8).

Fist To Five. A quick and easy way to gather formative assessment data, *Fist To Five* requires students to reveal their understanding and level of confidence about a topic by holding up anywhere from zero to five fingers that carry the following meaning:

- No fingers: I do not understand the topic at all.
- One finger: I heard of it, but I am not sure what it means or I don't know many details.
- Two fingers: I do know a little about the subject but would benefit from additional instruction.
- Three fingers: I basically understand the subject matter but need greater review and practice.
- Four fingers: I understand the subject very well.
- Five fingers: I can teach the topic to someone else.

Instructional Strategies

As with any part of the lesson, strategies used for the preteaching should be selected according to the needs of the students and the topic at hand. The following are a few basic strategies that generally can be incorporated into any pretaught lesson.

Preteaching Vocabulary

Based on their collaborative work, Isabel Beck, Margaret McKeown, and Linda Kucan (2013) promote a concise three-step approach that involves a "thoughtful introduction to a set of words, interesting interactions with the words, and assessments of students' knowledge of the words" (p. 364). Consider incorporating the following three steps when you preteach vocabulary:

1. Prepare student-friendly explanations for the words that make sense to students, which build on age-appropriate dictionary definitions but also consider students' prior knowledge and experience with the concepts.

2. Engage students in a range of meaningful activities that allow them to use the words in a variety of ways and in a variety of contexts.

3. Use formative assessments to gauge students' understanding as well as productive use of the target words. It's also beneficial to use self-assessment practices such as having students put their thumbs up, sideways, or down to show their levels of understanding for key words.

Video Clips and Web-Based Explorations

Carefully selected short video clips or high-quality interactive web-based resources, such as of virtual museums and other context-rich resources, may provide an opportunity for preteaching some necessary information for ELs. Another advantage of these resources is that students may watch, pause, or rewind a clip as often as needed or revisit websites to further explore a topic.

Picture Walks and Text Tours

To introduce a new book, you may take your students on a walk through a fiction or nonfiction book that is rich in illustrations. As you turn the pages of the book, call the students' attention to some key pictures, have the students point out important characters, features, or ideas represented visually, or describe briefly what the book is about through analyzing the visual clues and graphic elements. Invite ELs to discuss what they notice on the pages and how the illustrations may relate to the main ideas in the book.

Similar to a picture walk, take your students on a text tour. Put on your straw hat, hold up a flag, and pretend to be a tour guide as you take your students on a journey through the target text highlighting all the key illustrations that support the text. Briefly discuss the purpose and key features of each illustration while eliciting scaffolded questions from your students that you could respond to:

Who is in the photograph?

What does the caption say?

What country (city) is in the map?

What kind of illustration is that? What type of diagram is that?

After modeling this activity, make sure your students take on the role of the tour guide and explain the key text aides that appear in the same and additional nonfiction books.

A text tour is more frequently conducted on nonfiction articles, chapters, or books, especially in upper elementary, middle, or high school classes. During a text tour, remember to point out how the text is organized and what text features are important to pay attention to. Text tours are also effective when students encounter a new textbook and need to become familiar with the major sections of the book and the purpose of each section.

Anticipation Guides

Anticipation guides—sometimes called *anticipatory sets*—help activate students' prior knowledge or validate ELs' existing understandings. At the same time, anticipation guides also allow students to preview an upcoming lesson through a series of statements that are either true or false. Wood, Lapp, Flood, and Taylor (2008) note that anticipation guides build curiosity and stimulate student interest in the upcoming lesson, whereas Dodge and Honigsfeld (2014) observe that anticipation guides address all three aspects of working with background knowledge and help scaffold learning in multiple ways:

- They *assess* prior knowledge by having students evaluate a teacher-provided list of statements about the topic.
- They *activate* what students already know and make apparent the misconceptions that some students hold.
- They also *build* background in several ways: They preview key concepts and introduce vocabulary prior to reading; they provide a purpose for reading; they help students integrate and consolidate new learnings. (p. 22)

See Figure 7.3 for a template that would include teacher-provided statements based on the target lesson. Students read each statement prior to having access to the entire text and decide whether they agree or disagree with those statements. The statements are revisited after the lesson, when students have an opportunity to reassess the same statements. They may or may not continue to agree or disagree with the statements based on the new information gained from the readings.

Foldables (Zike, 1992). A twist on typical graphic organizers, foldables are two- or three-dimensional creations that are devised by folding 8 x 11 sheets of plain or colored paper for students to use to organize written information. The clever design of these easy-to-use manipulatives "provides even the most reluctant student with the incentive to write" (Dove & Honigsfeld, 2013, p. 50). There are seemingly endless ways to construct these paper marvels. They can be used in any grade or content class and can be scaffolded to suit the ability level of any student. One of the four-tab foldables is illustrated in Figure 7.4.

Each tab can be raised for information to be written inside. We suggest you visit Dinah Zike's website, www.dinah.com, for more information.

I-SEE Strategy. This activity helps students to break down big abstract ideas. It begins by asking students to picture what something looks like, such as democracy, freedom, revolution, conflict,

Figure 7.3 Anticipation Guide Template

Before Reading (Agree or Disagree?)	Statements	After Reading (Agree or Disagree?)
_____	1.	_____
_____	2.	_____
_____	3.	_____
_____	4.	_____
_____	5.	_____

Summary Statement:

Figure 7.4 Four-Tab Foldable

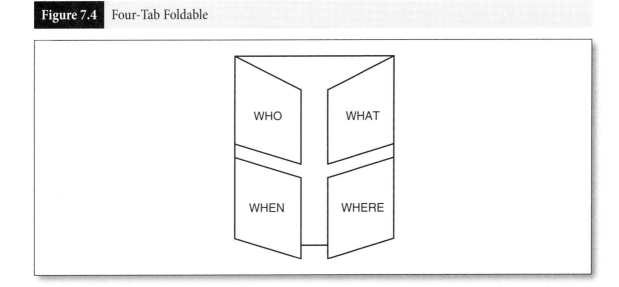

and so on, and illustrating it in one of four boxes. Next, students define the idea in one simple sentence. In a third box, students must elaborate on what they just stated, and in a final box, they give examples from their own experiences. Students then share their writings and illustrations with a fellow student to answer the question, "Do you see what *I see* when it comes to _____?" See Figure 7.5 for an example of the format.

Word-Analysis Frames. A common preteaching activity is to preview challenging vocabulary for English learners. Yet reviewing a list of words is often ineffective. This strategy supports student

Figure 7.5 I-SEE Strategy

I = ILLUSTRATE the idea	**S** = STATE in one simple sentence
E = ELABORATE on what was stated	**E** = EXAMPLES from experience

Figure 7.6 Word-Analysis Frame

Word: *prejudice*	Home Language: *prejudicar*	
Definition: *to form a negative opinion without any basis*	**Synonyms:** *animosity, bias, bigotry, enmity, discrimination*	**Illustration:**
Antonyms: *fairness, justice, goodwill, impartiality*	**Examples:** *racism, sexism, xenophobia, ageism*	
Sentence: *An American ideal is for all people to act without prejudice against one another.*		

learning with a more in-depth examination of vocabulary. It requires students to complete a series of tasks beyond the definition or its home-language counterpart by asking them to identify synonyms and antonyms, create an illustration representing the word, and compose a sentence. Figure 7.6 is an example of this strategy.

Pro-Prep Strategies for Model 5

The goal of preteaching English learners is to give students the opportunity to preview essential content and practice appropriate language skills before the main lesson. In this way, students will be more capable of understanding the subject matter and be more participatory during instruction of new material. The following strategies may take additional time to prepare for students, yet they will yield great benefits for your ELs.

Research via hand-held tablets. Becoming increasingly popular in K–12 classes, handheld tablets hold many uses for the instruction of English learners. The software on most of these devices includes applications for research, writing, and presentations as well as simple e-mailing.

Additional applications are readily available for the development of English-language skills. Students can take or find photographs to identify concepts and examples. They can also access the Internet for information, engage with specific software for language translation, and use specific tools for collaborating with other students. Other programs assist students to develop their reading and writing skills.

Videos. Consider the many advantages of building students' background knowledge using videotaped recordings. With various sites on the Internet that provide free resources to others available through paid subscriptions, videos bring literature, history, science, mathematics, and so on to life. For example, if you are teaching students about extreme weather, what better way to build their understanding about hurricanes, tornadoes, or blizzards than to actually show them each of these storms in action and the dangers they present. Many videos, offered in languages other than English, can support English learners to learn content through use of their home-language skills.

Songs and Lyrics. Songs and lyrics offer endless possibilities for students to build content information, academic vocabulary, grammatical structures, idiomatic expressions, fluency, and so on in the pretaught lesson. They also provide ways to motivate students to learn and achieve. According to Genia Cornell (2014)

> Song lyrics make great mentor text to use to teach theme, author's message, character traits, visualization, inferring, and more. Students who may not connect with a book or article in class just may connect with a popular song they are familiar with when you make it part of instruction . . . the trickiest part to using music lyrics as part of your instruction is finding popular, relevant songs that are school- and age-appropriate. (para. 2 & 3)

Talk Moves. Developing students' ability to use academic language to answer and ask questions and to speak with one another is an important part of pretaught sessions. In these groups, English learners often feel better able to take risks and are less self-conscious about misspoken words. To foster students' use of academic language, teachers can create a series of sentence frames that are either projected on an interactive whiteboard or displayed on table tents. When students ask or answer a question, these sentence frames support their ability to use more complex structures and academic vocabulary. See Figure 7.7 for some examples.

Figure 7.7 Sample Sentence Frames

I agree with what you said because _____.
I respectfully disagree with your point of view because _____.
I would like to emphasize that _____.
Based on the text, I can infer that _____.
One critical attribute of the character is _____.
I would like to add to what _____ said.
I can connect with what you said because _____.

SAMPLE LESSONS: TWO GROUPS: ONE PRETEACHES, ONE TEACHES ALTERNATIVE INFORMATION

The following lessons illustrate how co-teachers use preteaching for co-taught instruction, dividing students from data gathered from preassessment activities.

Lesson 1—Teaching Inferencing With "Magic" in Second Grade

This lesson segment focuses on prereading strategies students will need in order to develop and practice inferencing as a comprehension tool with the picture book *Sylvester and the Magic Pebble* by William Steig (2004), a tale of a donkey who finds a magic pebble and how one wish leads to terrible consequences. Second-grade students were divided according to their understanding of vocabulary and certain concepts contained in the text. Students selected for preteaching were English learners who had some facility with English, as well as English speakers who were struggling readers. English learners who were more advanced in their proficiency were not part of the pretaught group. The pretaught group—seven students—was gathered at the half-circle table on the side of the room under the direction of the ESOL teacher. The rest of the students formed teams of four at desks clustered throughout the room and were guided by the second-grade teacher.

The ESOL teacher began the preteaching component by conducting a picture walk of the text. She asked students to verbally identify items in the pictures and used a hand-held erasable whiteboard to make note of some common vocabulary and idiomatic expressions students needed to know. Next, the concept of magic was discussed and related to students' understandings of and connections with magical items in common fairy tales and familiar movies such as magic mirrors, wands, lamps, words, and so on. Subsequently, the ESOL teacher introduced a short list of vocabulary words she preselected for review—*remarkable, startled, panicked, bewildered,* and *frantic.* Students were guided to sentences in the text containing each word, and the meaning of each sentence was discussed supported by the pictures in the text. The last part of the pretaught session was spent on introducing the concept of inferencing. The teacher modeled as well as guided students to inference using several examples from the text, which gave students a preview of the main instructional objective. This part of the lesson lasted approximately fifteen minutes.

Meanwhile, the second-grade teacher engaged the other students to explore a theme present in *Sylvester and the Magic Pebble*—consequences—without having students read the text. She shared a personal anecdote with this group about a time when she decided to wear a light sweater instead of her warm coat; she continued, telling how the weather turned cold and rainy, and she regretted her earlier decision to just wear the sweater. After the brief story, she introduced the concept of consequences and told students the consequence of her actions was that she caught a bad cold. She then invited students to first think about a time when they made a bad decision and then share it with a partner or their team at their table. Students were then engaged in an activity to write in their journals about a time they made a bad decision and the consequences that resulted from it. Following this introduction, the second-grade teacher circulated among the students, who were writing and offered them her assistance and support.

Continuing the lesson, both teachers brought the students together as one group (Model 2), and the story was read through a shared reading. While one teacher read aloud, the other teacher would think aloud, discussing different aspects of the text with one another and modeling the strategy of inferencing for students. The lesson continued with both teachers guiding students to practice inferencing with different parts of the text.

An analysis of the lesson segment. This co-teaching pair used Model 5—one preteaches, one teaches alternative information—to introduce a text before a shared reading by previewing challenging vocabulary and exploring concepts with one group of students while the other group explored a greater theme of the text—consequences—and engaged in a writing activity. The lesson objective, to develop an understanding and ability to inference, was the objective for both groups of students. For this reason, both teachers planned to have the ESOL teacher focus on the lesson's objective with ELs and other struggling students during the pretaught component while the second-grade teacher provided students with the exploration of consequences, one of the themes related to the inferences that could be drawn from the text. It is important to note that the students being taught alternative information were not kept as one group as the classic Model 5 describes. Instead, students were divided into multiple groups and worked in part in pairs or teams. All in all, the entire class was made ready for the read-aloud and the development of the identified objective.

Lesson 2—Engaging All English Language Arts Students in Grade 11

Mr. Biondi and Ms. Mitchell make sense of using this model of instruction (Model 5) in combination with an additional model (Model 7) in their eleventh-grade English ELA class in Hicksville, New York. Here, they share their lesson in their own words:

Our English 11 co-teaching class consists of fourteen English learners and fifteen proficient speakers of English. The majority of the ELs are Spanish speakers, but there is also one Urdu speaker among them. Their abilities range from entering to nearly reaching English proficiency. Some ELs have been in the United States only several months; none of them have been here more than three years. We see the students once a day in period 9, the last one on their schedule. All of the students in class seem to get along, which creates an inclusive and friendly class environment. We are true believers in peer teaching and group work. Usually, we pair entering students with a bilingual student to provide for low-anxiety peer teaching.

Using Model 5 in which one preteaches and one teaches alternative information allows us time to build ELs' background knowledge in terms of literary characterization and facilitate their understanding characters in general. This type of learning opportunity was particularly apparent in a lesson we created about F. S. Fitzgerald's The Great Gatsby. *While the ESOL teacher was presenting a minilesson on the concept of direct and indirect characterization in literature, the ELA teacher set up a nonfiction reading assignment about F. S. Fitzgerald. During the practice stage of the lesson, the ELs identified types of characterization in short passages provided by the ESOL teacher while other students independently read a reading passage with biographical information about F. S. Fitzgerald followed by comprehension questions similar to those on an English state exam. Thus, both sets of students were engaged in meaningful instruction aligned with the course objectives of English 11.*

At the end of the lesson, ELs were assigned to read a specific passage from either chapter 1 or 2 of the text. They were furnished with a graphic organizer based on the characters introduced in the opening chapters as well as receiving an infographic on the same characters featuring relevant biographical information and significant details of characterization. Each EL was assigned a specific character to study to build his or her background knowledge and increase each student's ability to contribute during the cooperative learning activity on the following day. Our intent was to implement the philosophy of the "flipped classroom" while also fostering a sense of comfort and inclusion for English learners to work in cooperative groups with native speakers.

During the lesson on the following day, student groupings were based on the characters preassigned to English learners so they could be evenly integrated into the cooperative learning groups. Additionally, ELs received page numbers and scaffolded questions to guide them to the most pertinent passages in the novel. While the class worked on the group task, both teachers circulated among the student groups providing feedback and formative assessment (Model 7). Upon completion of the task and after every group had conferenced with both teachers, a representative from each group shared out their character analysis using the interactive whiteboard.

An analysis of the lesson segment. This lesson provided eleventh-grade English learners with the opportunity to fully participate alongside their English-speaking peers. During the pretaught segment, the ESOL teacher was able to work with ELs to build their background knowledge about direct and indirect characterization. At the same time, the ELA teachers took the opportunity to have the other students explore the author's life and practice writing answers to questions that are similar to those students will encounter on state tests. The teachers also used the concept of the "flipped classroom" to have ELs complete certain assignments at home in preparation for the next class. These assignments were effective in bolstering their participation to complete group tasks the previous day. In short, using Model 5 for preteaching was the key for ELs' successful engagement in the main lesson.

MODEL VARIATIONS

In our work with co-teachers, we have repeatedly come across class scenarios in which instead of a handful of students, larger groups of ELs and some of their English-speaking peers needed opportunities for foundational skill building, activating prior knowledge, or building background knowledge. The following model variations respond particularly well to these cases.

One Preteaches, One Monitors and Teaches

When a group of students is in need of a preteaching and background-building activity, the rest of the students can be engaged in an independent task that is monitored by the other teacher. The goal of the independent learning activity may vary from practicing a hard-to-master subskill to creative application of a recently mastered skill.

Both Teachers Preteach One Group of Students

At times, students are familiar with the concepts—they know that rain and snow are examples of precipitation, they just do not know the scientific vocabulary describing the phenomenon. When both the concept and the vocabulary are unfamiliar, such as Manifest Destiny or isotope, preteaching key concepts—especially through concrete, hands-on, or experiential learning opportunities—to all students will help facilitate the reading of complex text by unpacking the meanings of unfamiliar words before students encounter them.

Authentic background-building experiences that students can benefit from while in a large-group setting include inviting guest speakers to demonstrate a particular skill (such as showing colonial crafts), parent and community volunteers to share about their jobs, or traveling to specific locations via field trips (a natural history museum, a local farm, a planetarium, etc.). What is critical for each of these experiences is that all students are able to build their background knowledge of curriculum topics.

Preteach to Most Students, Alternative Information to Some

We have found that co-teachers sometimes have a greater number of students—up to two-thirds of a class—assigned to the pretaught group. This reversal of group size has been noted in classes where there are large populations of ELs or students whose lived experiences do not match the upcoming academic content. If needed, plan a preteaching session for the majority of students while a smaller group receives enrichment or an opportunity to extend or transfer a previously taught skill.

Preteach in Alternate Space

When preteaching a specific skill or content is better accomplished outside the regular classroom, do not hesitate to take a group of students outside in the school yard or hallway for a kinesthetic activity, the computer lab for keyboarding or technology skill building, to the library for research skills, or to an alternate classroom that maybe available.

Both Preteach Two or More Groups

Both teachers may engage in preteaching the entire class or part of the class as they work with two or more groups, thus assigning a specific purpose to Model 7 (multiple groups taught by two teachers). Using differentiated instructional materials, one teacher may introduce foundational concepts and skills, whereas the other focuses on different parts of the curriculum that need to be pretaught.

MODEL COMBINATIONS

Model 5 (Two Groups: One Preteaches, One Teaches Alternative Information) may be easily connected to several other models, especially to Model 3 (One Group: One Teaches, One Assesses).

Based on formative assessment data gained in an earlier lesson, you may decide that some or most of your students need some additional opportunities for preparing for a new lesson or unit. You can build content background or foundational skills for one or more groups of students, thus moving between Model 5 and Model 7 (Multiple Groups) as needed.

While this model works best when it is carefully preplanned and intentional, you and your co-teacher may wish to capture a teachable moment and offer immediate intervention to some students, thus shift into Model 1 (One Group: One Leads, One Teaches on Purpose) or Model 2 (Two Teachers Teach the Same Group). Preteaching or frontloading for one group could also allow another group to receive enrichment, thus everyone receiving instruction at their readiness level.

INSPIRATION FROM THE FIELD

Read what colleagues—ELD/ELL and classroom teachers as well as building and district administrators—shared with us from around the United States and see how they reflect or add to your own experiences.

First, let's hear from Katie Toppel, English language development specialist in Tigard-Tualatin School District, Oregon. See how she reflects on one of her most successful co-taught lessons in a kindergarten classroom, where preteaching played an important role in getting English language learners (ELLs) ready for the lesson.

I would consider myself a co-teaching newbie, as my colleagues and I just recently replaced pull-out ELD instruction with co-taught lessons at the kindergarten level. However, even though we are relatively new to the structure, I can definitely pinpoint one lesson that stands out as being a great success. My kindergarten colleagues wanted to conduct a lesson focusing on the five senses, which they had previously studied, in conjunction with candy canes for some hands-on holiday fun. For the language component, I pretaught adjectives students could use to describe what candy canes look, taste, smell, feel, and sound like. I began the lesson by presenting students with pairs of adjectives displayed on cards that included both the written word and an image representing the word (e.g., rough, smooth). Opposite pairs were intentionally created so that one of the adjectives described the candy canes and the other did not. Students had quiet time to think and then responded chorally to indicate the appropriate adjective. I then asked students to help me place each adjective next to the appropriate sense (represented by icons) in a pocket chart.

While I led the language portion of the lesson, the kindergarten teacher monitored ELL students to make sure they were participating and verbalizing answers. After all of the adjectives were matched with the appropriate sense, students used the sentence frame "I ____ a ____ candy cane" (e.g., I see a striped candy cane) and the pocket chart visual to share complete sentences describing candy canes with their partners. While students worked with their partners, both the kindergarten teacher and I listened to student responses, with a particular focus on ELL students. After that, the kindergarten teacher took over the lesson and guided students toward independent practice in which they used the app Book Creator on their iPads to record one complete sentence for each of the five senses, while I checked in with ELL students at their tables. After they recorded five sentences, students listened to their recordings and used sound spelling to write the adjectives they chose on the hard copy of their worksheet. While students were recording sentences and writing *adjectives, both the kindergarten teacher and I circulated around the room, helping students and informally assessing their work. I focused my support on the five ELL students in the classroom during this portion of the lesson and listened to all of their recordings to see if their sentence production required any additional instruction.*

Next, let's visit Hicksville Public School, New York, where a range of technology tools are implemented in co-taught classes, partially to prepare ELLs for mastering complex content. See what Lisa Estrada, supervisor of English as a new language, world languages and activities, has observed about technology integration to support ELLs.

Hicksville Public School ESOL teachers Justina Ketyer, Kyrstin Stehle, and their co-teaching partners, Susan Farrell, and Catherine Carey regularly use technology to enhance language instruction in the co-teaching classroom. Together, they have found innovative ways to foster digital literacy and provide ELLs with targeted, student-centered instruction. As their supervisor, I observe these teachers use technology as a support to create, deliver, and assess learning experiences to engage ELLs.

One digital tool used to accommodate the diverse needs of English learners is EDPuzzle. The teachers use this video curation tool to embed comprehension questions and edit videos found on sites like YouTube and National Geographic. Videos are often used to support ELLs in their receptive skills during whole class, paired, and individual activities. By listening, reading, and viewing videos, ELLs take in, interpret, and relate information to their own personal experiences.

As co-teaching partners, they utilize platforms that streamline their workflow. Google Docs and PlanBook.com are regularly used to collaborate and plan for co-teaching. The teachers have found ways to address the challenges of limited co-planning time within our program. Well-planned lessons and instructional resources are accessed through Google Classroom and Google Docs on the students' iPads. The scaffolded worksheets and materials provide opportunities for ELLs to interact and learn using technology. Other digital resources such as RAZ Kids, BrainPop ESL, and Learning A–Z are used to target language development that supports ELA instruction in the classroom. For example, leveled books on RAZ Kids reinforce skills learned during ELA by making the difficult content from their readers more accessible.

The ESOL teachers and their co-teaching partners have also found ways to inform their instruction by surveying the class with Kahoot! The students use their iPads to answer questions that transmit the answers directly to the teacher's device. These teachers have found ways to enrich and redefine instruction for ELLs.

Mariola Krol, secondary ESOL teacher in Sewanhaka Central High School District, New York, remembers a successful lesson in which an anticipation guide along with other preteaching and background-building activities were infused into the lesson for all students' success.

In preparation for discussing a challenging topic, the homework assignment was to write a paragraph opening with "I have never been more frightened than the time . . ." The aim of the lesson was to identify and discuss the major concepts and themes present in Night *by Elie Wiesel. During the Do Now, students were to define 'justifiable' and finish the sentence starter:* Telling a lie is justifiable when _____. *After several minutes of reflecting and writing, students shared their sentences with their classmates. My co-teacher then asked the students to take out their books* Night *and their anticipation guide, which included statements such as:*

1. *Revenge is a justifiable emotion.*

2. *All is fair in love and war.*

3. *Misery loves company.*

4. *Survival should always be the primary goal.*

5. *Lying is justifiable when it's for the right reasons.*

I explained that students would be working in their already assigned groups and discussing whether they agree or disagree with the statements. All the students received the same anticipation guide, and they supported each other in their heterogeneous groups to come up with the answers. As students worked in their groups, my co-teacher and I circulated around checking students' progress and offering support as needed. Each group selected a spokesperson to present their responses. With each of the statements, a brief discussion was held regarding morals, right and wrong, and how love can change a person. The goal of this activity was to build background and activate prior knowledge, followed by an interactive PowerPoint about the author, Elie Wiesel's, life. Next, I led a discussion about the author and shared how I met him at a conference. I also displayed a map of Europe to show where the concentration camps were located. It was important to review the difference between the words memoir *and* autobiography, *asking the students to define the meanings of the two words and giving examples. I wrote down the information on the board, using a graphic organizer (T-chart). With a few minutes remaining, my co-teacher handed out a green exit card and students wrote two things they learned in class about the Holocaust and one new vocabulary word. I modeled the assignment, and several students shared their responses before the bell rang.*

Next, we hear from Leah Tweedy, ELL teacher at Iowa City High School, as she explains how the class composition and the nature of the curriculum help determine whether or not preteaching and reteaching are appropriate choices with high impact on student learning.

In my ten years of teaching ELLs, I have co-taught in the middle and high school settings in a variety of subject areas. Based on the subject area and student background, the models of co-teaching my co-teachers and I employ vary significantly. However, in each situation, a few models always arise as the natural fit to meet our classroom's needs. Currently, my science co-teacher, Phil Lala, and I co-teach a sheltered Foundations of Science class for beginner and intermediate ELLs. We have approximately thirty students following a curriculum that is required for all first-year science students at City High. Since our class is sheltered with only ELLs of similar language levels, we are able to modify the assessments and teaching to fit their needs.

On any given day, we flow through co-teaching Models 1 through 4 and 7. For example, we often use Model 2 as Phil focuses on the content objectives of the lesson and I lead the teaching of the language objectives. Model 4 is sometimes incorporated when we want the intermediate ELLs to have slightly different language expectations on a lesson than the beginners. In such situations, we split the class, with Phil taking the beginners, teaching and modeling the language expectations for them, and I do the same with the intermediate students. This way, students are expected to meet the same content objectives but use language that is appropriate for their level. Model 7 is a natural fit on lab days. Recently, we studied light and sound waves. The laboratory was set up with a variety of sound stations at which groups of students conducted experiments, with a total of two sets of five stations. Phil and I circled the labs, clarifying, monitoring, and assisting the students as necessary. Selecting the appropriate co-teaching model has become an easy process: one always fits naturally into that day's learning goal.

The two models we employ least with our students with relatively similar language needs are Models 5 and 6. However, those are the two models I used most often in nonsheltered co-teaching experiences. In my former district, we had a much smaller ELL population and didn't have the numbers to support sheltered classes. I would co-teach in secondary classes with just a few ELLs and the rest English speakers. The teachers and I would often sit down and discuss the big understandings and standards students needed to meet for each unit. For our limited-English students, we would identify the areas likely to be confusing or unnecessary, and therefore ideal windows of time for more focused instruction for beginner or intermediate ELLs. As we reached those parts of the lesson, we would split into groups and I would take my students to either preteach the needed vocabulary for the next activity or unit (Model 5), or reteach any areas of confusion the students demonstrated in formative assessments (Model 6). These two models were the greatest help to my students in a nonsheltered environment, especially the preteaching of background and vocabulary. I could instantly tell a difference when my students went into a unit prepared with language and content background. They exuded more confidence and often needed less help and reteaching as the unit progressed. So what's the optimal co-teaching model? The one that fits the students' needs and the classroom environment!

Finally, let's hear from Cynthia Valdez, ELL content coach in Mesa County Valley School District, Colorado, who describes a mixed-level high school ELA class where a variety of co-teaching models and grouping strategies have been used.

The ELA 10 class consisted of about 40% ELLs who were at different language levels (high 2s–5 WIDA levels; a few Monitor and Exit students were also mixed with mainstream English native students). The classroom methods of teaching were diverse, and the groupings changed often to give everyone a chance to work together, which included all four communication domains (L, R, S, W). I did many preteaching and background-building activities for various groups and extensions of the same for ELLs who lacked background. The curriculum mixes historical documents with other readings, so ELLs without U.S. history background would get very confused by the assumptions made in the curriculum, especially when comparing and contrasting to formulate a cognitive evaluation. The content teacher built some background for all students through short historical videos, but the video language was too fast for even Monitored ELLs (WIDA levels 5–6). I would reteach by playing the videos over and over and stopping as needed for ELLs to write the needed words on the fill-in-the-blank worksheet that went with the video. The ELLs would work together to listen and record their answers, which gave them practice with the content language. After the ELLs finished the video and worksheet, I would ask questions to formatively assess their understanding of the event or concept. I would often assess that many ELLs still did not understand enough to make good cognitive choices about the theme or topic, so I would preteach more background in various forms. Our co-teaching helped all students as while I was preteaching or reteaching, the content teacher was able to deepen the understanding and add more information with the other students to meet their middle- and higher-level learning needs. All students were served well within our co-teaching class, and everyone learned together in a safe and effective classroom environment for all. The ESL programming for this high school was targeting English ninth- and tenth-grade English classes to support high school ESL students and to build their skills to be successful in LA eleventh and twelfth grades, as well as all other contents. This plan showed great success, as more ELLs passed English classes the first time taken and throughout their high school years than ever before. Targeted ESL programming mixed with co-teaching has been successful for all our district high school ELLs.

TAKEAWAYS

In this chapter, we present Model 5 (Two Groups: One Preteaches, One Teaches Alternative Information) as an approach to activate students' prior knowledge to build background knowledge and skills as needed. We have revisited the role formative assessment plays in making decisions in the co-taught classroom, especially when preteaching or reteaching a lesson. Finally, we share several vignettes focusing on Model 5 contributed by co-teachers and their supervisors who had tried this particular model in their own classrooms with success.

QUESTIONS FOR FURTHER DISCUSSION

1. Why is it important to incorporate preteaching into your co-teaching repertoire?

2. Which three preteaching strategies can you see trying in your classroom? Why did you choose them?

3. How can you justify taking a group of students to alternate instructional areas for Model 5?

4. What are some of the challenges you anticipate as you try to implement Model 5? How will you overcome them?

8

Model 6—Two Groups

One Reteaches, One Teaches Alternative Information

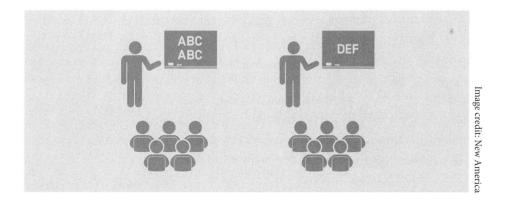

Image credit: New America

AN INTRODUCTION TO THE MODEL

In this chapter, we continue the discussion of grouping strategies to support English learners (ELs) in their content attainment and language and literacy development. More specifically, we address why and how ELs will benefit from extended opportunities to practice carefully selected dimensions of the content curriculum and key language skills that will advance their linguistic and academic progressions.

When co-teachers incorporate Model 6 (Two Groups: One Reteaches, One Teaches Alternative Information) into their practice, they begin to devote more attention to the development of critical skills through reviewing and practicing what has already been taught, as well as afford ELs—and others who need it—more explicit teaching of target skills. Through this model, co-teachers also create the time and place for more individually guided assistance for some while simultaneously challenging students who need extension or enrichment activities within the regular instructional time.

Using formative and summative assessment data, co-teachers determine which students most benefit from additional support or extensive personalized assistance, including scaffolding and explicitly reteaching what the student had not grasped previously. Some students will need extra time to practice new learning until progression to the next skill level or mastery of new content is reached. At the same time, assessment data will also reveal which students would do better if instruction expanded upon what they already know and can do provided enrichment were a regular part of the classroom.

English learners in the co-taught classroom are faced with the task of acquiring English language and literacy skills while also making reasonable progressions with grade-level content. Recognizing this challenge is particularly important when you work with entering- or emerging-level students. As also noted by Martinez-Wenzl, Perez, and Gandara (2012):

> The research is consistent in finding that it takes students significantly longer than a year or two to become proficient in academic language. As a result, students who are in mainstream classes before they have developed the requisite language skills to fully participate are not in fact being afforded equal access to the curriculum. Nor are students being provided with an adequate education if they are denied grade level instruction in academic content while they learn English. Moreover, the research is now clear and overwhelming that trading off the instruction of academic content by focusing on instruction about English does not result in superior outcomes even for English acquisition. (pp. 25–26)

Many educators and researchers agree that ELs must develop language and literacy skills necessary for acquiring the K–12 core curriculum, which in turn helps them achieve academic success in school and beyond. However, language and content should not be perceived as sequential: first language, then content; instead, language and content are integrated in the co-taught classroom.

Within an advocacy framework, Staehr Fenner (2013a) invites educators to reflect on a series of self-evaluation questions, one of which focuses on whether or not ELs have "access to a challenging, high-quality and developmentally appropriate curriculum aligned to the state's standards within and across content areas" (p. 87). It is believed that all ELs, even those who are recent arrivals or demonstrate entering or emerging levels of language proficiency, can and must be supported to learn the content. The grade-appropriate curriculum serving as a road map in English language arts (ELA) and all content areas must be translated into meaningful instructional experiences for ELs through curricular *adaptations* and *acceleration*.

Adaptations may take the form of accommodations or modifications. Accommodations offer access to the grade-level curriculum without altering the standards through the use of scaffolding tools. On the other hand, modifications result in fundamental changes to the grade-level expectations and are needed when the standards are not attainable by an EL due to disabilities or other factors. Reteaching plays an important role in ensuring a rigorous curriculum for all.

Acceleration, on the other hand, requires careful selection and instruction of key competences ELs will need to be successful in their current grade-level curriculum. Rollins (2014) advocates for the acceleration model by "putting key prior knowledge into place so that students have something to connect new information to" (p. 6). She cautions that instead of focusing on everything students do not know, teachers must strategically select and teach the specific prior knowledge and skills that will help students meet the standard. Model 5—Two Groups: One Preteaches, One Teaches Alternative Information—discussed in Chapter 7—is most suitable to accomplish this type of instruction. However, Model 6—Two Groups: One Reteaches, One Teaches Alternative Information—discussed in this current chapter—is also critical to the success of an integrated, accelerated approach to teaching ELs by providing the necessary practice of essential skills. Hern and Snell (2013) advise against equating accelerating the curriculum with remediation; accelerated curricula offer foundational skill-building and support for students' social-emotional needs while developing critical thinking skills and ensuring sustained, low-stakes practice.

We also look to Walqui and van Lier (2010) for validating the need for Model 6 (as well as the other co-teaching models), who suggest five specific design factors to be included in a quality curriculum for ELs:

(1) setting long-term goals and benchmarks,

(2) using a problem-based approach that include interrelated lessons with real-life applications,

(3) *creating a spiraling progression that includes necessary preteaching and reteaching* [emphasis added],

(4) making the subject matter relevant to the present lives and future goals of the students and their communities, and

(5) building on students' lived experiences and connecting to the students' funds of knowledge. (p. 99)

The spiral kind of teaching suggested by Walqui and van Lier (2010) designates a central place for preteaching and reteaching, thus co-teachers can ensure progression in the content curriculum and in meeting language and literacy goals as well. Spiraling (thus the idea of utilizing Model 6) is likely to be welcomed by all teachers who have ever worked with students who may not completely grasp a new concept or fully develop a new skill the first time around, but by having repeated experiences with the concept or skill, they reach mastery!

A CLOSER LOOK AT MODEL 6

English to speakers of other languages (ESOL) teachers throughout the United States have noted how some English learners feel marginalized in their schools. Similarly, Yoon (2008) indicates, "the main reason for students' anxiety, silence, and different positioning has much to do with being outsiders in the regular classroom context" (p. 498). Feeling a sense of belonging is critical for students to be academically successful. It is certain that students tend to engage more when they feel they are valued; however, if students believe the people around them do not care about them, they tend to lose motivation to connect with others as well as with what is being taught (Hewitt, 1998). For this reason, beware of automatically placing ELs in preteach or reteach groups; it may perpetually contribute to them feeling as outsiders and make them believe they are less capable than their peers. Instead, regularly collect meaningful formative assessment data and strategically use the information gained from your data collection to help better determine who needs reteaching and what methods should be used.

You may be surprised to find from time to time that ELs have mastered certain information, skills, or strategies, whereas it is their English-speaking peers who need additional support, or it is a combination of both groups of students who have not attained set objectives. More often than not, we have found that Model 6 leads to creating mixed groups of ELs and non-ELs for the most effective interventions, further supporting the notion that both co-teachers are teachers of all children in the room.

The Reteach and Enrich (R&E) model has been showcased as a schoolwide success story (Nobori, 2011), in which every child receives either a reteach or enrich intervention during strategically scheduled class periods when students from different classrooms are gathered to receive a best-match learning experience. As we uncover Model 6 in this chapter, we suggest an adaptation of R&E to be purposefully selected for the co-taught classroom.

Model 6 is especially well suited for co-teachers to diagnose and respond to each individual student's challenge with the curriculum, including both ELs and non-ELs, and to create multiple opportunities for meaningful experiences with the curriculum and the academic language and literacy skills and strategies that lead to student success. Let's examine a three-fold approach to determining what may be retaught while incorporating Model 6 (see Figure 8.1) into co-taught instruction. First, we will consider grade-level content attainment, then language and literacy skills, and finally, learning strategies that help students become self-directed, independent learners.

Focus on Grade-Level Content Goals

Within the context of a content-based co-taught classroom, Model 6 is a safety net for some students and an opportunity for enrichment for others. Note we did not say safety net for ELs and enrichment for their English-speaking peers. We, in fact, agree with the argument so poignantly presented by Deborah Palmer and Ramón Antonio Martínez (2013), that "bilingual learners have much the same needs and strengths as monolingual learners; they simply have a greater potential to work and learn in two (or more) languages" (p. 273). Similarly, Claude Goldenberg (2013) concludes that most instructional strategies that work with the general student population are likely to have a positive impact on ELs. When preparing lessons for reteaching and teaching alternative information, co-teachers should consider the checklist in Figure 8.2 inspired by Goldenberg (2013) when preparing lessons.

When we looked for a well-researched and well-established framework for offering effective instruction for all students (both ELs and English-speaking peers), Universal Design for Learning

Figure 8.1 A Three-Fold Model of Reteaching/Enriching

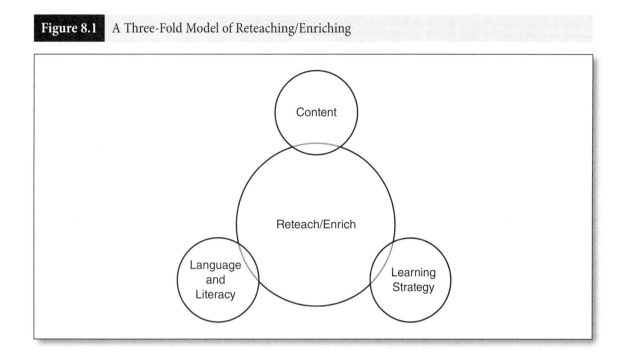

(UDL) appeared to be best suited for consideration. While UDL is primarily considered a curriculum design process (Novak, 2014), its principles and key practices are helpful for planning co-taught lessons (see Stein, 2016; www.udlcenter.org for more information). Since the three primary principles of UDL are to provide multiple means of representation, action and expression, and engagement, differentiation is integral to this framework, thus readily applicable to the co-taught classroom. See the three principles of UDL with a brief explanation and key strategies you can implement in the co-taught EL classroom.

Figure 8.2 Checklist for Planning Model 6

Reteach and Teaching Alternative Information (Enrichment)

- Have we set clear goals and learning targets for both groups of students?
- Does each group have challenging yet differentiated material suitable for their needs?
- Have we clearly designed instruction and tasks that are based on already established class routines?
- Have we developed appropriate instructional activities to engage all learners?
- Do our plans contain sufficient time for modeling and/or demonstrating?
- Have we planned for sufficient time for practice and feedback?
- Do our plans create opportunities for students to SWIRL (speak, write, interact, read, and listen)?
- Have we prepared appropriate formative assessments?

The Three Principles of UDL Applied to Reteaching

1. Representation—present the content of the lesson in multiple formats to ensure that all students can access it and transfer it to new knowledge:

a. Use multiple perceptual modalities (auditory, visual, tactile, kinesthetic) infused in the lesson;

b. Offer language-based visual or symbolic presentation of content including native language resources; and

c. Provide a variety of opportunities for comprehension.

2. Action and Expression—during the lesson, students need to have options for expressing and demonstrating what they have learned and can do:

a. Include physical involvement and movement during the lesson;

b. Provide choice opportunities for responding to the content of the lesson (tools and multimedia) including native language or home responses or translanguaging, which allows students to simultaneously tap into and use all linguistic repertoire (native language, additional dialects or languages, as well as English); and

c. Purposefully use learning strategies and a variety of instructional resources.

3. Engagement—students must be motivated and engaged in the lesson in multiple ways:

a. Plan authentic and relevant learning experiences building on students' funds of knowledge and funds of identity;

b. Foster collaboration and communication especially across cultural and linguistic groups; and

c. Encourage student goal setting, self-assessment, and reflection about the learning process.

When the UDL principles are used specifically for Model 6, strategically employ instructional practices and materials that make the reteaching accessible to all students in multiple ways. See Table 8.1 for a collection of ideas you can tap into while all your students can benefit from the UDL approach to instruction.

While UDL offers a sound framework for working with diverse students of all abilities, the strategies in Table 8.1 are merely a sample selection to begin with UDL. What to keep in mind is that in the co-taught classroom, ELs will be uniquely positioned to benefit from multiple opportunities to participate in academic conversations with peers and structured written activities guided by teachers to build new knowledge, to expand their vocabulary and language use, and to engage in meaningful learning.

Focus on Academic Language and Literacy Skills

Academic language has been receiving well-deserved growing attention in recent years. It is defined by World-Class Instructional Design and Assessment (WIDA, 2011) as

the language required to succeed in school that includes deep understandings of content and communication of that language in the classroom environment. These understandings revolve around specific criteria related to discourse, sentence, and word/phrase levels of language. (p. 1)

Table 8.1 UDL-Based Strategies and Materials

Representation	Action and Expression	Engagement
Home language/bilingual resources	Act out	Guided notes
PowerPoint or Prezi	Tactile learning	Interactive games
Graphic organizers	Kinesthetic learning	Peer tutoring
Audio or video clips	Think-aloud	Cooperative learning teams
Three-dimensional (3-D) models	Interactive read-aloud	Creative expressions
Manipulatives	Quick write/Quick draw	Web-based tools and apps
	Graphic organizers	Websites

With this definition in mind, consider when reteaching how you may focus on the relationship between content and language as well as the need for using academic language—at the word, sentence, and text level—to communicate complex ideas. See Table 8.2 for a summary of possible language targets for a lesson on natural disasters. These targets will always be based on student assessment data, so consider the examples as representative samples of what may be necessary to reteach.

Table 8.2 Language Targets at the Word, Sentence, and Text Levels

Word-level work	Sentence-level work	Text-level work
Content vocabulary:	Passive voice:	Nonfiction text features:
Tornado	Hurricanes <u>are formed</u> . . .	Title and subtitle
Hurricane	Modal verbs:	Headings and subheadings
Volcano	Wildfires <u>can</u> . . .	Words/Phrases that are bold, underlined, in italics, or highlighted text
Generic academic vocabulary:	People should . . .	
Prepare, preparation	The government needs to . . .	Illustrations and captions
Disaster	Description Frames:	
Form	The _____ is a kind of _____ that _____.	
Erupt	(The tornado is a kind of violent storm that happens over land.)	
Rescue		
Effort		

A word of caution: While words are the building blocks of academic language, do not overemphasize vocabulary only when reteaching ELs. Focusing on words in isolation or emphasizing lists of words and their definitions will not get the kinds of results with academic language development that you are hoping for in the co-taught classroom. Although students may learn some meanings for content vocabulary, they may not understand or be able to express their ideas with the same vocabulary while reading and writing (Goldenberg & Coleman, 2010). Going beyond vocabulary teaching, particularly when reteaching, will expand students' productive language skills.

Another way to organize the reteaching of academic language is to consider its four key uses—discuss, explain, argue, and recount through the mnemonic device "DEAR" (or by rearranging the four initials "DARE"; Gottlieb & Castro, 2017) and how they can be authentically and meaningfully practiced via using Model 6. In a smaller group setting, co-teachers can revisit certain language features and offer a more in-depth opportunity to practice these critical language uses (see Table 8.3).

Table 8.3 Key Language Uses with Examples Across the Core Content Areas

Key Language Uses	ELA	Math	Science	Social Studies
Discuss	• Author's word choice • Specific language use in target text	• Real-life applications of math problems	• Authentic examples of scientific concepts	• Cultural and lived experiences related to the content
Explain	• Character development • Setting	• Key elements of a word problem • Own pathway to arriving at a solution	• Steps to follow in forming a scientific hypothesis	• Roles of the three branches of the government • Key historical events
Argue	• Own opinion about a piece of literature • The key turning point in a story	• Own mathematical reasoning • Own pathway to solving problems	• Different positions on key scientific issues • Taking a stand for or against an issue	• Different points of views • Arguments and counterarguments
Recount	• Story plot • Sequence of events	• Step-by-step directions to solve problems	• Safety rules in the lab • Steps in a science experiment	• Key historical events • Political trends

An additional challenge in the acquisition of academic language is that students need not only develop their receptive language skills (having opportunities to comprehend academic English by listening to or reading challenging language input) but also to build their productive language skills by creating sentences, paragraphs, and longer academic texts both orally and written. In sum, students need both explicit instruction in academic language and sustained, meaningful opportunities to continue to acquire and develop the necessary language skills. During reteaching time, ELs are going to develop stronger language skills when they are engaged in activities that help them make meaning and use the language with a purpose.

Focus on Learning Strategy Instruction

Time ELs spend in Model 6 can be structured in a way that co-teachers strengthen their students' language-learning strategy use. Learners of all ages can develop effective strategies that aid in their social and academic language use as well as continued language development (Oxford, 2017). The following strategies are organized in three broad categories: vocabulary-learning strategies, literacy-learning strategies, and communication strategies. While these are just a sampling of learning strategies, we suggest you begin with some of these key strategy-building activities:

Vocabulary-Learning Strategies

- Emphasize the value of the home language by looking for cognates (*difference* vs. *differencia*—words that sound the same or similar and mean the same or something similar). Don't forget to point out false cognates as well, when the word meanings are not aligned (such as record vs. recordar, meaning write down vs. remember).
- Explicitly model and teach word-learning strategies by showing students what word parts—prefixes, suffixes, and root words—make up a word.
- Encourage students to develop tolerance for ambiguity by exposing them to short complex texts that are slightly above their language proficiency levels and help them experience that even if they do not know every single word in a paragraph, they can make sense of it.
- Practice looking not just inside but outside the word as well (Fisher & Frey, 2008b). Search for context clues to unlock the meaning of new words.

Literacy-Learning Strategies

- Practice previewing text and making educated guesses and predictions about the readings.
- Model and practice skimming (looking for main idea) and scanning (searching for specific details).
- Examine and compare text types, text features, and genres to help students build their literacy schema.
- Model note-taking and text annotation strategies.

Communication Strategies

- Encourage students to ask for help or clarification by teaching them how to approach the teacher or their peers if something is not clear. Key phrases and sentences (Can you repeat/ explain that please?) or sentence starters (What does _____ mean?) can be available on anchor charts, bookmarks, and tabletop tents until students internalize them.
- Support students by teaching them how to use resources, both their own resources such as their home language and literacy skills, and existing language skills in English as well as outside resources such as print and electronic dictionaries, Apps, and computer programs that are available to them in and out of school.
- Model and practice the use of circumlocution, or expressing yourself without using a key word you cannot recall (saying what you want to say using different words).
- Practice self-monitoring and self-evaluation strategies, thus fostering your students' meta-linguistic awareness. Remember, you want them to be able to monitor how they use the language, check their own written work, or reflect on how well they expressed themselves.

This model configuration provides a plausible place for students to reflect more personally (Fisher, Frey, & Hattie, 2016):

- o What am I learning?
- o Why am I learning this?
- o How will I know that I have learned it?
- Nurture risk taking so students can develop into self-directed, independent learners who understand that making mistakes is a natural part of language acquisition.

VIDEO 8.1: Model 6—Two Groups: One Reteaches, One Teaches Alternative Information

http://resources
.corwin.com/
CoTeachingforELs

The importance of strategy instruction is well supported by decades of research by Rebecca Oxford (1990, 2017), who also notes that "deepening strategy instruction to make it more personally valuable for autonomy could be transformative for learners" (p. 2). Helping students become self-directed, self-regulated learners is a critical part of educating ELs.

ADVANTAGES

The most apparent advantage of the model is affording ELs with multiple meaningful opportunities to learn grade-level content, to attend to individual needs, to recognize cultural assets that students bring to the classroom, and to practice academic language. At the same time, students who have reached higher levels of competency may also extend their learning and remain highly engaged. The teaching-learning cycle is only effective if what teachers teach, learners actually learn. We often confuse teachers we work with when we tell them not to cover the curriculum, but instead, uncover the curriculum. Deep learning can only take place if English learners engage in meaning-making, which takes time and requires patience and persistence, both from the teachers and the students. Deep learning is also more likely to happen if there are increased opportunities for student-to-student as well as student-to-teacher interactions and higher levels of engagement in a smaller group.

With Model 6, all students benefit from a lower teacher-student ratio, which leads to supporting a natural learning progression. You and your co-teachers must have felt hesitant to continue with a unit unless students developed foundational understanding or essential skills. With Model 6, you have another opportunity to communicate clearly what and how students are expected to learn, and bring a choice of resources and strategies for some students to differentiate learning for all. At the same time, the smaller group setting and the extended time lends itself to further establishing how what is being taught is relevant to students' lives—transferring skills introduced in the large-group setting to new context and engaging in a deeper exploration of a particular concept or skill. For example, reteaching time allows for more in-depth text-to-self, text-to-text, and text-to-world connections to be made; sometimes, not all three would fit into the lesson.

During the implementation of Model 6, co-teachers may agree to monitor student progress and also collect assessment data that will help inform instruction. Additionally, new resources may be introduced that were not appropriate for whole-class instruction to vary instruction and offer new entry points into the learning target. Ajayi (2008) suggests a range of resources such as "reports, newspapers, pictures, songs, manuals, textbooks, narratives, procedures, legal documents, spoken or written words, and the different text types associated with electronic multimedia" (p. 209).

Multilingual resources as well as new technology tools that you might not want to introduce to the entire class at the same time might be piloted. Since co-teachers will take their own groups, face-to-face co-planning time can be reduced. In sum, Model 6 helps you meet students where they are (rather than going ahead in the curriculum), thus providing access to differentiated learning, additional practice, and enrichment.

CHALLENGES

There are a few challenges associated with this model. It should not be implemented and perceived by ELs or other students as remediation. If ELs are consistently separated into the same small groups, they may perceive themselves as less capable than others. Consider this: How can something be remediated if it has never been built? Instead, it should be recognized as valuable time offered to all students to practice and extend their understanding and skills. The challenge for teachers is to ensure that all students get equitable opportunities for learning and equal access to high-quality curriculum.

We gleaned from teachers that finding time for preteaching seems to be easier than for reteaching. The pressure to move to the next unit and to get through the curriculum is a frequently cited challenge we hear in the field. One successful planning strategy is to set up a weekly schedule in which opportunities for practice, reteaching, and enrichment are consistently included.

Another challenge of this model is data collection and data management. For this model to be effective, co-teachers need a system to continuously collect valid and reliable formative assessment data based on which students will be grouped as well as data that will inform you when you are ready to move on. Managing time, the noise level, instructional resources, and the available classroom space while you and your co-teacher work in two separate groups may also present a problem. See Table 8.4 for a summary of the advantages and challenges of Model 6.

INSTRUCTION USING MODEL 6

Low-Prep Strategies for Model 6

This model's main purpose is to allow for reteaching and enriching all students. Some instructional choices that require minimal preparation include reviewing previously taught materials through power words and power sentences, chunking, and text mark ups.

Power Words

The *power word* strategy is one way to help students remember key words and concepts of the lesson. Since the power word is the most important word in a sentence, paragraph, or even a text, you can offer some additional modeling and think-alouds to help students find power words in text titles, in introductory sentences, and later in carefully selected short paragraphs. Focusing on power words will help students to use essential words or precise academic vocabulary in their own speech and writing as well.

Table 8.4 Summary of Advantages and Challenges of Model 6

Model 6: Two Groups: One Reteaches, One Teaches Alternative Information	
Advantages	**Challenges**
A reduction in the student-teacher ratio can boost the content and language learning of ELs.	Since the two groups are working off different materials, equity and access to rigorous curricula for all learners must be considered.
An increase in opportunities for student interaction and engagement in a smaller group.	Sound levels in the co-taught class may be distracting for both students and teachers.
Attention might be more easily paid to differentiate instruction.	Some students might enjoy more enrichment learning opportunities than others.
Individual learning needs and aspects of cultural diversity for learning can be better met.	Some grouping strategies might segregate students or characterize them as less able.
This approach to co-teaching might facilitate a reduction in face-to-face co-planning time.	Creating flexible groupings for instruction can be confounding and time consuming for co-teachers.
The smaller group size gives teachers a better opportunity to gather data by conducting informal assessments.	Co-teachers do not always have equal access to classroom spaces or material resources with this model.
Positive student-teacher relationships may develop more readily.	Implementation of this model is a challenge in middle and high schools due to classroom space and logistics.

A *power sentence* is a student-friendly definition or summary account that often follows an established pattern. A power sentence can frequently be derived from the text. It may be the topic sentence or summary statement that also tends to offer a good linguistic model for analyzing and imitating. Another way to approach this strategy is for co-teachers to model sample sentences that follow a particular pattern and then have students develop their own power sentences about the text or topic (see samples in Figure 8.3).

Figure 8.3 Power Sentence Samples

Sentence Frames

(Verb+ing) IS (adjective) BECAUSE (reason).

(Verb+ing) + noun phrase IS (adjective) BECAUSE (reason).

Examples:

Playing with matches is dangerous because they can cause fire.

Having a fire safety plan at home is helpful because it can save lives.

Reading about fire safety is important because you learn fire safety tips.

Adapted from Dove & Honigsfeld, 2013

Chunking

Chunking, or breaking a concept, a task, or complex information into smaller units of meaning, is a frequently used critical strategy for all learners. It serves as a scaffolding technique by helping students focus on a shorter piece of the lesson, task, or text, reducing the cognitive and linguistic load, making the task more manageable, thus leading to success and a sense of self-efficacy. During reteaching, you can help teach the strategy of chunking, as well as model and practice how to make sense of a part of the lesson or text, how to practice a key subskill, how to monitor one's own learning, recognize language and literacy development progression, and so on.

Text Mark Ups

During whole-class instruction, even with two teachers in the room it may be hard to monitor how students work with complex text. Stephanie Harvey and Harvey Daniels (2009) suggest active reading strategies including text coding or text monitoring (see Figure 8.4). During a reteach lesson, read short selections with students as they learn to use the following notations on the margins or Post-it notes. Introduce text coding through modeled reading and text monitoring one or two codes at a time, gradually building up to all eight codes.

Figure 8.4   Text Codes

✓ = I know this

X = This is not what I expected

* = This is important

? = I have a question about this

?? = I am really confused

! = This surprises me

L = I have learned something new here

RR = I have to reread this section

As a result, students will understand and deconstruct more complex texts. When students internalize the strategy of text mark ups or text annotation, they become more engaged in reading and focus more carefully on the content and structure of the text.

Another approach is to explicitly teach and practice the different ways in which students can mark and label a text as well as write marginal notes to highlight important information, identify an author's claims, and gather evidence that is apparent in the details of the text. Porter-O'Donnell (2004) suggests some of the ways to annotate text as follows:

- *Before Reading*: Mark the titles and the subtitles; examine the print and highlight any bold or italicized words; consider the illustrations and highlight any important information found in the captions.
- *During Reading*: Circle the names of individuals, events, or ideas; place a box around words or phrases; underline important information; write margin notes to summarize, make predictions, form opinions, ask questions, and make connections.

- *After Reading*: Review annotations and draw conclusions; reread the introduction and the summary to derive something new; consider if there are any noticeable patterns or repetitions and determine what they might mean; write a journal entry that identifies the author's claims and the found evidence to support them.

Pro-Prep Strategies for Model 6

Some lessons used within the framework of Model 6 will require more preparation. Depending on the learning target for each group, resources that reinforce learning or challenge students' thinking may serve the purpose. Here, we introduce three key strategies: reference sheets, graphic organizers, and inquiry circles.

Reference Sheets

We have earlier introduced the idea of one-pagers (see Chapter 3); a variation of a one-pager is a reference sheet (or "cheat sheet," though we prefer the former) that is designed to give a quick overview of some key information or a collection of language-based tools the student can refer to. Some reference sheets are prepared ahead of time by the teacher, others may be co-constructed with the students in class or in the small-group setting Model 6 affords, or may be prepared by one group of students as an extension or enrichment activity to be used by the other group at a later time. For example, one teacher may work with one group of students on synthesizing knowledge (What are the causes of the collapse of the Roman Empire?) while the other group is collecting linguistic resources for a particular task (math chart with all key words found in word problems related to addition, subtraction, multiplication, and division). The reference sheet may contain an annotated timeline, key steps to complete equations, guidelines for writing in different genres, lists of transition words or phrases (*above all, meanwhile, first and foremost*), and so on. See Table 8.5 for an example of a Signal Word Reference Sheet.

Graphic Organizers

Graphic organizers help students become familiar with different text structures through a range of reading and writing activities as presented in this book previously. They will also aid learners in applying their understanding of how ideas are organized in different genres by gathering information and organizing ideas using a visual tool. A favorite note-taking graphic organizer is depicted in Figure 8.5 showing prompts for key ideas, details, and summary/evaluation of the source.

Additionally, see www.thinkingmaps.com for eight graphic organizers that promote analytical thinking while providing visual support. Examples from ELA, science, and social studies lessons are presented in Table 8.6.

Graphic organizers are ideal tools to be differentiated for multilevel classes since they can be presented blank or with various amounts of pre-entered information depending on the amount of support students need to complete the task.

Table 8.5 Signal Word Reference Sheet

Text Type	Description	Signal Words
Description	To describe a topic by listing characteristics, features, attributes, and examples	• for example • characteristics • for instance • such as • is like
Sequence	To list items or events in numerical or chronological sequence	• first • second • third • later • next
Comparison	To present how two or more events, concepts, theories, or things are alike and/or different	• however • nevertheless • on the other hand • but • similarly
Cause and Effect	To present ideas, events in time, or facts as causes and the resulting effect(s) or facts that happen as a result of an event	• reasons why • as a result • therefore • because • consequently
Problem and Solution	To show the development of a problem and one or more solutions	• problem is • dilemma is • if/then • because • so that

Figure 8.5 Structured Note-Taking Template

Key Points	Details
Summary and Evaluation	

Table 8.6 Thinking Map Examples

Thinking Map	Purpose	Examples from ELA, Science, and Social Studies Lessons
Circle Map	Contextualization (adding a Frame of Reference)	Create a frame of reference for Katniss Everdeen, the protagonist of *The Hunger Games*
Tree Map	Classification	Summarize the achievements of the Mayan civilization
Bubble Map	Description	Describe Cassie Logan in Mildred D. Taylor's *Roll of Thunder, Hear My Cry*
Double Bubble Map	Comparison and Contrast	Compare and contrast animal cells and plant cells
Flow Map	Sequence or Order of Events	Describe the steps taken in a science experiment
Multi Flow Map	Cause and Effect	Discuss what events led to the Boston Tea Party and what events followed it
Brace Map	Part-Whole Relationships	Identify the major systems of the human body and the organs found in each system
Bridge Map	Analogies	Explore the analogies in Walt Whitman's "O Captain! My Captain!"

Adapted from Honigsfeld and Dove, 2013

Inquiry Circles. Similar to literature circles, to offer enrichment opportunities, your students can engage in meaningful, deep conversations focused on content-area topics within the framework of inquiry circles. Stephanie Harvey and Harvey Daniels (2009) suggest a sequence of three guiding questions to help students discuss content-based readings. They named the three types of questions as (a) definition, (b) consequence, and (c) action questions. See generic and content-specific examples in Table 8.7. Students can be invited to generate the discipline or topic-specific questions based on the generic guiding questions so they develop an even more enhanced ownership of the discussion.

To scaffold this activity, consider giving students model questions in which to generate topic-specific questions or sentence frames that require students to fill in the blank spaces of partially completed questions.

Table 8.7 Guided Questioning for Inquiry Circles

Question Type	Generic Guiding Questions	Examples From a Lesson on Climate Change:
Definition Questions	What is it? What is taking place?	What is climate change? What is happening to Earth's oceans?
Consequence Questions	Why does it matter? Why is it important?	Why should we learn about climate change? Why does it matter if the Earth's temperature rises?
Action Questions	What can be done? What actions should be taken?	What choices do we have as individuals? What actions can we take individually and as a community?

SAMPLE LESSONS: TWO GROUPS: ONE RETEACHES, ONE TEACHES ALTERNATIVE INFORMATION

The following lesson segments portray co-teachers as they separate students into two groups for reteaching. Paula Barnick, ESOL teacher in Valley Stream Union Free School District 13, New York, shared with us how students are selected for reteaching during a co-taught writing lesson:

Co-teaching during half of the students' literacy block finds the classroom teacher and I intentionally interspersing grammar lessons and writer's craft lessons while using student notebook entries as the greatest authentic indicator . . . It was evident that one group of students needed reinforcement . . . as a result of the conferencing sessions that we had. The flexibility of having two teachers present in the classroom made a difference in ensuring that students understand before moving forward with instruction, while not holding other students back . . .

Inspired by Ms. Barnick and her co-teacher's use of data gathering and purposeful grouping for both remediating and extending students' ability to write, we selected the following co-taught craft lesson, developed from a framework by Fletcher and Portalupi (2007), to further support small groups of first graders to write longer and more complex stories.

Lesson 1—A Two-Day Lesson to Support First-Graders' Writing Craft

This two-day co-taught lesson is primarily for a first-grade class that contains both English learners and English speakers. The challenge of its delivery is to balance instruction for students who are entering and beginning English learners with those students who are already working at or above grade level. This balance is accomplished by incorporating multiple ways to configure the class for co-taught instruction on day one and focusing on reteaching on day two.

Day One. The lesson begins with the co-teachers using Model 2—One Group: Two Teach the Same Content. In this way, all students receive the same initial instruction with the support of both teachers in front of the class. While the whole class is seated in the carpeted area of the room, both teachers sit in front of them with a chart easel between them.

On the chart paper is displayed a graphic organizer that has three boxes labeled *Beginning*, *Middle*, and *End* (see Figure 8.6). Pointing to the chart, one teacher explains that all stories should have a beginning, middle, and end. She continues by giving an example from one of her favorite stories the class recently read, *The Little House* by Virginia Burton, and describes how the story opens, what happens in the center of the story, and how the story is finally resolved. The other teacher does the same—shares a story with students they all commonly know, revealing the three targeted parts of the story.

Next, working together, both teachers read the picture book *Fireflies* by Judy Brinkloe, and they invite students to think about how the story begins, what happens in the middle, and how the story ends. Each teacher takes a turn reading while the other teacher thinks aloud about the story and asks students questions. At intervals, students are invited to turn and talk to a partner to share different parts of the story. During the turn-and-talk time, both teachers step into the group to assist entering and beginning ELs with their conversations about the story and to gather some formative assessment information (Model 1—One Leads, One "Teaches on Purpose," and Model 3—One Teaches, One Assesses). At the end of this part of the lesson, the graphic organizer is completed—its contents determined by a culminating question-and-answer period led by both teachers with the whole group of students.

Students are now charged with completing their own stories in their writer's workshop notebooks that have a beginning, middle, and end. They return to their seats to begin the task and are offered graphic organizers (see Figure 8.6) that replicate the one on the chart paper the class used together to guide their writing. During writer's workshop, students sit in teams and both teachers circulate among the class to check for student understanding, assist students' writing, and assess their outcomes (Model 7—Multiple Groups: Two Monitor/Teach).

Through conferencing with the students and reviewing their writer's workshop notebooks and graphic organizers, both teachers gather and share their data about each student's

Figure 8.6	Writing Organizer

Name: _____	Date: _____
Beginning	
Middle	
End	

progress before the end of the class period. These data are the basis for grouping students during the next day's lesson.

Day Two. The lesson begins with both teachers together in front of the whole class. They display the chart from the previous day and tell students they will continue writing today with the same focus of creating stories with a beginning, middle, and end. The teachers explain that some students will work with one teacher while the remaining students work with the other. At this point, the students are divided for instruction.

The group designated for reteaching is seated at a round table together with their notebooks and are handed new graphic organizers that support student writing through storyboarding (see Figure 8.7). Students are guided step-by-step to visualize and illustrate the beginning, middle, and end of their stories in order to present students with a clear guide for their writing. With this task, storyboarding encourages students to grow their ideas and clarify story details. In this way, students have an additional opportunity to explore writing a more complex narrative that is organized through the use of the three designated story parts—beginning, middle, and end.

In the meantime, the other group of students is given the opportunity to elaborate on their stories from the previous day. These students are provided with a three-page stapled blank book and are charged with writing the beginning, middle, and end of their stories, using one page for each part of the story.

An analysis of the lesson segment. This lesson truly exemplifies Model 6—One Reteaches, One Teaches Alternative Information—in that it illustrates how co-teachers use multiple models for instruction before students are grouped for reteaching. Teaching partners often expose all students to the same initial lessons, thus allowing ELs the opportunity to learn alongside their peers and demonstrate their understanding and application of new strategies, skills, or information. This pattern of using multiple co-taught models before reteaching allows teachers to incorporate the use of data for the flexible grouping of students and eliminates the practice of segregating all ELs for additional instruction. For this lesson, three student groups might be needed, providing one group with reteaching, one group with the use of the three-page stapled books, and a third group with extra time to complete their original stories in their writer's notebooks.

| Figure 8.7 | Storyboarding |

Name: _____

Date: _____

Picture	☐	First, _____ _____ _____ _____ _____
Picture	☐	Next _____ _____ _____ _____ _____
Picture	☐	Last _____ _____ _____ _____ _____

Lesson 2—Women in History in a Grade 11 Social Studies Class

This eleventh-grade co-taught lesson focuses on Lily Ledbetter, whose fight for equal pay for equal work eventually led to the involvement of all three branches of government. For this lesson, the co-teaching team plans a series of opportunities for reinforcement/reteaching for their ELs both before and during the lesson to support students' acquisition of challenging vocabulary and concepts, and to promote their oral and written discourse.

To prepare ELs for the social studies lesson, the ESOL teacher reinforces and reviews students' understandings and knowledge of the vocabulary and concepts involving past lessons such as the three branches of government, the Supreme Court, the judicial process, the legislative process, and so on, in a stand-alone English language development/English language learners (ELD/ELL) class period that occurs just prior to the social studies class. ELs also preview selected scenes from a documentary film that will be shown again during the co-taught lesson.

In the social studies class, the lesson begins with all students viewing the documentary film *A Call to Act: Ledbetter v. Goodyear Tire and Rubber Company* (Imbriano, 2010). To support the large group of Spanish-speaking ELs in the class, the co-teachers decide to display subtitles in Spanish while the documentary is shown. All students are charged with completing a structured note-taking graphic organizer during the viewing in which they must jot down pertinent facts relayed by the film (see Figure 8.5 earlier in the chapter). The teachers pause the film at certain intervals to ask students guiding questions and allow students time to reflect on what they have already seen and heard as well as complete parts of their note taking.

After the film, students discuss the issue of gender roles and equality as it relates to the film and share their completed graphic organizers in teams of three. Students consider the following questions in their teams:

1. Which gender generally does the following jobs: secretary, bus driver, train conductor, airline pilot, taxi driver, ship's captain, carpenter, doctor, teacher, and nurse?

2. Which jobs do you think only men should do? Which jobs do you think only women should do?

3. To what extent do women have the same opportunities as men? To what extent is women's pay today the same as men's for the same work?

At this time, both teachers circulate around the room, listen in on students' conversations, and review their structured note taking. For brief intervals, one of the teachers might join a team's conversation to guide students toward a better understanding of the topic or to promote more active oral discourse among the team members.

Following the team discussions, students are asked to individually write a reflection in their journals in response to the following prompt: *Considering the film and the issue of gender equality, reflect on the status of gender equality in the United States today.* Based on each teacher's review of students' work in their teams, the co-teachers quickly confer with one another, and some students are chosen to work at a table with the ESOL teacher. At this time, certain aspects of the film are reviewed, team discussions are clarified, and the journal-writing task is more readily guided via step-by-step questions and prompts.

An analysis of the lesson segment. In this social studies lesson, we catch a glimpse of how Model 6—One Reteaches, One Teaches Alternative Information—is interpreted differently. In their conception of this lesson, these co-teachers have devised a plan for ongoing support for their ELs that involves review of subject matter previously taught in the stand-alone ELD/ELL class as well as using ongoing formative assessment during the co-taught lesson to determine when an immediate intervention should take place. This reoccurring reinforcement, review, and support were apparent during team conversations as well as in the course of the written assignment. There was not a great deal of teaching alternative information as this model generally suggests. Instead, reinforcement and review were carefully intertwined while both co-teachers maintained the same lesson content and pace with ample support from both teachers.

MODEL VARIATIONS

The hallmark of this model is that the class is divided into two groups. Each group is taught by one of the co-teachers, and they share the same classroom space; they differentiate instruction based on student needs. One frequently observed variation is when both groups receive reteaching (simply targeting different subskills or different resources), or alternately, both groups are exposed to enrichment and extension activities. One other variation we have seen is when the two teachers each take a small group for reteaching/enriching but the majority of the students work independently or in preestablished stations. As with all previous models, the various configuration modifications must be devised to accommodate different teaching goals and students' needs.

You can also approach Model 6 and make instructional decisions about reteaching or enriching by considering the following four scenarios and reflecting on these four questions:

(1) Should co-teachers reteach the *same* information, skill, or strategy using the *same* approach?

At times, students need more time to process new information or to hear what has been presented previously once more before their understanding is solidified. Revisiting a previously taught lesson using identical steps may offer reinforcement for students who need it.

(2) Should co-teachers teach the *same* information, skill, or strategy using a *different* approach?

At other times, students benefit from exposure to the content or language already presented in a new way. You may choose to reteach a previous lesson via using alternate resources, taking a fresh approach, experimenting with new technology, enabling ELs to learn grade-level content in their primary language, and so on.

(3) Should co-teachers teach *new* information, skills, or strategies using *previously implemented* approaches?

When students are ready to apply what they have mastered to a new context, Model 6 is most appropriate to offer extension or enrichment activities for some students and further opportunities for practicing content concepts and skills or language and literacy skills for others.

(4) Should co-teachers teach *new* information, skills, or strategies using a *new* approach?

In this scenario, students who have mastered the curriculum and demonstrated at or above grade-level skills receive enrichment. The challenge is to make sure the alternate information allows for deep learning, targeted skill practice, and enrichment opportunities rather than moving forward in the curriculum.

MODEL COMBINATIONS

By virtue of focusing on reinforcement and review in Model 6 (Two Groups: One Reteaches, One Teaches Alternative Information), it may be naturally connected to Model 3 (Two Groups: One Teaches, One Assesses) or any other models that allow for collaborative assessment data collection. Model 6 may also lead to being expanded into Model 7 (Multiple Groups: Two Monitor/Teach) if co-teachers decide that instead of two groups, multiple groups need to be set up, some of which might be engaged in an independent extension activity, thus freeing up the teachers to offer focused, individualized interventions to those who need them most. After an intervention is offered through Model 6, co-teachers may introduce new material via Model 2 (One Group: Two Teach the Same Content) while infusing information from the retaught lesson to continually reinforce key concepts, strategies, and skills.

INSPIRATION FROM THE FIELD

Read what colleagues—ELD/ELL and classroom teachers as well as building and district administrators—shared with us from around the United States and see how they reflect or add to your own experiences.

In Chapter 7, we saw how Cynthia Valdez, secondary English language learner (ELL) content coach, and her co-teacher in Mesa County Valley School District, Colorado, use a variety of co-teaching models, including Model 5. Here, let's see how she and her co-teacher achieved success with a particular student who began to thrive after a teach-reteach approach was introduced in the co-taught classroom.

We shared a dual-identified ninth-grade student who struggled especially in reading and writing. He did most of the classwork with the class as we supported him by differentiating and giving support as needed. However, he was unable to write the four essays expected within the ELA 9th coursework, so the plan was for him to write one very well. He chose the second one presented through classwork, and I worked with him mostly as a reteach with many scaffolds. For example, I would ask him what he learned and what he knew about the text. He was reluctant to write much at first, so I would record his thinking as he spoke about it. After listening to him and recording his thinking, I would ask him what he believed about the situation and I helped him identify a claim. From that information, we used the appropriate Thinking Map to chart his thinking. He put his thinking on the map while I asked questions and gave prompts that produced language, which he also wrote on the map. He found his evidence within the text and put it in the appropriate place on the map. I asked more questions until he stated the warrant and then he wrote it down as well. I created a formatted electronic essay with color coding for the different parts. He would take his language off the maps and type them in the correct place in the essay format. We did this for all the essay paragraphs, and he began to realize where the parts would go by himself. Once he had all of the essay parts entered, we deleted the formatting and turned it into essay writing. We included all the parts of his learning when he turned it in to the content teacher with the essay on top. We co-teachers were able to help him throughout the semester to obtain this learning to become a successful essay writer at the level of his peers through teach and reteach methods.

Next, let's see how Nicole Foley, elementary ESL teacher in Norristown Area School District, Pennsylvania, manages multiple co-teaching models and how Model 6 plays a critical final step in her co-teaching routine.

In our co-teaching classroom, we usually start out using Model 2 (Two Teachers Teach the Same Content), and we both fly out to help students who are struggling when needed. We do a lot of formative assessment, so we are both usually doing some type of assessing during our whole-group teaching. We will make notes or call each other's attention to particular students to see if they notice the same thing.

We then move into Model 7 (Multiple Groups: Two Monitor/Teach). This part changes each year depending on our students. We each teach something different, but each group sees each teacher at least twice per week. Our lowest-proficiency-level students are seen in small group daily. This year, I taught small-group reading and my co-teacher taught small-group writing. The students also worked in small cooperative groups, working in several areas, and each group would complete each activity once per week: (1) Spelling and high-frequency words, (2) Writing independently, (3) Reading independently or listening to stories, (4) Computer work—enhancing reading skills, and (5) Dramatic play—using language (vocabulary from our reading units—science and social studies based) to interact with each other. We would then move into Model 6 where one of us reteaches a concept to students needing it and the other teaching alternative information. It has been very successful, and the students have made incredible progress academically.

Let's visit with Jennifer LaLima, Garden City Union Free School District, New York, ESOL teacher, who shares some reasons why she appreciates what Model 6 offers.

One of my co-teachers, Madelyn Fisher-Fogel, fifth-grade teacher, had a great classroom with many stations and areas. She made these areas to be very inviting and almost like a home. This benefited our instruction and our students, especially when we would use Model 6 because I could work with a smaller group in one of these sections without giving the impression that this group was separate at all. The inviting sections of the classroom were fun for the children to work in, so for them it felt more like they were taking a quiet break from the large group and learning in a more comfortable setting. This is an extremely important model for all classrooms because it allows the teachers to differentiate and truly meet the needs of the students. Contrary to what I've heard again and again, ELLs do not need 'simplified' curriculum; they need enriched language and amplified curriculum. This model helped me to have the opportunity to reteach, check for understanding, go deeper, and provide enrichment for the language we were using. Meanwhile, my co-teacher was able to work with another group, in a different way that met the needs of her group.

Next, let's hear from Matt Cope, ESL teacher, and Carl Chaney, history teacher, at Cary High School in Wake County Schools, North Carolina, who are mindful of assessing and responding to their ELs' needs through choosing the most appropriate model.

Students of all levels want their instruction to feel personalized. They also want to know that their ideas will be heard in a safe environment. As with Models 4 and 6, the Two Group Reteach Model allows teachers and students to engage in a platform that is inherently more individualized and low risk. It allows us to be more flexible to needs of the students and more intentional in our targeting of how to meet those needs.

As we reflect on our students and their work, we often ask: who is struggling, and who is meeting expectations and needs to be challenged? Providing these focused opportunities to reteach in needs-based groups allows us to provide more focused instruction and instantaneous feedback. This works for those struggling and excelling in equal part. We have also seen that this model enhances engagement because struggling students feel cared for and successful while keeping excelling students motivated through more individualized enrichment. The Two Group Reteach Model has given us the flexibility to better differentiate our classroom as we strive to help both struggling and excelling students. These smaller group environments allow more focused attention on each individual student while providing them with a more low-risk environment that facilitates participation and immediate feedback. Engaging students in this way does not only increase student participation but also provides for more accurate assessment and responsive feedback.

In Chapter 2, we learned how Thad Williams and his colleagues collaborate in a culturally, linguistically, and economically diverse public high school in the Pacific Northwest. Here, you can learn about the two co-teaching models that are frequently chosen for their after-school co-taught biology tutorial program.

One of our instructional collaborative activities was co-teaching. We approached this entire endeavor with the goal of co-teaching the weekly thirty-minute biology ELL tutorial. We felt this was the best way to help students with challenging biology content and science practices, as well as increase the biology and ELL teachers' capacity to work with ELL students. On average, twenty English learners attended the after-school tutorial. These students ranged in English language proficiency levels from newcomer beginner to intermediate to advanced ELLs. Occasionally, non-ELL students would come to help work in groups and be additional science and language supports for students. We adapted the co-teaching approaches and used one of the two approaches depending on what students were doing in the biology classroom. We called the first approach One Group: Two Preteach. The second approach was One Group: Two Reteach. As you can imagine, they are similar but depend on whether or not we are preteaching students content before they are going to see it in a biology lesson or lab, or we are reteaching students content after they have struggled with it in class. We chose to keep it one group because of our ability to co-plan and work closely together in the facilitation of this tutorial. We also felt that staying in one group increased our ability to see what each other was doing and learn from each other through the modeling of certain strategies, and supporting the other with either biology content or language strategies.

**VIDEO 8.2:
Co-Teaching
Reflections:
Danielle and
Nicole**

http://resources
.corwin.com/
CoTeachingforELs

TAKEAWAYS

In this chapter, we explore the ways in which two teachers can deliver differentiated instruction using Model 6 (Two Groups: One Reteaches, One Teaches Alternative Information) in a co-taught class. We emphasize that student assessment data will help co-teachers make informed decisions about what their students need and how to maximize impact on student learning. We also note the dual purpose of Model 6: providing reteach and enrichment opportunities to all. We recognize that some students cannot continue successfully with a unit of study unless they develop foundational understanding and skills and have multiple meaningful opportunities to interact with the content, whereas others may become bored and disengaged if they are not challenged and motivated through extension and enrichment opportunities. A final word of caution: Reteaching affords ELs and other students extended time for practicing challenging content concepts and language or literacy skills. Yet reteaching may be easily misunderstood and misused, and ELs may become stigmatized if the same group of students gets placed in the intervention group.

QUESTIONS FOR FURTHER DISCUSSION

1. How do you ensure that Model 6 does not lead to further well-sanctioned segregation of ELs?

2. What are the potential benefits of Model 6 for all your students?

3. What challenges do you anticipate co-teachers will need to overcome to succeed with Model 6?

4. Which strategies from this chapter are you most interested in trying? Why?

9

Model 7—Multiple Groups

Two Monitor/Teach

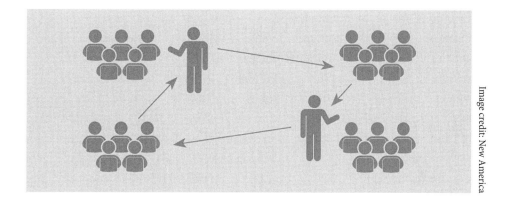

Image credit: New America

AN INTRODUCTION TO THE MODEL

One of the most important aspects of co-teaching for English learners (ELs) is that it provides students at various levels of English language proficiency targeted instruction to develop their language and literacy skills along with content knowledge. This model—creating multiple student groups for instruction—is truly the most versatile; it can accommodate individual needs in an almost unlimited number of ways. It is often the model of choice for novice and experienced co-teachers alike. It allows for the planning and implementation of differentiated instruction through the development of various learning tasks and activities. This model sets as a priority the cooperation or collaboration of students learning together in teams under the supervision of one or more teachers, or small groups of students working under the direct instruction and guidance of one of the teaching partners.

The effects of small-group instruction are evident in the strategies used for cooperative learning, a mainstay of this model, which has been widely researched and shown to have notable, beneficial gains in students' academic achievement (Johnson, Johnson, & Stanne, 2000; Kagan, Kagan, & Kagan, 2016). Cooperative learning refers to the tasks set for teams of students who work in tandem to complete assignments, such as brainstorming, problem solving, responding to questions, finding textual evidence, analyzing a political cartoon, completing a step-by-step process (a science experiment or a simple recipe), and so on. Felder and Brent (2007) identify the many benefits of cooperative learning as follows:

> Cooperatively taught students tend to exhibit higher academic achievement, greater persistence through graduation, better high-level reasoning and critical thinking skills, deeper understanding of learned material, greater time on task and less disruptive behavior in class, lower levels of anxiety and stress, greater intrinsic motivation to learn and achieve, greater ability to view situations from others' perspectives, more positive and supportive relationships with peers, more positive attitudes toward subject areas, and higher self-esteem. (p. 34)

Cooperative learning provides an avenue for English learners to work alongside their proficient English-speaking peers as a team yet still be held accountable for their own work. Some teachers assign specific "jobs" to team members—leader, scribe, materials manager, vocabulary/spell checker, time keeper, graphic designer, tech person, and so on—in order for each student to have a specific stake in the final product. With each new activity, job assignments can be rotated so that students have opportunities to take on several different responsibilities for the team.

There are certain aspects of cooperative learning that enhance its effectiveness; having guidelines in place leads students to understand what is expected. Students need to know how to contribute to the learning of the team—they should readily participate, learn the basic concepts being explored by the group, and be held accountable for their role and the resulting group product. Johnson, Johnson, and Smith (2006) have determined five key elements of successful cooperative learning teams—positive interdependence, individual accountability, face-to-face promotive interaction, interpersonal and small-group social skills, and group processing. We have interpreted these elements for this model of instruction in the co-taught class as follows:

1. **Positive Interdependence.** Each team member understands the importance of everyone's contribution for the completion of the task. Co-teachers foster positive interdependence by setting common goals for task completion, assigning roles and responsibilities, offering rewards for exceeding expectations, and assuring students share resources.

2. **Individual Accountability.** Each student is assessed according to how much and how well they contributed to the task. To support English learners to do their share of the work when their language skills are just beginning to emerge, co-teachers must carefully consider how to differentiate the task, scaffold information, and foster students' use of their home language skills with team members.

3. **Face-to-Face Promotive Interaction.** Students support each other's learning through their shared understanding of cooperative work combined with their individual roles on the team. Some co-teachers assign students to be leaders or "encouragers," giving them the responsibility to invite all students to participate before decisions are made. Team members are expected to "teach" one another so that all students come to a common understanding of the topic and the task.

4. **Interpersonal and Small-Group Social Skills.** Co-teachers support students' communication skills by offering sentence frames or stems for students to use in order to work together in a positive social environment and to support for English learners to develop oral language skills. Co-teachers offer students the language of how to agree or disagree in ways that are respectful yet allow them to share their understandings, experiences, and ideas honestly. Students are asked to address each other by name and use accountable talk stems (Fisher, Frey, & Rothenberg, 2008) during discussions. The following are some examples of accountable talk:

   - Can you tell me more about _____?
   - I would like to add to what _____ said.
   - I agree/disagree with you because _____.
   - This reminds me of _____.

5. **Group Processing.** This element identifies the process and importance of group reflection—to have students review, mediate, and even celebrate how well they completed the task together to achieve the goals set for the team. Co-teachers can support this process by asking students to reflect on specific aspects of the work the team completed as well as monitoring student discussions and offering their own feedback.

Collaborative teamwork differs from cooperative learning in that the group does not work together to complete one project. With collaboration, students share and discuss their individual ideas with one another but ultimately must accomplish the task with their own ideas that may or may not have been influenced by the group discussion. The value of this activity is for students to be aware of different perspectives. There is also a variation of collaborative teamwork we have observed with this co-teaching model we might call *collaboration as needed*. Students work on independent tasks sitting in groups and confer with one another if they have questions or are not quite sure how to proceed. We have found this type of group work is supportive yet may not create the optimum situation for English learners to develop their English language proficiency. In this situation, conversation is haphazard, and we find ELs rely on bilingual dictionaries and home-language discussions with those who speak a common language most prevalent. Although students gain content knowledge, they do not always have opportunities to speak, write, interact, read, and listen (SWIRL) in English.

Another very common use of this model is to have students rotate between learning centers or stations under the guidance of the teaching team in the room. Magnuson (2010) identifies the importance of learning centers for young children—"areas within the classroom where students learn about specific subjects by playing and engaging in activities" (para. 5)—giving them opportunities to observe, listen, talk, make decisions, discover, problem solve, cooperate with others, and share. Learning centers allow preK–Grade 2 students to express themselves by experimenting with materials, taking risks, directing their own learning, role-playing, and developing communication skills. *Learning stations*, the term most often used for the same strategy with older students, are also incorporated in the co-taught class using this model in Grade 3 and up. Stations are frequently designed to accommodate the different levels of language proficiency for ELs, and the same activity is differentiated to contain multiple degrees of difficulty to address students' content and language learning needs accordingly.

Considering all the abundant and rich learning experiences this co-teaching model can offer, there is little wonder why so many co-teachers rely on it for instructing English learners. Yet like all co-teaching approaches, this model needs careful planning through the consideration of individual student assessment data and often requires a great deal of time to prepare materials. On the other hand, once strategies and resources are fully developed, the instructional activities for group work can be saved and duplicated or refined year after year.

A CLOSER LOOK AT MODEL 7

In the classic setting for this model, also known as *station teaching* for its use in special education inclusion classes (Friend & Cook, 1996), students are divided into three groups. Each teacher works with one of the groups, and the final student group works independently. After a set amount of time, each group rotates to a different teaching station, either working with the other teacher or working on their own. Typically, both teachers are seated at separate tables or among a group of desks designated for their group of students; these designated spaces are generally an ample distance apart to reduce the possibility of distraction.

In a departure from the classic configuration, in co-taught classes for English learners, we have observed various ways to set up multiple group instruction with this most adaptable model. Co-teachers often arrange groups—as many as needed—according to the following criteria:

- The content to be mastered
- The objectives to be met
- The space provided
- The learning activities created and differentiated
- The proficiency level of the students
- The materials being used
- The individual needs of the learners

For this reason, the preparation for instruction using this model may appear to be labor intensive—requiring a great deal of time to create activities for students at various levels to learn the same content or to practice language and literacy skills. However, the versatility of this model allows for the use of both low-preparation strategies as well as those strategies that take time to prepare and execute. In addition, both teachers are engaged in the preparation of lesson materials, which significantly lessens the workload.

To promote the acquisition of grade-level subject matter, we have also observed this model used to help entering and beginning English learners explore rigorous content and concepts. In particular, one lesson in a middle school science class focusing on the nitrogen cycle involved students investigating different aspects of how nitrogen gets into the soil to support plant growth. In teams, students moved from station to station with the two co-teachers and a bilingual aide offering support when needed in order for students to complete the fact-finding task. All students were well engaged in the learning and successfully completed the assignment with varying amounts of assistance and support from both teachers and fellow students. In a follow-up interview with the co-teachers, the science teacher expressed how he initially had concerns about the content being introduced to these students as it became more rigorous. To his amazement and through the co-teaching partnership, scaffolding of and modifications to the general-education readings and assignments provided ELs with the support they needed to thrive in a rigorous, content-rich learning environment.

High levels of student engagement are critical to the successful implementation of this model. In a meta-analysis of over 75 research studies, Marzano (2007) concludes that students enrolled in classes where there were highly engaging activities consistently outperformed students taught in more traditional settings via direct instruction. According to Marzano, "keeping students engaged is one of the most important considerations for the classroom teacher" (p. 98). The promotion of student engagement with this model is equal to the tasks that are set for student learning. For this reason, we highly recommend creating learning centers or stations that provide opportunities for students to discover new information, experiment with new materials, engage in discussions about text, use manipulatives to solve problems, explore their greater community, and so on. In contrast, having students complete worksheets, engage in handwriting practice, writing spelling words five times each, and so on, will not bring about the levels of engagement that lead to the acquisition of new language skills and, ultimately, the mastery of skills and content.

Model 7 also promotes student-led classes or student-directed learning. Working in teams, youngsters engage in various hands-on activities—analyzing, constructing, dissecting, measuring, probing, speculating, scrutinizing, and so on—under the supervision and guidance of the co-teaching team. Merryweather (2014) describes this type of learning as follows:

> Student-lead learning is exactly as it sounds. Although teachers remain in the classroom to provide guidance on subject areas and to oversee quality, the control of the learning experience is handed over to the students. They are encouraged to teach themselves and their peers by undertaking their own study and research, then sharing their findings with others. (para. 2)

Ultimately, student-directed learning promotes English learners to be more motivated and engaged in learning—tapping into prior knowledge, exercising higher forms of cognitive functioning, and developing new language skills through the application of speaking, writing, and reading tasks.

In elementary schools, this model is frequently used to develop reading competencies ranging from direct skill building through teacher-led guided-reading instruction to teams of students rotating through established literacy centers that are either purchased or teacher created.

Math centers also are designed for students to investigate specific concepts or for real-world exploration and application. In this way, students have the opportunity to practice and apply strategies and skills that have been demonstrated during whole-group or minilessons.

In grades such as kindergarten, literacy centers might be permanent stationary places in the classroom such as listening or writing centers in which new material is added and subtracted according to the objectives of a particular learning segment. In upper elementary grades, learning centers are often more portable, although there are sometimes designated spaces in the classroom—a table, an area rug, a computer station, and so on—where activities are conducted. Using learning centers in combination with this co-teaching model provides opportunities to meet the needs of all ELs at various levels of English proficiency. Learning centers also help young learners enhance their self-efficacy and develop a sense of autonomy.

In secondary classes, learning stations can be invaluable for English learners. Not only do they often promote the four language skills—speaking, writing, reading, and listening—they also can make content more accessible and comprehensible for students who lack English language proficiency. We have frequently observed this model being used in science classes; the hands-on nature of science investigations and experiments provides the context for co-teachers to use various grouping strategies for students to engage in the learning process. Learning stations can also be successfully developed in any content class. Malefyt (2016) suggests learning stations also support teachers to conduct formative assessment to assist in future planning and drive instruction. He recommends the following strategies for station teaching in the secondary classroom:

- **Station-Progression Maps.** Co-teachers can maintain an outline of how student groups progress from station to station using a progression map. Spaces for teacher review and signatures upon completion of tasks on theses maps allow for greater student responsibility and accountability.
- **Varied Involvement.** Although routines are important in the co-taught class, consider engaging students in diverse activities with learning stations incorporating varied modes of learning (kinesthetic, tactual), use of technology, creative writing (songs, poetry), photography, and so on.
- **Free-Choice Time.** Allow students to have some unscheduled time to complete project work or extend a project that was initiated by a learning station activity. In this way, students get to manage their own time and opportunities to build on their areas of interest.
- **Resource Management.** Some instructional resources such as laptops or tablets may be limited in number and therefore impossible to use with whole-class instruction. Station teaching provides the vehicle to incorporate such learning tools into the co-taught class.
- **Anecdotal Notes.** While circulating within the class, consider carrying a clipboard and jotting down information on individual student progress. Station-teaching time is ideal for gathering information on the academic and linguistic development of ELs.
- **Critical Conversations.** Station teaching provides opportunities for teachers to have one-on-one conversations with students, which help to clarify information, extend ideas, support reading and writing activities, and strengthen the student–teacher relationship.

Grouping strategies play a significant role in the organization and execution of this model as well as many others in the co-taught class. Although we have discussed in detail various grouping strategies in previous chapters, we would like to emphasize their importance and share the following considerations for grouping students to increase their learning experiences from Fisher et al. (2008) in Table 9.1.

Accordingly, Fisher et al. (2008) outline additional information when forming groups with English learners:

> When your classroom includes English language learners, you must be keenly aware of their proficiency levels in English as well as their understanding of the content of the task. Placing one student who is new to English in a group of proficient students may seem like a good idea, but in actuality, that student is likely to participate more with students whose level of proficiency in English is closer to his or her own . . . (p. 102)

In sum, this model has multiple applications in K–12 co-taught classes. Students can be configured both heterogeneously and homogeneously in small groups of various number and size to accommodate the learning of English learners and English speaking students within the confines of one classroom.

VIDEO 9.1: Model 7— Multiple Groups: Two Monitor/ Teach

http://resources .corwin.com/ CoTeachingforELs

| Table 9.1 | Grouping Strategies |

Strategy	Description
Language level	Students may be grouped homogeneously according to their language proficiency or heterogeneously to be supported by learners with various levels of English ability.
Home language	English learners collaborate with those who speak the same home language to discuss ideas and information.
Skill ability	Youngsters are placed together to practice and learn a similar skill or learning strategy.
Curiosity	Students are grouped according to their selected interests.
Persistence	Persistent pupils are used to model positive learning behaviors and are strategically placed in various groups.
Content knowledge	Students may be grouped heterogeneously or homogeneously to possibly work directly with one of the co-teachers according to his or her knowledge of the content.
Strategy knowledge	Similar to content knowledge, learners may be grouped heterogeneously or homogeneously to share strategic knowledge.
Assignment	Youngsters are grouped according to how an assignment or activity is differentiated for their learning needs.
Roles	Student leaders, like those who are more persistent in their work, are strategically placed in various groups.
Design	Using random ways of selecting students gives them the opportunity to collaborate with various members of the class.
Choice	This strategy gives students the opportunity to work with a group of students of their choosing.

ADVANTAGES

Drawing on our insights from working with teachers to develop collaborative teaching practices over the past 10 years, this model—Multiple Groups: Two Monitor/Teach—is one that remains popular with and often preferred by co-teaching teams. Beyond its versatility, this model provides a considerable number of advantages for teaching English learners.

First and foremost, the flexibility of this model provides ELs with comprehensible input—a way of teaching that makes content understandable for students with various levels of English proficiency. Lightbown and Spada (2013) identify how comprehensible input continues to be the unyielding support all students need to acquire a new language. By grouping students in multiple ways for instruction, small-group learning can provide opportunities for tiered reading lessons, scaffolded discussions, application of strategies (manipulatives, visuals, realia, props), and so on— for entering or beginning ELs and the direct teacher support to make lessons accessible.

Grouping strategies, addressed earlier in this chapter in connection with station teaching and with some detail in Chapter 6, also come into play with this model of instruction when considering its advantages. Whether students are placed together heterogeneously or homogeneously, careful selection of participants and activities for small-group learning can yield high levels of interaction and engagement for all students. It is imperative that co-teachers interact directly with student groups as well as facilitate their active learning with one another so that language and literacy skills are continually developed. Given that student engagement is most critical to successful learning (Dove, Honigsfeld, & Cohan, 2014), this model can provide multiple opportunities to motivate students to attend to tasks, spark their curiosity, and support them in developing their language skills.

Another significant aspect of student teamwork is that it promotes SWIRL—an emerging practice in collaboratively taught classes in which co-teachers focus on providing opportunities for students to speak, write, interact, read, and listen every day. We often compare language acquisition with learning how to ride a bicycle or progressing as a swimmer. If you never get on a bike or go into the water, you will have little, if any, chance of developing these skills. Similarly, language learning is a skill-building endeavor. Giving students ample time to practice their language skills— using student-to-student interactions as the vehicle within this co-taught model—is a positive step toward ensuring ELs have a rich language-learning environment.

Guided student interactions in the co-taught classroom can also create favorable learning experiences to build multicultural awareness. Considering the general increase in the ethnic, racial, and linguistic diversity in schools across this country, co-teachers that conduct classes that have both native English-speaking students and English learners are well-positioned to incorporate group activities and discussions that inform students about multicultural issues as well as learn about the diverse nature of the cultural backgrounds of students represented in the class.

Another advantage of this model is that it can create possibilities for ELs and other students to learn essential academic content, strategies, and skills by way of differentiated instruction to meet individual needs. In this way, academic rigor may remain uncompromised; even if the content is modified to afford students access to information or additional practice, the process or the product may meet grade-level and curricular benchmarks in the group-learning environment. Expectations can remain high when ongoing evaluation and feedback to students provide the support they need and guide the design of meaningful learning activities. As Tomlinson and Imbeau (2010) suggest, a focus on differentiated learning gives teachers the impetus to continually reflect on the following question: "What does this student need at this moment in order to be able to progress with this key content, and what do I need to do to make that happen?" (p. 14). Within a multigroup instructional model, individual student needs can often be readily served.

Maintaining curricular integrity is at the heart of the integrated co-taught classroom. With an innovative teaching approach such as this one, contemporary or revised materials might indeed be incorporated as well as the adoption of new pedagogies (Fullan, 2016) to fully realize this co-taught model. Yet we want to preserve the consistency and adhere to the curricular fundamentals that are presented in any class on the same grade level and/or content. This delicate balance can be maintained with this model of instruction. Grouping students for learning can provide authentic, multi-level instruction while maintaining curricular coherence.

The consideration of learning styles, a composite of cognitive, affective, and physiological factors, has provided some teachers with insights into students' learning preferences to address individualized instruction. Evidence of the positive effects of using learning-style strategies has sparked the interest of some teachers to implement learning-style approaches to enhance student achievement. Common elements associated with learning styles include individual preferences for how new material is learned—auditory, visual, tactual, or kinesthetic—as well as the environment of the classroom—formal versus informal seating or bright light versus low light settings. By providing flexible groupings and varying team activities, students have a better chance of having their individual preferences for learning met.

Last but not least, educators, researchers, and policy makers are seemingly abuzz with the idea of student-led classrooms, in which activities are designed to guide students in their own information gathering, discovery, and problem solving. In turn, teachers take on the roles of facilitators, mentors, and coaches. In student-led lessons, it is the students, generally in small groups, who lead in-depth discussions about selected topics and who incorporate technology—iPads, Chromebooks, laptops, and so on, to have ready access to information. Advocates of student-led classes that promote this type of learning believe it provides children and adolescents with the strategies and skills for lifelong achievement. If you subscribe to this trend in instruction and co-teach ELs in an integrated setting, the use of multiple groups of students should certainly be a go-to model to support this approach to learning.

CHALLENGES

With any approach to learning, there are always challenges that need to be addressed, although with this model of co-teaching, there may be fewer challenges due to its versatility and inherent opportunities for the flexible grouping of students for instruction. The following are common concerns teachers face when incorporating this co-taught model into their regular instructional practices.

First off, not all students prefer to work, or work well, in teams. Despite numerous studies on the benefits of collaborative learning, some students, like some teachers, do not appreciate this mode of learning. One reason might be that the benefits of teamwork are not obvious to some students who have had disappointing experiences with the practice, including the frustration of unresolved student conflicts, the lack of productivity on projects, or the takeover of a group by one or two students without regard to its other members or contributors. To overcome this issue, co-teachers must set clear directions, have an organization in place so that all team members participate, carefully monitor group work, and offer feedback and guidance on a continuous basis. With those who are younger or less experienced with teamwork, take the time to have them review and practice the necessary strategies and skills that make for functional and productive group learning.

In classes that have a large number of students, even the presence of two co-teachers in the room may not be sufficient to quell all off-task behavior. Consider how you can incorporate individual accountability measures so that there will be an assessment for the group's effort as well as each member's contribution. Self-assessment tools or peer-rating scales can support students to remain on task (see Figure 9.1 for a sample self- and peer-rating form). In addition, rules and procedures for teamwork that are established by co-teaching partners from the onset of group activities provide students with overall expectations for working with others.

Although we have repeatedly cautioned against segregating students by labeling and grouping them into EL and non-EL groups, some co-teachers find this practice in conjunction with multiple-group work not only supports the instruction ELs need to be successful in the co-taught class but also provides the (ELD/ELL) teacher with better or easier access to ELs to offer guidance and feedback. In our opinion, this fixed type of grouping is more for the co-teachers' benefit and not for the students. It allows for a division of labor in the co-taught class with each teacher being responsible only for his or her own student group(s). This practice will not serve English learners; they need to work alongside their English-speaking peers to have meaningful and constructive experiences using English. To ameliorate this concern, try to balance the occasions in which students are grouped homogeneously, according to their language and literacy proficiency, with opportunities to be grouped heterogeneously, combining both ELs and non-ELs for instruction and practice.

When preparing activities for multiple student groups, beware of creating learning centers or stations that amount to busywork. The most powerful use of this model is when all students are involved in true collaborative group tasks that require meaningful discussions, analysis of issues,

---

Figure 9.1 Self- and Peer-Rating Form

Rate Yourself and Your Team Members				
Your name: _____ Date: _____ Team: _____				
Directions: On a scale of 1–5, with 5 being the highest score and 1 being the lowest score, rate your team members as indicated below.				
Team Members	**Contributed to group discussions**	**Completed individual role/ part**	**Worked with others respectfully**	**Supported the work of others in the group**
My name:				
Name:				
Name:				
Name:				

problem solving, choice making, discovery learning, experimentation, hypothesis testing, opinion sharing, and so on. Yet we have observed classes where, due either to low expectations or lack of understanding of what ELs can do, these students are placed in groups for activities that require copying, cutting, pasting, and coloring—even in secondary classes! The work of all students must be purposeful, meaningful, and help all students make progress toward meeting grade-level benchmarks.

It is important to note that preparing instruction for multiple groups of students that is scaffolded, differentiated, provides tiered reading content, supports different learning styles, and so on is not a simple task. This model at times will be quite labor intensive to organize, coordinate, prepare, and deliver. Table 9.2 summarizes the advantages and challenges of Model 7. In spite of the time needed for its preparation, the benefits of this model for developing both language and content skills are found in the high levels of student motivation, engagement in learning, and academic achievement of English learners.

Table 9.2 Summary of Advantages and Challenges of Model 7

Model 7: Multiple Groups: Two Monitor/Teach	
Advantages	**Challenges**
Small-group learning can provide students with comprehensible input.	*Not all students prefer to work, or work, well, in teams.*
Careful selection of participants and activities can yield high levels of student engagement.	*The presence of two co-teachers in the room may not be sufficient to quell all off-task behavior in large-sized classes.*
Teamwork can promote SWIRL—opportunities for ELs to speak, write, interact, read, and listen every day.	*The segregation of students by language proficiency into EL and non-EL groups will not serve English learners.*
Student interactions can foster experiences that build multicultural awareness.	*Some teacher-created learning centers or stations may amount to busywork for ELs.*
Differentiated instruction meets individual needs while academic rigor remains uncompromised.	*Preparation might be labor intensive to organize, coordinate, and deliver instruction for multiple student groups.*
Authentic, multilevel instruction maintains curricular coherence.	
Students are better able to have their individual preferences for learning met.	
This model supports student-led classes.	

INSTRUCTION USING MODEL 7

Most likely, the strategies presented in previous chapters for other co-teaching models might very well be adapted for this multifaceted model. For example, the concept webs, partially completed graphic organizers, and use of realia, and manipulatives featured in Chapter 3 could most easily be incorporated into group work in learning centers or stations for this model. For this reason, we invite you to review the strategies identified in previous chapters and adjust them for this configuration. The following are additional strategies that can be used in purposeful and meaningful ways for multigroup instruction.

Low-Prep Strategies for Model 7

The great appeal of this model is in its adaptability, and at times teachers will take advantage of this aspect of the model to provide opportunities for student interactions that take little or no time to prepare. For this reason, we present some ideas for simple yet effective group work.

Rolling rounds. With this strategy, students seated in groups are presented with a category such as *invertebrates*. Students must then take turns going around the table naming items that belong in that category. An adaptation for English learners is to provide them with a list of choices or a word list accompanied by photographs or illustrations to select from during the round.

Writing rounds. A variation of rolling rounds, this activity gives students the opportunity to think and write their answers for a set category before they are shared with the group. This strategy allows for additional wait time and provides students the opportunity to check resources or seek the advice of a peer or one of the co-teachers before the group work takes place.

Story rounds. Another around-the-table activity, this one involves students' writing in cooperation with others. Each student in the group is given a blank piece of paper and asked to write one sentence about a given topic. Next, students pass their paper to the person seated on their right. Now, students must continue writing about the topic using their group-member's paper. After they write a sentence on the paper that was passed to them, the papers are shifted to the right again. This practice continues for three or four rounds until eventually, students end up with their original papers. Students then read their papers aloud within their groups, and selected ones are shared with the entire class. This activity can be used for creative writing, to summarize information already taught, or as a prereading activity to determine what students already know about a topic.

Numbered heads together. This strategy affords ELs greater participation in class discussions and supports them to answer questions in front of the whole class. To begin, four students sit as a team, and each team member is designated a number from one to four. Teachers present the class with a question or a prompt, and students must collaborate together in their teams to come up with a response. When the specified time is up, teachers call a number and all students with that number must raise their hands. From these students, one of them is called on to answer, and the discussion continues through several rounds in the same manner. This activity allows for wait time, discussion of responses, and provides all students with plausible answers before they are called on to respond, thereby ensuring the participation of English learners.

Jigsaw. This group approach gives students the time they need to read, discuss ideas, listen to one another, and write. Teachers direct individual students to move from one group to another and then back again with the set purpose of completing certain tasks that build knowledge and understanding of a set topic within a framework for cooperative learning. To implement this strategy, arrange students in groups of equal size and designate those groups as their "home" groups. Next, take one student from each home group to create "expert" groups. Students read and discuss a certain part of a set topic by reading a portion of an article or book chapter. In turn, other expert groups read, discuss different parts of the text, and jot down essential information. When time is called, students return to their original home groups and use their notes to share with their home group members what they learned in their expert groups.

Pro-Prep Strategies for Model 7

Group work sometimes needs a great deal of preparation, as one of our sample lessons, Learning About Separating Mixtures in Grade-Five Science, illustrates later in this chapter. Here, we highlight a few of the many strategies that take some time to prepare yet yield powerful learning experiences for all students.

Guided Reading. This practice supports student reading during small-group instruction. It was first introduced as component-balanced literacy or Four-Blocks framework (Cunningham, Hall, & Defee, 1991). Generally speaking, students are grouped according to their instructional level in reading. In each group, students read the same text as the teacher guides them through the use of minilessons, pointed questions, building background about the topic, uncovering new vocabulary, and so on. This reading strategy provides students with needed skills they can later apply when they read independently (Dove & Honigsfeld, 2013).

In the co-taught class, each co-teacher might take one group of students for guided reading while other groups work on different aspects of building their literacy skills; the groups could rotate from independent work to one of the co-teachers so that each group would have some time for direct literacy instruction. Another approach to this activity is for one teacher to remain stationary and support students' reading development while the other teacher circulates around the room to guide students' independent work.

To be most effective, preparation for guided reading should include a thorough review of the texts students will read; an analysis of the difficulties ELs might have with vocabulary, idiomatic expressions, cultural references, and sentence structures; and a list of questions that follow a framework such as Bloom's taxonomy to assure critical thinking skills are being addressed. Additionally, guided reading provides opportunities to note students' abilities in developing their literacy skills and to keep records of their progress (see Figure 9.2).

Tea Party. Often used as a prereading strategy, this activity offers students a preview of their reading through examination and discussion of pieces of text as well as further analysis of content and prediction of general themes, settings, information, and so on through group work using the data obtained by individual students.

In preparation for this activity, teachers print phrases and/or sentences from the reading on strips of paper and distribute one to each student. With soft music playing in the background, students walk around the classroom, reading as many of the sentences they can from their fellow

| Figure 9.2 | Guided Reading Record |

Guided Reading Record	
Date:	Students:
Reading Selection:	
Minilesson Focus:	
Vocabulary:	
Observations:	
Follow-Up:	

students, discussing what each short piece of text means, and taking notes; clipboards can facilitate this part of the activity. Next, students get into their predetermined cooperative learning groups and share their notes with their teams. Together, group members write and submit a prediction about the text with as many details as possible. This activity ends with students coming back together as a whole class and teachers reading and discussing the collected predictions.

Coffee Klatch. This activity combines elements from both the Tea Party and Jigsaw strategies. It gives students the time to gather, analyze, evaluate, and summarize information from a number of sources. In order to begin, teachers prepare readings—articles that cover different aspects or points of view about the same topic, idea, or event—and materials for each student group. These readings can be tiered to accommodate students' different reading levels. Chart paper, markers, and index cards are also distributed to each team.

In their groups, students read the articles they were assigned either silently or taking turns reading aloud. In the co-taught class, one teacher might work with one group of students while the other teacher circulates to support other teams. Each student is charged with completing index cards that contain information from the readings; students should place only one or two pieces of information per card, and all students on a team should have different information they have noted. For this reason, team members need to consult with one another as they complete their cards. Next, students are asked to walk around the room, read as many cards from other teams as they can, and take notes. When time is called, students regroup into their original teams and share their information.

As a culminating activity, students prepare a graphic representation of the total information they have gathered on the topic using the chart paper and markers. Finally, each team presents their findings to the rest of the class. As we have seen with many strategies for use with multigroup instruction, this activity provides for a SWIRLing classroom in which students must speak, write, interact, read, and listen to fully participate.

The Proof Is in the Pudding. Students truly enjoy when instruction takes a turn away from ordinary pencil-and-paper exercises. This activity, developed originally for elementary grades, has students working in teams to create a no-cook recipe for pumpkin pudding (see Figure 9.3 for the ingredients). For secondary classes, consider how this strategy might be adapted for lessons in which students must follow a set of complex directions to complete a task, solve an authentic problem, or create something new. Using the maker education philosophy, "teachers act as guides for inquiry-based approaches to the development of knowledge and thinking processes" (Kurti, Kurti, & Fleming, 2014, p. 8), students can form teams to develop expertise in a shared topic of interest.

In preparation, purchase the ingredients for making the pudding, gather sufficient mixing bowls, measuring cups, and utensils, and prepare a recipe card for each team. For the activity, divide students into heterogeneous groups. Have students "pick out of a hat" a specific role they will have on their "cooking" team—kitchen manager, head chef, sous chef, junior sous chef, line cook, and so on. Make sure each person on the team has a task related to his or her title. Students complete the activity by carrying out their specific role to make the pudding. After students enjoy the pudding, they are charged with describing in writing the step-by-step process they undertook to put together the recipe.

Figure 9.3	Pudding Ingredients

Pumpkin Pudding Recipe

1 pkg. (5 oz.) instant vanilla pudding

1 can (12 fl. oz.) evaporated milk

1 can (15 oz.) pumpkin

1 tsp. pumpkin pie spice

Whipped topping

Directions: Combine the pudding mix and the evaporated milk in a large bowl. Slowly add the pumpkin until it is mixed thoroughly. Blend in the pumpkin pie spice. Spoon into separate bowls or cups. Top with whipped topping. Each recipe yields 7 one-half cup servings.

SAMPLE LESSONS: MULTIPLE GROUPS: TWO MONITOR/TEACH

We have observed countless lessons using this model for co-taught classes; the versatility and flexibility of this model makes it one which co-teachers use frequently. The following two lessons showcase this model and exemplify its advantages when used in co-taught content lessons.

Lesson 1—Learning About Separating Mixtures in Grade 5 Science

This co-taught science lesson has been developed for an integrated fifth-grade class that contains both English learners and English speakers. During this lesson, students work to meet content benchmarks by making observations and predictions as well as collecting and discussing data as they discover how some mixtures may be separated based on the properties of substances. The language focus for students is to use oral and written discourse to discuss, make predictions, and draw conclusions.

The lesson begins with students completing an anticipation guide (see Figure 9.4). Some students complete the guide individually, reading each statement quietly and marking if they agree or disagree with what is written. During this time, the fifth-grade teacher sets up learning stations around the perimeter of the room that will be used for the next part of the lesson. At the same time, the ELD/ELL teacher invites students to come to the side table with her if they would like support in completing the anticipation guide. This invitation is open to all students, both ELs and non-ELs alike.

Several students work with the ELD/ELL teacher. She reads each statement aloud, reviews vocabulary, brings up visuals of certain concepts on a laptop computer, and gives students time to reflect on each statement. Students who have already completed their anticipation guides individually are asked to read a brief article on solutions and mixtures using their Chromebooks on the website chem4kids.com. When all students have completed their anticipation guide, the class comes back together to view a brief video.

The video reveals information previewed in the anticipation guide. Both teachers lead a discussion about students' answers to the statements in the guide once the video has ended.

Figure 9.4 Anticipation Guide

Anticipation Guide: Mixtures and Solutions

Name:_____ Date:_____

Directions: Place an A next to statements with which you agree and a D next to statements with which you disagree.

_____ Chemistry is a branch of science that deals with how matter is composed.

_____ Chemistry involves the ways in which substances interact, combine, and change.

_____ Chemistry connects other sciences to each other.

_____ Chemistry can help you better understand the world around you.

_____ A new substance can be made by mixing other substances together.

_____ Changes in substances can always be controlled to produce new substances.

After the lesson preview, students are introduced to the purpose of the lesson—the objectives are displayed on a PowerPoint slide—as well as have explained what they will be doing during science lab today. Additional PowerPoint slides are shown that identify different types of matter and the different properties they maintain—weight, height, density, and so on. After this brief introduction, the co-teachers describe for students the steps they will take to complete the tasks set for the science lab.

Students are divided into small groups; they are directed to take their clipboards and their science lab observe/predict/conclude sheets (see Figure 9.5) and are assigned to a learning station. The ELD/ELL teacher remains with one group of students to guide them in completing each task while the grade-level teacher supports the other fifth graders. Students observe the materials, engage in conversations with their lab group members, jot down notes about the properties of the materials on their lab sheets, and make predictions about what will happen when the material is combined and when it is filtered.

Finally, students conduct the experiment. They combine the material with water, make additional observations, and then try to filter the mixture with a screen. They further discuss what occurs and write their conclusions. Students then rotate to the next learning station.

After the lab activity, students return to their seats and the whole class engages in a debriefing exercise with both teachers. They review key ideas and preview the upcoming science lesson.

An analysis of the lesson segment. From the onset, the co-teaching partners establish equity for their students when all students—not just the ELs—are invited to join the support table to review

Figure 9.5 Observe/Predict/Conclude

SCIENCE LAB: OBSERVE/PREDICT/CONCLUDE

NAME: _____ DATE: _____

LAB PARTNERS: _____

	What are the properties of the material I observed?	What do I predict will happen?	What is the conclusion (what really happened)?
Station # _____ Materials: _____ _____		When mixed with water:	
		Can it be filtered?	
Station # _____ Materials: _____ _____		When mixed with water:	
		Can it be filtered?	
Station #____ Materials: _____ _____		When mixed with water:	
		Can it be filtered?	

the anticipation guide, and for themselves when both teachers lead the anticipation guide debrief. Model 7—Two Teachers Monitor/Teach—is well incorporated into this lesson as a collaborative, hands-on science activity and is conducted with the support of both teachers. Here, we see strong evidence of SWIRL—*students are speaking with one another, writing their observations and predictions, involved in purposeful interactions, reading information and directions, and listening to each other.*

Lesson 2—Analyzing Propaganda Posters in Grade 12 Social Studies

In this twelfth-grade social studies class, students are invited in groups of four to sit at a table of their choice. Each table has a propaganda poster taped to the middle of a large piece of chart paper along with directions for how students may respond to each poster (see Figure 9.6). The social studies teacher turns on music and invites students to respond to the propaganda poster in front of them by writing on the chart paper. All students at a given table are asked to write on the chart paper at the same time. In the meantime, both teachers circulate around the room, respond to students' questions, support their responses, and take anecdotal notes. When the music stops, the social studies teacher invites students to find a seat at a different table, and the activity is repeated several times, lasting about 20 minutes.

Students are then engaged in a debriefing activity in which they share some of the writings on the chart paper at their present tables and make predictions about what the lesson's objective will be using the propaganda posters as a guide.

Figure 9.6 Propaganda Poster Mark Up

MARK IT UP!

There are several ways to react to a piece of text or illustration. Consider the following questions and respond to the text/illustration at your table.

- What information does this text/illustration reveal? What event, if any? When did it take place?
- What are the words/images trying to say?
- What is the setting? Why might it be important?
- What is the theme?
- How might you make a personal connection to the text/illustration?
- What are you wondering about?
- Who do you think is the intended audience?
- How would you describe this piece of text/illustration? Does it evoke strong emotions? What are they?
- What type of impact does this text/illustration have on today's society?

An analysis of the lesson segment. Although this lesson requires some preparation, this segment is truly student driven. Students select where to sit and how to respond to the various propaganda posters. They may also respond to what other students have said on the chart paper. Students remain anonymous—they are not asked to sign their names; in this way, they can feel comfortable about writing their thoughts, ideas, and opinions. In the debriefing, students are welcome to share someone else's writing as well as their own. The magic of this lesson is in the planning and the preparation. Once it is set, the students lead their own learning. Both teachers support English learners as they circulate within the room. Even entering- and beginning-level students will be able to react to an illustration if given additional support and guidance. Use of students' home language and additional grouping strategies might also benefit some students to be successful in completing the task.

MODEL VARIATIONS

The variations for this model are as many as the imagination can devise. Being the most versatile way to configure classes for co-teaching, we could not possibly identify them all. Therefore, here is a sample of the ways in which students can be arranged for teaching multiple groups—three or more.

Both Teachers Rotate to Monitor and Teach

Set up as many learning stations or centers as the learning targets require. Once each center and station is introduced and the students are ready to work in their stations collaboratively or independently, both teachers move around the room and offer support to all the students who need it.

Both Teachers Rotate to Monitor and Teach

Similar to the previous configuration, as teachers move from station to station, they collect observational data on student task completion, academic interactions, and any of the learning targets established for the lesson.

One Teaches One Group, One Rotates to Monitor Other Groups

If students are grouped for intervention or if a particular group needs direct teaching, this configuration is an ideal choice. One teacher offers the focused intervention while the other teacher moves from group to group to support student learning.

Two Teachers Are Stationary

When using this approach, two groups are always with their designated teacher, while two or more groups work independently. When time is called, groups rotate from independent stations to teacher-guided or facilitated learning stations.

Two Teachers Are Stationary, All Students Work Independently

In a variation of the previously presented option, two groups work with their designated teachers while the rest of the class completes an independent project or assignment. This approach allows for an extended amount of time for conferencing, guided practice, interventions, or enrichment with select students.

MODEL COMBINATIONS

Model 7 occupies a unique position in the co-teaching context since it may be combined with all of the other models. On the one hand, you may decide to begin the class together (be it Model 1, 2, or 3)—thus, whole-group instruction is used to introduce the multiple group portion of the lesson. For example, the entire class is learning about the difference between mixtures and solutions using a variation of Models 1, 2, and 3 followed by six stations the teachers set up around the classroom for groups of four students to rotate and complete the station experiment. Model 3 is also well suited to collect formative assessment data to determine which group students should be placed into. On the other hand, you may begin the lesson by first dividing the entire class into two groups. Based on the purpose of the two groups, students receive differentiated instruction further enhanced when additional groups are formed for Model 7.

INSPIRATION FROM THE FIELD

First, let's see how Stacey Kevelos, South Country Central School District, New York, elementary ESOL teacher has expanded her co-teaching time during the literacy block to include Model 7 or multiple groups while also maximizing the impact of her co-teacher and a teaching assistant in the room.

One of my most successful co-teaching experiences has been with kindergarten teacher Heather Nolan. This is only our second year co-teaching, but things worked out so well last year we decided to continue this year—and I've even added additional co-teaching time. Last year I was in her room Monday through Friday at the 9:30 time slot—for only one period. This year, I stay for a double period on Monday, Wednesday, and Friday. During this time of day is when the class has Reader's Workshop.

After the morning message and word wall activity, Mrs. Nolan and I take turns running the minilesson, which usually last about 10 minutes. While one teacher is sitting in the rocking chair with the students' attention, the other teacher is usually on the rug with the students. Both teachers feel free to interject during the lesson for the benefit of all students. For example, if Mrs. Nolan is running the lesson and I see confusion on some of the students' faces, I will jump in and paraphrase what she is talking about, say it in a different way, or give an example. We both do this daily. If one teacher does the morning message/word wall time, the other does the minilesson. Although one teacher is technically running the minilesson, both participate in the execution.

After the minilesson, the students usually participate in independent work or partner work. While the students are working, both teachers walk around the room and conference with individual students. We take very specific anecdotal notes as to what the lesson was and whether or not the student was able to follow through on his or her part. Notes are an integral part of our teaching because they document student growth. The second session is when the students break up into groups for center work. This is the time the students do guided reading, word work, and so on. I run a small group, Heather runs a small group, and there is a teaching assistant in the room at that time who runs a group as well. There is usually an independent group also. The groups are based on academics/running records. The whole class is mixed together, and all students get to meet with each teacher in each center.

Angela Tarquinio, the only ESOL teacher at South Side High School in Rockville Centre Union Free School District in New York, discusses why and how Model 7 is utilized in her practice.

Model 7 has taken a natural role in the co-teaching classroom for my teaching partners and me. The ELs love having me in their classrooms, and my colleagues are very receptive to my suggestions and show much respect for my expertise. Model 7 allows me to connect with all students while I am able to assist anyone in need. I love that all students accept me as part of the class and come to me with questions and advice about their work.

How we use it: *We have used this model when teaching character analysis, analyzing passages, annotating excerpts, how literary devices are used, finding quotes, and providing textual evidence to support opinions.*

What it looks like: *The class begins as a whole group, then gets broken up into four to five groups. Each group usually has a specific task. After students convene into their groups and share their knowledge or complete the task, the whole class then listens to what each group has prepared.*

What benefits the model offers when we use it with ELs: *ELs benefit from this model because they are forced to use the language and work with others in their group. The fact that I'm present allows them to take risks and reach out to the other students or even share their work. Although some ELs are still extremely shy and self-conscious, I have seen a big improvement among them speaking up and participating.*

In Chapter 4, Janeen A. Kelly, director of the Department of English Language Learner and World Languages, Washoe County School District, Nevada, discusses how teachers use Model 2. Here, she shares how Model 7 proved to be more effective for a certain group of youngsters.

Kindergarten and first-grade teachers in our district were anxious to participate in the collaborative model for co-teaching. As we met with the teams, it became very clear that the co-teaching Models 2 and 4 that we had implemented in Grades 2 through 5 were not as effective for kindergarten and first grade. We shifted our thinking from whole-group to small-group teaching using two teachers focused on language needs in content to a station-to-station model using at least two teachers as well as a teaching assistant. This would assist our team in providing more focused language instruction and practice opportunities in smaller groups. It also allowed us to scaffold and differentiate for all students as they moved through the stations. An important factor to consider was that the stations were to be tied to both content standards as well as language standards, and that strategic planning occurred among the teaching team involved in delivery of the instruction at the station. One teacher commented, "We used to just create work stations that would keep the students busy. Now we critically think about what is the purpose of this station and how will it enhance learning and language opportunities for our students."

The schedule for an additional teacher and assistants to work in our kindergarten or first-grade classroom was staggered throughout the day. For example, my classroom would have the EL teacher, the special education teacher, and the kindergarten assistant come into my room from 9:00 am to 10:30 five days a week. Another teacher would have this support from 10:30 to 12:00 five days a week. We were able to stagger our grade-level schedules so that every teacher on the team had an opportunity to have the additional language support. One teacher commented, "I had never thought much about how language was a critical focus for instruction with my students. I was so focused on them learning the content that I had ignored the language of the content that needed to be modeled, as well as practiced by the students in meaningful ways."

As a result of our careful planning and implementation, we were able to target students who were not making progress and pull them for additional help, and we were able to carefully observe during learning to assist them with any obstacles or prompt them with questions that allowed them to explore more deeply a concept being learned. One teacher commented, "We were amazed at our student language progress when the English Language Proficiency Assessment (ELPA) results were returned. Almost all of our students made progress, some moving from emerging language to developing language proficiency in one year. However, even more surprising was that we had been exiting less than ten students every year. After one year of using a collaborative teaching model, we exited at least twenty students that year in kindergarten."

Finally, let's find out how Alyson Konsker, English teacher, and Faith Tripp, ESOL teacher, agree on Model 7 to serve their purposes best in their integrated English 9 class at West Hempstead High School, New York.

Throughout the year, we have experimented with various co-teaching models in our integrated English 9 class. One model that we have found great success with is two teachers teach multiple groups. We have established a routine that incorporates vocabulary instruction and assessment of both content and language. For each work of literature that we read with the class, students engage in a variety of activities that promote collaboration, higher-order thinking, and reading, writing, listening, and speaking.

Vocabulary is carefully selected from each chapter, and prior to reading, students are introduced to each word by viewing a related image and discussing its meaning in context. In a later lesson, using these same words, students will engage in a collaborative activity in which they match each word to its image and its definition and write an original sentence for each word. These word-picture-definition matches are displayed around the room throughout the duration of the teaching unit as anchor charts.

In order to assess content knowledge, we have established a carousel activity that incorporates all the language domains as well as comprehension strategies. First, we chunk the chapter based on major events. Next, we separate the class into small groups that may be heterogeneous or homogeneous. Then, we provide each group with a selection from the text and they must read, discuss, and illustrate the selection. Their illustrations must include crucial dialogue as well as characters' thoughts and feelings. The teachers rotate and meet with each group as facilitators. After the illustrations have been completed, the chart paper is placed around the room in various stations. Student groups rotate from station to station, observing and discussing what is presented on each chart and responding to higher-order questions. The question sheets are differentiated so that some provide language frames or cloze passages while others simply state the question. Again, the teachers rotate from station to station checking in on students' discussions and listening for both language and content mastery.

VIDEO 9.2: Co-Teaching Reflections: Kerry and Bernadette

http://resources .corwin.com/ CoTeachingforELs

TAKEAWAYS

In this chapter, we introduce the final co-teaching model, which invites co-teachers to divide the class into multiple small groups. We explore multiple ways Model 7 can be an effective approach to differentiated instruction to include more ELs to engage in a SWIRLing class—actively involved in speaking, writing, interaction, reading, and listening. We emphasize the versatility of this model, which translates into its many advantages when incorporated into co-taught programs for ELs. We also note that at times, preparation for this model may be labor intensive, so we do suggest that co-teachers share the work when planning lessons. We recognize that when two teachers jointly support a class of students with diverse academic and linguistic needs, strategically grouping students makes a lot of pedagogical sense: All students can be better served when two teachers implement tiered, multilevel instruction.

QUESTIONS FOR FURTHER DISCUSSION

1. What do you perceive to be the greatest challenges of implementing Model 7?

2. What is your ideal number of group setup for Model 7?

3. If you choose to run one or more independent groups, how do you ensure high levels of engagement and self-directed learning for students who work independently?

10

Collaborative Assessment

Undoubtedly, we are greatly privileged to have had so many wonderful opportunities to visit co-taught classes for English learners (ELs). By watching teams of teachers throughout the country, we have learned much about this growing practice for ELs. On rare occasions, we have had the pleasure of sitting in with teaching partners while they co-assessed and reflected together, and watched how those two activities influenced their co-planning—targeting individual students for specific teaching approaches for upcoming lessons. Interestingly enough, when teachers effectively co-assess, they are able to identify the multidimensional learning characteristics of the ELs they share. This intimate knowledge of the learning needs of students is due to co-teachers' routine practices for examining student work together.

While co-assessment is one of the last chapters in this book, it has been noted how important it is for co-teachers to engage in the entire collaborative instructional cycle—co-planning, co-teaching, co-assessing and co-reflecting—which is the blueprint for successful co-teaching. The cyclical nature of this type of teaching suggests that assessment, in fact, needs to inform the initial stages of lesson planning, a notion also advocated by Wiggins (1998), who places assessment practices at the center of instruction. Following Wiggins's work on backward design, you and your co-teacher would begin with the end in mind and establish the end-desired results by examining appropriate language development goals and/or content standards and then planning your instruction based on the evidence of learning identified by the standards (Wiggins & McTighe, 2011). Co-assessment therefore is critical in determining how well students have performed in order to plan the necessary language and content learning targets to help all students meet grade-level expectations.

The general purpose of co-teaching is to help all learners be equipped to meet the desired outcomes both in language development and content achievement. Without co-assessment practices, lesson planning for co-taught instruction may not fully focus on the learning needs of all students. As also affirmed by Howard and Potts (2009),

Assessment should be addressed in the initial stages of planning to help structure the activities and experiences to ensure learner success. . . . Both teachers should discuss the standard and how they will assess whether the students learned what was being taught. Teachers should think about both formative and summative assessments and should be sure that their common definition of assessment extends outside of tests and quizzes to include projects, presentations, verbal questioning, permanent product, and other forms. (p. 4)

In other words, all forms of assessment are integral in determining how to select and organize learning opportunities in a co-taught class for English learners.

STANDARDS AND ASSESSMENTS

Co-teachers' shared understanding of assessment is critical. Therefore, what is the role of standards-based expectations and grade-level content goals versus students' individual needs as they set out or continue on the path of language development and academic achievement? First and foremost, co-teachers must determine what drives instruction for English learners, since it will guide the teaching and assessment decisions they make. Figure 10.1 illustrates how various drivers interact to propel instruction and assessment. While the content standards are pictured as the largest gear representing the vast amount of academic content ELs have to master followed by the English language development (ELD) standards, the smallest gear labeled as *student needs* will move the machinery forward. Specifically, assessment practices that provide co-teachers with accurate achievement data and insight into students' language and content learning needs should be the main drivers of instruction.

English learners have to meet dual standards to demonstrate adequate progress: language development standards and core content standards. When teachers examine both sets of standards together, they can create a blueprint of targets and rigorous yet reasonable expectations for ELs. Yet English learners have unique and varied backgrounds, so their individual needs also need to be considered. Our belief about instructional and assessment practices is closely aligned to the six principles developed by members of the Understanding Language Initiative at Stanford University (2013):

1. Instruction focuses on providing ELs with opportunities to engage in discipline-specific practices that are designed to build conceptual understanding and language competence in tandem.

2. Instruction leverages ELs' home language(s), cultural assets, and prior knowledge.

3. Standards-aligned instruction for ELs is rigorous, grade-level appropriate, and provides deliberate and appropriate scaffolds.

4. Instruction moves ELs forward by taking into account their English proficiency level(s) and prior schooling experiences.

| **Figure 10.1** | The Drivers of EL Assessment and Instruction |

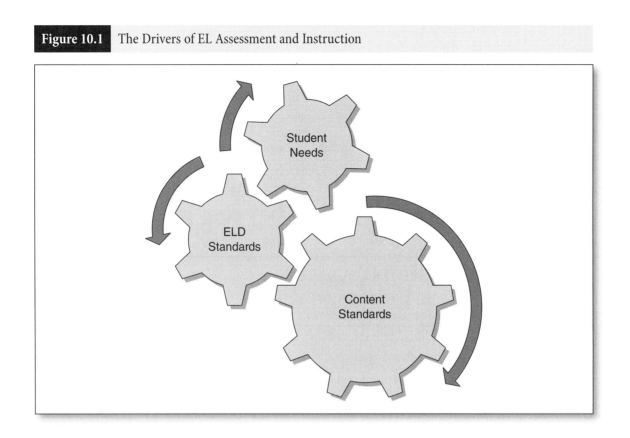

5. Instruction fosters ELs' autonomy by equipping them with the strategies necessary to comprehend and use language in a variety of academic settings.

6. Diagnostic tools and formative assessment practices are employed to measure students' content knowledge, academic language competence, and participation in disciplinary practices. (p. 1)

These principles align directly with the standard practices we have observed in successful co-taught classes for English learners, which include integrating lessons with both language and content goals in mind, maintaining high expectations and rigorous instruction, back mapping and forward mapping the curriculum to tailor instruction to students' individual needs, incorporating specific strategies that support EL learning, and giving ELs multiple meaningful opportunities to demonstrate what they know and have learned.

In a comprehensive research project, Tung and her colleagues (2011) have examined the intersection of curriculum, instruction, and assessment in select high-performing and significantly improving urban schools for English learners. The following four themes emerged as consistent practice:

- Designing and implementing a coherent, standards-based curriculum specially adapted for ELs
- Explicitly teaching all aspects of the English language and giving ample opportunities for students to use them authentically

- Utilizing ELs' native language strategically to ensure that students understand tasks, vocabulary, and metacognitive strategies
- Using multiple forms of assessments that inform teachers' instruction and advance student learning

Standards-based instruction and ongoing, carefully aligned assessment practices are among the prominent findings. All teachers of ELs must learn and implement instructional and assessment strategies that advance students' language, literacy, and academic development.

THE PURPOSE OF CO-ASSESSMENT FOR ELS

Teachers have been assessing students through one method or another for decades. So what makes co-assessment for ELs so integral to the collaborative instructional cycle? To begin, it stems from how co-teachers create and gather data from assessments that genuinely reveal student learning. These assessments include culturally responsive practices and the use of multiple formats for students to share what they know. In addition, when two teachers review students' work, they bring their own personal perspectives to evaluate students' performance. In turn, student outcomes are often identified through multiple dimensions and by equitable means to provide a clearer picture of EL achievement.

Although there is much written on co-assessment for students with disabilities, there is little in the literature specifically for this practice with ELs. For this reason, we detail here the purpose of assessment for ELs overall, including equitable measures and the importance of formative as well as summative assessments, as a guide for co-teachers.

The reason for assessing ELs goes beyond obtaining an achievement score. O'Malley and Valdez Pierce (1996) note six purposes for assessing ELs: (1) screening to identify ELs, (2) placing ELs in appropriate language support programs, (3) reclassifying ELs or exiting them from language support programs, (4) monitoring ELs' progress, (5) evaluating English language development/English language learner (ELD/ELL) programs, and (6) providing data for accountability measures. Staehr Fenner (2013a) and Hauck, Wolf, and Mislevy (2013) identify several overarching reasons why equitable assessment practices—ones that are valid, reliable, and fair—are essential for accurately gauging English language development and academic achievement:

1. Correct identification, classification, placement, and reclassification of ELs based on their language proficiency levels. Valid and reliable assessment measures will ensure this.

2. Effective instruction. If both general-education and ELD/ELL teachers have meaningful, accurate, and actionable assessment data about their ELs' language development and content attainment, they can plan more effective lessons, differentiate instruction more purposefully, and integrate content learning with language development opportunities across the four domains of listening, speaking, reading, and writing.

3. Transparent accountability. Since data on ELs are integral to school, district, and state accountability systems, they must accurately document ELs' development both in language proficiency and academic attainment.

The data received from these types of assessment are essential for co-teachers to share with one another. So what does it mean when ELs are identified as *beginning* or *developing* on an English language proficiency test? What do their achievement data in reading, mathematics, and other content on standardized tests reveal for the purpose of developing accessible lessons?

In addition to identification and summative assessment, formative assessment is central to the co-taught classroom. Fisher and Frey (2007) make a compelling case for checking for understanding and conducting formative assessments that inform instruction. Among others, Gottlieb (2006, 2016), Guskey (2014), Guskey and Jung (2013), Jung and Guskey (2012), and Staehr Fenner (2013a) recommend a multiple-measure assessment system to be established that includes formative and summative assessment measures. These assessment practices will need to address both content and language development with the types of accommodations that are most conducive to the students' language proficiency level.

Hattie (2012) cautions teachers to know their impact and concludes that offering specific feedback may have one of the highest influences on student learning. He also emphasizes the importance of the teacher's interactions with the learner. He eloquently writes,

> The art of teaching, and its major successes, relate to what happens next—the manner in which the teacher reacts to how the student interprets, accommodates, rejects, and/or reinvents the content and skills, how the student relates and applies the content to other tasks, and how the student reacts in light of success and failure apropos the content and methods that the teacher has taught. (p. 2)

Hattie talks about the importance of each teacher's ability to recognize the need for thoughtful and impactful assessment practices. Taking it a bit further, we assert that you can double the importance and impact of student assessment when you co-teach and collaborate with a partner. Moreover, we suggest that you also embrace the notion by Tonya Ward Singer (2014) that teachers are data gatherers and problem solvers, and as such are "always shifting the level of scaffolds they provide to balance support with rigor, foster independence, and engage every learner every time" (p. 16).

THE ARCHITECTURE OF CO-ASSESSMENT PRACTICES

We liken establishing a collaborative assessment system to designing, building, and enjoying a house. In the following sections, we elaborate on laying the foundation of the house, crafting and installing its frame, wiring the house, furnishing and inspecting it, and then moving in. As this metaphor unfolds in greater detail, it will fully capture the complexity of assessing ELs and the need for sustained collaboration.

Essential Considerations (Laying the Foundation)

A shared foundational understanding of assessment for ELs is essential for co-teachers to have for optimum outcomes. Building upon Tonya Ward Singer's (2014) suggestion to establish problems of practice and inquiry questions, we encourage you and your co-teacher to begin co-constructing your co-assessment practices by critically reflecting on and coming to a joint agreement regarding the following three key questions as well as their respective supporting questions:

1. **What are our shared goals for student learning?**

    a. Where are our students today, and where do we want them to go?

    b. How are we planning for content and language development?

    c. How do we measure student growth in both content and language development?

    d. How do we ensure sharing responsibility for student outcomes in both content and language development?

2. **How will all students, including ELs, on every level of proficiency demonstrate success?**

    a. What is our definition of success for ELs (and non-ELs)?

    b. How do we differentiate instruction and assessment for all levels of ELs?

    c. How do we set attainable goals for all our students yet remain mindful of the grade-level benchmarks?

    d. What assessment tools and measures are we going to use that are fair, meaningful, and equitable?

3. **What instruction will we provide collaboratively to ensure success for all our students?**

    a. How do we integrate content and language instruction?

    b. How do we scaffold and support learning?

    c. How do wc gradually incrcase student autonomy?

    d. How do we ensure active student engagement?

Engaging in structured conversations or collaborative protocols like this one enhances the effectiveness and outcomes of collaborations. However, we have always viewed collaboration as a fluid and creative process, so the tools we offer in this chapter should be adapted and modified as needed.

Building a Framework for Co-Assessment (Framing the House)

Collaborative conversations that create a common frame of reference for assessing ELs are a critical step for successful co-assessment. Here, we borrow Margo Gottlieb's (2016) three-pronged framework that defines assessment for ELs from three different perspectives: assessment *as, for,* and *of* learning (see Figure 10.2). Let's examine and expand this framework for co-teachers' collaborative engagement in these assessment practices:

Figure 10.2 Framework for Co-Assessment: Assessment *as, for,* and *of* Learning

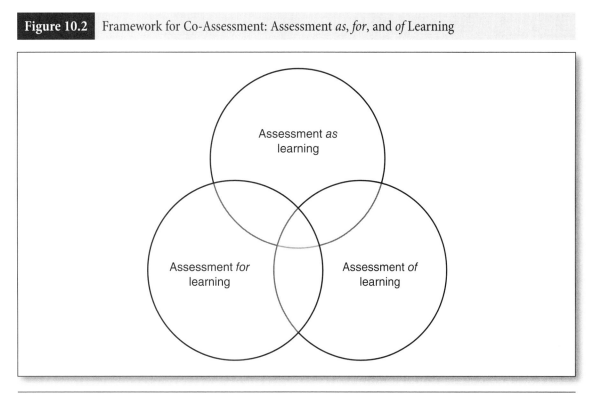

Gottlieb (2016). Used with permission.

---

1. *Assessment as learning* is student self-assessment. It suggests that—when supported by two teachers—English learners can be meaningfully included in this assessment process. As Rothstein and Santana (2011) also found, "students who are aware of themselves as learners and who can name and monitor their own learning strategies can more easily apply knowledge obtained in one context to another" (p. 18). ELs develop agency and become more self-directed, independent learners when they are regularly invited to engage in self-assessment and reflection by co-teachers. As a result, ELs learn to do the following:

   a. Set their own goals

   b. Monitor and reflect on their progress

   c. Make choices of assessment tasks and projects when offered

   d. Develop, maintain, and reflect upon their own work-sample portfolio

   e. Participate in the assessment process in many other ways

Transparency and shared decision making regarding student goals is well represented in Figure 10.3, which is an example of a weekly goal-setting template that Cathy Marketos of North Merrick Union Free School District, has used with her ELs. Every Monday, specific goals are collaboratively set with each student and shared with the classroom teacher, which in turn are reviewed and assessed at the end of the week.

Figure 10.3 Weekly Goal Setting

NORTH MERRICK UNION FREE SCHOOL DISTRICT

EL Goals

When applicable will include ELA and Content Area Language Development

Student: _____   School: _____

Grade: _____   Classroom Teacher: _____

ENL Teacher: _____   Level of Language Proficiency: _____

Frequency: _____

Goals	Summary of Progress	Assessment Tools
READING Vocabulary		
WRITING Grammar		
LISTENING		
SPEAKING		

Figure 10.4 Vocabulary Self-Assessment Tool

Vocabulary	My Knowledge of Key Words			
	I have never heard of it	I have heard of it, and I think I know what it means	I know it very well	I can tell or write a sentence with it

Self-assessment tools may also focus on targeted skills and be designed to offer specific information about students' language, literacy, or content-based skills or knowledge. For example, if you want to help raise students' awareness about word knowledge, try a cross-cutting strategy that may be used in all grade levels and content areas, such as the Vocabulary Self-Assessment Tool in Figure 10.4. It is a simplified version of a classic by Beck, McKeown, and Kucan (2002).

Figure 10.5	K-W-L Chart on the Dust Bowl

What I KNOW about the Dust Bowl	What I WANT to Know about the Dust Bowl (Use question prompts below or write your own questions)	What I LEARNED about the Dust Bowl (Save for end of viewing activity)
Who?		
What?		
When?		
Where?		
Why?		
How?		

Developed by Geeta Vir and Gioia Scharfschwerdt, Patchogue-Medford Schools, NY. Used with permission.

Some self-assessment tools may be highly specialized to focus on the target lesson. See Figure 10.5 for a Know, Want to Know, and Learned (K-W-L) chart developed for secondary ELs linking a video viewing activity (http://www.pbs.org/kenburns/dustbowl/educators/lesson-plans/) to self-assessing background knowledge, generating their own questions, and documenting new learning about the Dust Bowl and the Great Depression.

2. *Assessment for Learning* refers to the process that both classroom teachers and ELD/ELL specialists may employ on a regular basis. Teachers collect evidence of what learning targets their students have mastered, are in the process of mastering, and what they have yet to attain. Assessment for learning consists primarily of a formative process, and as such, it helps inform instruction and offer feedback to students. It has been recognized by many that "integrating instruction and assessment, formative assessment is a continuous cycle that entails gathering evidence of and judging student learning; providing feedback to students about their learning; and using assessment data to adjust subsequent instruction as needed" (Alvarez, Ananda, Walqui, Sato, & Rabinowitz, 2014, p. 2).

Based on the formative assessment data collected, co-teachers may make adjustments to their teaching immediately or plan on reteaching a given skill or concept during the following class session. Heritage (2010) notes that

teacher feedback is most beneficial when it assists students to understand their current learning status and provides hints, suggestions, or cues for them to act on. It is this, rather than offering general praise or total solutions, that enables students to assume a degree of responsibility for their learning. (p. 18)

To establish a successful routine or structure for assessment *of* learning, we have adapted a five-step protocol from Margo Gottlieb (2016). We encourage you and your co-teacher to use this

Principles of Formative Assessment

Through formative assessment practices, co-teachers will

- promote student learning in a continuous, ongoing manner;
- elicit evidence of learning in a variety of ways (on the fly, preplanned, curriculum aligned, language focused) through a variety of assessment tasks;
- change the roles of teachers and students by placing students and their needs at the center of instruction and assessment;
- set learning goals and use tools that indicate progressions to monitor learning;
- offer meaningful feedback to students and adjust instruction to improve learning for students; and
- help students self-assess and become self-directed, autonomous learners.

Adapted from Alvarez, L., Ananda, S., Walqui, A., Sato, E., & Rabinowitz, S. (2014). *Focusing formative assessment on the needs of English language learners.* San Francisco, CA: WestEd.

tool (Figure 10.6) as a way to engage in yet another collaborative conversation, answer the key questions we posed, and map out key steps you will take together. Decide on how some of the work will be divided up between the two co-teachers, what tools and measures you will be using along the way, and how you anticipate this process will impact student outcomes.

3. *Assessment of Learning* refers to processes that yield summative assessment data, including classroom assessments and standardized tests. We encourage co-teachers to carefully consider what types of summative assessment will provide the most valid and reliable information on whether the student has mastered the target content and language and literacy skills or not. Since summative assessments are used to determine how well students have met instructional goals of a specific learning segment that may range from a unit of study to a quarter or marking period or an entire academic year, they may be designed together by co-teachers or may be standardized at the school, district, or state levels:

   - End-of-unit tests or projects
   - Chapter reviews or tests
   - End-of-marking period or semester exams
   - District benchmark or interim assessments
   - State assessments

Co-teachers we have worked with and observed often opt for nontraditional, performance-based, or project-based summative assessments that encourage learners to demonstrate what they have learned in creative ways, often allowing for the use of multiple modalities rather than responding to traditional pencil-and-paper tests. Yet a caution is in order. The cognitive complexity of projects and the academic language demands associated with them must be both carefully scaffolded and aligned to the students' characteristics

Figure 10.6	A Five-Step Protocol for Co-Assessment of Student Learning

Steps to Follow	Co-teachers' Decisions
1. Create standards-based content and language objectives along with criteria for success.	*Key consideration:* How are we aligning content and language objectives? _____ _____ _____ _____
2. Match performance assessment to learning objectives and the criteria for success.	*Key consideration*: How are we defining criteria for success in content and language development? _____ _____ _____ _____
3. Collect and interpret evidence of student learning during instruction.	*Key consideration*: What data sources will be used, and how are we making sense of the data together? _____ _____ _____ _____
4. Provide criterion-referenced feedback based on the evidence.	*Key consideration*: How are we offering meaningful feedback to all students? _____ _____ _____ _____
5. Make instructional decisions based on student data that advance student learning.	**Key consideration**: How are we adjusting our instruction based on the evidence we have collected? _____ _____ _____ _____

Adapted from Gottlieb, M. (2016). *Assessing English language learners: Bridges to educational equity.* Thousand Oaks, CA: Corwin.

(Gottlieb, 2016); thus, collaborative work on designing assessment tasks and tools is critical in ensuring that assessments will be valid and reliable.

Creating an Assessment System (Putting Up All the Walls and Adding the Roof)

As co-teachers, you also need to agree on how ELs' assessment practices will fit into a comprehensive system that spans from daily assessments to collecting benchmark assessment data, and administering summative assessments including the inclusion of ELs in large-scale, high-stakes assessments. Begin by reflecting and answering the following questions with your co-teacher:

Daily formative assessments:

How do we collect meaningful assessment data about each student?

How do we use the data to inform instruction?

How do we provide immediate, useful feedback to students?

Benchmark assessments:

How do we monitor student progress and growth?

What common assessments are we going to develop or select?

How frequently are we going to collect data? In what ways will the benchmark data be used to make short-term and longer-term decisions about ELs?

Summative assessments:

What types of summative assessments are we going to utilize?

How do we account for variances in student characteristics (prior knowledge or lack thereof; cultural experiences with tests and exams or projects, or lack thereof)?

How do we ensure fair and equitable summative assessment tasks and measures?

Portfolios may accomplish multiple goals and serve as a comprehensive approach to assessment. If you decide on creating process portfolios for your ELs, periodically collect representative work samples that may capture language development and content attainment at given times and also document growth over time. If you choose to have your students develop end-of-year portfolios or product portfolios, these will serve as culminating collections of student work that represents their self-selected accomplishments, outstanding achievements, and highlights of the literacy and content-related activities. These portfolios are designed to demonstrate mastery of course content and contain only their best work (Venn, 2007).

For example, when you decide to create an end-of-year portfolio assessment for secondary English learners, consider including some of the following items:

- Letter to the reader introducing what is included in the portfolio
- Quotations that have special meaning for the student
- Select paragraphs that illustrate writing techniques and crafts
- Sample essays of various types (descriptive, narrative, explanatory, expository, persuasive, cause and effect, compare and contrast, and others)
- Written work from other classes (lab reports, speech outlines, summaries, essays, projects)
- Annotated student drawings or photographs that connect to the course content
- Graphic illustrations of course content (charts, graphs, concept maps, webs, timelines). (Adapted from Honigsfeld & Dodge, 2015)

Depending on the grade and language proficiency level, you will have to modify this list of items to include more relevant representations of student work.

Adding Technology to the Collaborative Assessment Plan (Wiring the House)

Technology-based tools are ideal for progress monitoring and sharing information about ELs. When collaborating teachers have editing rights to a (co-developed) form, they can have access to the data collected by each team member. Collaborative data collection and analysis help set consistent goals for ELs as well as support a more integrated approach to serving ELs.

See Table 10.1 for commonly used assessment practices that yield a range of important data that help improve instruction and student outcomes. Consider the three Ts of assessment practices, which include the *tools* co-teachers use, the assessment *task* the students complete, and the *technology* integrated (Parris, Estrada, & Honigsfeld, 2016).

Differentiating Assessment Practices for ELs (Furnishing Each Room)

English learners are a diverse group of students with a range of different needs. Among many others, Sandberg and Reschly (2011) acknowledge the challenges teachers face when creating curriculum-based measurements and assessing ELs. While differentiating instruction for ELs is becoming more widely accepted and practiced, when it comes to assessment, many teachers continue to assign identical projects, give the same quizzes and tests, and use the grading system designed for English-speaking students. We believe co-teachers must collaborate not only to differentiate instruction but to design differentiated assessment tools as well. We have found that co-assessment is a crucial, yet occasionally overlooked, element of the collaborative instructional cycle that also includes co-planning, co-delivering instruction, and reflection on one's teaching (Honigsfeld & Dove, 2010, 2015a).

Table 10.1	Technology Integration		
Assessment Practices	**Tools Teachers Use**	**Tasks Students Complete**	**Technology Integration**
Reading comprehension	Checklist or rubric	Reading and responding orally and in writing	Accelerated Reader 360 or Active Learning
Observation	Anecdotal records	Student-to-student interaction	Google Forms
Quizzes	Multiple choice or true and false questions	Select correct answers based on available choices	Kahoot Quizlet Plickers
Student questions	Student-led inquiries	Generate own questions	Padlet
Presentations	Checklist or rubric	Student presentation with interactive explorations	Screen-casting tools such as Explain Everything
Exit cards	Exit slip with prompts/questions	Short responses	Socrative
Projects	Checklist or rubric	Independent or group projects	Schoology
Portfolios	Self-assessment	Work sample collection	E-portfolio

If you are wondering how to differentiate assessment, consider the *who, what,* and *how* of assessments for ELs:

Who Does the Assessment?

While we often associate assessment as one teacher's responsibility, an important way to differentiate assessment practices is to have students either complete self- or peer- assessments or have both co-teachers assess. Role definition between co-teachers is essential for success: The ELD/ELL teacher will look for progression on and/or mastery of language development targets, whereas the classroom teacher will primarily focus on content attainment. It is also valuable to have multiple perspectives so students may self-assess as well as subject their work to peer and teacher review.

What Is Being Assessed?

In a co-taught class, an important point to negotiate is what will be assessed. *Equal* is not necessarily fair and equitable (see Rick Wormeli, 2006). For example, language assessment might be taking a backseat to measuring the degree to which ELs have mastered content learning targets. If we focus on content assessment, can we find alternate ways students can express their content knowledge that reduces the linguistic burden? Is there enough emphasis to also monitor and assess language and literacy skills? The ultimate question is whether or not we are assessing what we intended to assess, thus creating valid assessment measures.

	Level 1	**Level 2**	**Level 3**	**Level 4**	**Level 5**
Assessment Task: Retell key events related to the target topic	Draw and label pictures depicting the target topic	State key words and phrases associated with the target topic using visual support	Retell a short sequence of events associated with the target topic using visual support	Offer a scaffolded oral presentation on the sequence of events associated with the target topic	Offer an oral presentation using multiple sources on the sequence of events associated with the target topic

Figure 10.7 Differentiated Expectations

Adapted from WIDA, 2012.

How Are ELs Assessed?

As we noted earlier, a key decision to make is the selection of appropriate assessment tasks and assessment tools. If needed, assessment tasks may be adjusted to better align to what the students know and can do, and how they can best demonstrate their new learning. See a 5-level assessment task description based on the World-Class Instructional Design and Assessment (WIDA) standards showing how all students are working on meeting the same goals, but the specifics of the expectations will vary (Figure 10.7). Further, students may also be given varied assessment tools such as rubrics or checklists that are differentiated. The main concern here is whether our assessment tasks and tools are reliable, thus accurately and consistently measure what we intend to measure.

Willner, Rivera, and Acosta (2009) suggest that the entire school faculty learn about accommodating ELs during formal assessments. We use the term *accommodations* to refer to adjustments made to assessments that continue to measure grade-appropriate outcomes, whereas modifications indicate that the EL is multiple grade levels below expectations. We build upon the special-education literature when we recognize accommodations as "practices and procedures in the areas of presentation, response, setting, and timing/scheduling that provide equitable access during instruction and assessments" (Thompson, Morse, Sharpe, & Hall, 2005, p. 14).

According to Willner et al. (2009), there are at least five key aspects of accommodations to keep in mind. Let's see what these mean for co-teachers who design assessment tools and measures together, thus have to agree on accommodations as well:

- Focus on teaching grade-appropriate content to ELs:
  - While back mapping and teaching foundational skills are essential, jointly decide on what big ideas, key concepts, and skills students should be able to master regardless of language proficiency.
  - Use differentiated instruction throughout the unit for students to experience tiered instruction, content delivery, multiple entry points into the curriculum, and interest- and needs-based support.

- Use scaffolded instructional and formative assessment tools that offer linguistic, graphic, visual, and interactive supports (see Chapter 2).

- Provide accommodations that support ELs' linguistic needs:
  - Offer native language support such as dictionaries, glossaries, and/or a translated version of the assessment for those who are biliterate.
  - Reduce linguistic complexity without compromising.
  - Paraphrase directions in simplified English.
  - Use nonverbal cues such as graphic or pictorial support.

- Assign accommodations based on individual student needs:
  - Review the student profiles you created to understand student characteristics before deciding on accommodations (see Chapter 1).
  - Consider available assessment data about each student.
  - Decide on the most appropriate and valid and reliable approach.

- Use a team approach when making accommodation decisions:
  - Work in teams with content and ELD/ELL teachers to better identify what core knowledge and skills will need to be assessed and what might be omitted from an assessment that may be too lengthy for ELs.
  - Work with other ELD/ELL specialists to review past practices and establish most effective accommodations used with your ELs.
  - Establish a schoolwide policy regarding accommodations to be used with ELs in formal assessments such as unit tests, quarterlies, and so on, as well as to establish grading practices.

- Provide the opportunity to use the accommodations before the test:
  - Invite students to offer input into what accommodations help them do better on assessments.
  - Let students experience the accommodations in low-stakes context prior to a high-stakes assessment.
  - Let students evaluate the effectiveness of the accommodations you use.

Examining Student Data (The house is built, ready for inspection)

A successful beginning to the co-teaching partnership must include a shared analysis of ELs' performance on their latest language development assessment as well as an examination of students' academic performance data. Review available English language proficiency scores including subscores for language and literacy subskills to establish short-term and long-term goals. Analyzing student assessment data together will allow both teachers to better understand what students *can do,* what reasonable expectations and language acquisition and literacy development targets may be set for the students, as well as what ways students may be better supported through scaffolded instruction.

A powerful collaborative activity ELD/ELL and general-education teachers engage in is sampling and carefully examining representative work by ELs. Originally developed by members of Harvard's Project Zero, the Collaborative Assessment Conference (CAC) (http://www.lasw.org/CAC_steps.html) is designed to examine student work to uncover whether the student has reached mastery of the target curriculum as well as learn about the student as a learner as much as possible.

The three critical principles of the CAC process apply well to teacher collaboration for the sake of ELs:

1. Examine authentic student work and look for strengths and needs.

2. Examine the actual work—not what you hope to see—while also discussing how teachers can best support the child to make necessary progress.

3. Take a collaborative approach and invite colleagues to participate in this process.

To help teachers gain a more meaningful connection between their instructional practices and student learning to support the development of a culture of inquiry, Langer, Colton, and Goff (2003) have developed a framework called Collaborative Analysis of Student Learning (CASL), which is "a teacher development system that helps educators develop a culture for collaborative inquiry" (p. 3). Colton, Langer, and Goff (2016) recently revised and updated their structured framework of collaborative conversations and shared inquiry, and based on their over a decade-long work with CASL, they have concluded:

> Facilitated structured collaborative inquiry into how students learn complex academic standards helps teachers relentlessly and effectively pursue, discover, and apply responsive approaches for learning so that each and every student, regardless of students' backgrounds or interests, reaches standards of excellence. (p. 4)

The five phases of a CASL inquiry adapted for co-teaching for ELs

Phase I: Establishing a Focus for CASL Inquiry

What aspects of the target curriculum and what elements of language acquisition and literacy development are most challenging for ELs?

What aspects of the target curriculum are most challenging for non-ELs?

Phase II: Defining Teachers' Professional Learning Goals

Which ELs and non-ELs would be most fruitful to study over time so that we may discover equitable responses?

Phase III: Inquiring Into Teaching for Learning (3–5 months)

Which approaches are most responsive to ELs' vs. non-ELs' strengths and needs?

Phase IV: Assessing Learning Progress

What progress have our students made? Who needs further assistance?

Phase V: Integrating Learning Into Teachers' Professional Practice

What have we learned about ourselves and our teaching, and what might we need to learn more about?

Adapted from Colton et al. (2016). *The collaborative analysis of student learning: Professional learning that promotes success for all.* Thousand Oaks, CA: Corwin.

With the use of preestablished protocols, the goal is for participating teachers to work toward shared decision making. To achieve that goal, co-teachers must systematically do the following:

- Identify and analyze students' strengths and weaknesses
- Design the most appropriate intervention strategies that will respond to the patterns of learning challenges ELs face
- Generate possible explanations for student performance levels from multiple points of view
- Discuss research-based best practices and promising strategies they wish to implement
- Plan coordinated interventions

When implemented with fidelity, collaborative assessment is highly structured and cyclical—each time new data are collected from students, their performance is reassessed. In this process, teachers have the opportunity to continue to reflect on their students' academic learning as well as socioemotional and linguistic development when it comes to diverse learners. Co-assessment coupled with shared reflection time and co-planning can also help determine whether the modifications and accommodations co-teachers planned and executed offered the necessary support or not, and what additional interventions are needed. The literature on the co-assessment of student work offers several different protocols to follow when examining student work (see for example Blythe, Allen, & Schieffelin Powell, 2008), as well as those that specifically examine work by English learners—their cultural and linguistic challenges as well as academic and language development (e.g., Honigsfeld & Dove, 2010). In our work, we have found it helpful to customize the protocol for examining student work by focusing on challenges shared by ELs and their teachers. We call our protocol *Sampling Work by English Language Learners* (SWELL). See the Co-assessing Student Work textbox for the entire protocol.

Grades for ELs (Monitoring the House)

Schools need to establish a collaboratively developed, fair, and equitable class and school grading and reporting policy that has a clear purpose, is aligned to standards, and is supported by research (Guskey, 2014). No small feat to accomplish! When ELs and non-ELs are together in the same class, to develop such policy requires careful considerations. Key questions to consider about grading ELs in the co-taught class include:

- Will all ELs at all levels of language proficiency receive grades?
- Will letter grades or number grades be used or are we going to develop a standards-based reporting system?
- How can we effectively report to parents about their children's progress on academic and linguistic skills?

To ensure that all stakeholders can understand and appreciate what is expected of students at a particular grade level or content area, it is recommended that you include measures to report both student growth in language development and academic attainment as well as core content achievement in relation to grade-level standards and/or benchmarks (Gottlieb, 2016). Co-teachers

Co-assessing Student Work

As you collaboratively examine student work samples produced by English language learners, consider the following questions organized in four subcategories.

1. Linguistic Development

    a. What stage of second language acquisition is evident?

    b. Which linguistic features has the student mastered and is using systematically?

    c. What are two or three prominent linguistic challenges the EL's work demonstrates?

    d. Other comments:

2. Academic Needs

    a. What are two or three examples of successfully acquired content-based knowledge and/or skills?

    b. What are some noticeable gaps in the EL's prior knowledge?

    c. What are some gaps in the EL's new content attainment?

    d. What content-specific skills does the EL need to work on?

    e. Other comments:

3. Cultural Experiences

    a. In what ways are the EL's own cultural experiences reflected in his or her work?

    b. Is there any evidence that the EL was faced with new cultural experiences?

    c. Other comments:

4. Social-Emotional Aspects of Learning

    a. Is there evidence of motivated, self-directed learning in the EL's work sample?

    b. Has the EL been engaged in the task?

    c. Is there evidence of task-persistence?

    d. Is there evidence of being engaged in cooperative learning (peer editing, etc.)?

    e. Other comments:

Adapted from Honigsfeld, A., & Dove, M. G. (2010). *Collaboration and co-teaching: Strategies for English learners.* Thousand Oaks, CA: Corwin.

also must be keenly aware of whether or not their assessment and measurement practices offer ELs attainable goals or lead them to frustration and lack of success.

Dave Nagel (2015) suggests a five-step process to prevent student failure he calls SI2TE (Support, Intervention, Incentives, Time, Evidence). Here is the adapted version for co-teachers to implement in support of ELs:

SI2TE for ELs (Support, Intervention, Incentives, Time, Evidence)

Support: Help build resilience in students by offering support, encouragement, and reminders that "academic struggles are not permanent" (Nagel, 2015, p.103).

Intervention: Use the co-teaching structure to frequently review assessment and offer interventions right away.

(Increasing) Incentives: Focus on positive feedback with a special focus on "incentivizing student input (efforts) versus outputs (proficiency)" (p.104).

Time: Recognize that ELs need additional time to complete many tasks and to show the desired outcomes, so adjust the time needed for students to work on assignments and to reach success.

Evidence: ELs need varied opportunities to show evidence of new skills and mastery of new content, so be flexible and creative about the ways you gauge student learning.

Adapted from Nagel, D. (2015). *Effective grading practices for secondary teachers: Practical strategies to prevent failure, recover credits, and increase standards-based / referenced grading.* Thousand Oaks, CA: Corwin.

Use Data (Enjoy Your House)

What do you do with information you have about your students' language literacy and academic development? At the instructional level, data gleaned from these assessment measures will inform instruction as well as guide student growth. John Hattie and Helen Timperley (2007) have analyzed the power of feedback given to students and established the purpose of feedback as a way to reduce the discrepancy between what students' existing understanding or performance is and what the desired goal would be. They also have suggested that effective feedback answers three questions for the learner:

As a learner, where am I going? (Co-teachers offer *feed up* or help define learning goals or targets)

As a learner, how am I doing? (Co-teachers offer feedback on work or performance)

As a learner, what are my next steps in learning? (Co-teachers offer *feed forward* or scaffold new learning)

Hattie and Timperley (2007) also share four levels of feedback: (a) task or product, (b) process, (c) self-regulation, and (d) personal, and identify four major types of feedback that all teachers can give:

- Feedback on task or product,
- Feedback on process,
- Feedback on self-regulation, and
- Feedback on self.

The first three types of feedback help students move from giving the correct answer or demonstrating procedural knowledge to becoming self-directed, independent learners who also demonstrate high levels of self-confidence and self-efficacy. English learners certainly need all that! The final type of feedback according to Hattie is largely useless and may even become counterproductive; yet for English learners, it may serve a special purpose of relationship building. Since English learners' needs are absent from their discussion of student feedback, we have adapted their framework and augmented it to be specific to co-teachers' work with ELs (see Figure 10.8).

Co-assessment is a complex endeavor, with its fair share of challenges, yet it is well worth the effort. The collaborative process that goes into co-assessment will result in more meaningful data about ELs and better decision making regarding the information gained from each type of assessment. In sum, see Table 10.2 for a summary of the various student data sources and their uses.

**VIDEO 10.1:
Collaborative
Assessment**

http://resources
.corwin.com/
CoTeachingforELs

Figure 10.8   Levels of Feedback and Their Implications for ELs

Level of feedback	Purpose	What it sounds like	Implications for ELs
Task or product	How well the task is understood and whether the work is accurate or not	*That's correct, you had to read the paragraph before trying to answer the questions!* *The past tense verbs are all correctly formed in your essay, except in the last sentence.*	Immediate feedback is offered on what the EL was able to do.
Process	How effective and successful the learner is in completing a task	*Before you move on to the next draft, let's review the steps of the writing process.*	ELs become more confident language learners and language users when they understand the linguistic and academic processes that they need to master.
Self-Regulation	How well the student is able to monitor his or her own learning process and outcomes	*This self-editing checklist will offer some key suggestions on how to improve your writing.*	This type of feedback is highly beneficial to ELs who need to develop self-management and independence.
Personal	How the student is perceived as a learner	*You are a wonderful writer!* *You are a great artist. I love the way you add illustrations to your writing!* *You are doing a fantastic job in this class!*	ELs need to hear words of acknowledgement. Though this type of feedback is generic, it continues to be relevant to ELs, even though it may often be dismissed as superficial for general-education students.

Table 10.2   Summary of Student Data Sources and Their Uses

Types of Student Data	How to Obtain Data	What Information to Gain
Home Language Survey or Questionnaire	Students' permanent records/files, parent/guardian interview	Home and English language use for communicative purposes and literacy attainment
Initial Screening/Intake Results	Students' permanent records/files, interview with parents/guardians	Length of U.S. residence and prior schooling experiences in home country and United States
Academic Transcripts	From previous schools attended in country of origin and/or previous schools in the United States	Students' prior academic achievements and credits accumulated for graduation
Standardized Language Assessments	State and local standardized assessment measures	Levels of language proficiency, specifically in speaking, writing, reading, and listening
Teacher-Generated Assessment: Formative and Summative via Tests and Quizzes	Grade books; student files; portfolio assessment folders; online data tools	Progress in and mastery of content and literacy development; students' current learning challenges; data for future curricula and lesson development
Formative and Summative Assessments via anecdotal note taking, checklists, peer and self-evaluation, electronic surveys, etc.	Teacher anecdotal notebooks; student files; portfolio assessment folders; online data tools	Successes and challenges with language and content as it pertains to speaking, writing, reading, and listening; students' self-efficacy

INSPIRATION FROM THE FIELD

Read what colleagues—ELD/ELL and classroom teachers as well as building and district administrators—shared with us from around the United States and see how they reflect or add to your own experiences.

First, we invite you to read Pushpanjali Sengupta's reflection on the impact of co-teaching on student learning. She is an EL an facilitator/ELD instructor and LAP facilitator/ interventionist at Cherry Crest Elementary, Bellevue Schools, Washington.

You know when you look at the setting sun and you are in awe of what is happening in front of you . . . well, that is how I feel every day at work. The Kindergarteners in Pam Lawlor's class and first graders in Melissa Hayfield's class have proved beyond doubt that every student is capable of performing to the standards with the appropriate support and rigor, and this has been possible with co-teaching and collaboration with these teachers. I have been co-teaching with them on a regular basis, and the results have been amazing. I hear students using claim and evidence to solve an engineering challenge in Science and to talk about a book they are reading. They encourage each other to ask and answer questions using phrases such as: Can you explain why . . .? I claim this . . . Using evidence from the text, I conclude . . ., etc. It gives me goosebumps to hear the students use academic language in the class without being prompted by teachers. With our increasing demand on students to produce more academic language, it is really important to teach in a way where the content is comprehensible by each student in the class, whether they are ELs or struggling readers. Co-teaching has given us the opportunity to take equity into consideration. With the co-teaching model in place, we have been able to address the academic as well as social-emotional needs of all students. It has made each of us a better teacher and has resulted in building a classroom community where we are all part of the team. Using a variety of research-based strategies in the class, our team has been able to build the academic capacity of the students.

It has taken time to build the trust and rapport with teachers, and this learning process has been really valuable! As a result of the change in mindset, students are embracing the challenge and taking pride in learning new things and applying what they have learned in other areas. They are giving feedback to us about our teaching and asking us to teach them using the 'team assignments.' Parents are seeing the difference and encouraging us to continue with the team teaching. Other staff members in the building and from the district have come in to observe co-teaching lessons and have taken an active interest in learning more about the process. Administrators have been supportive and eager to co-teach in the classroom. I owe this success to the fact that now we are not teaching in isolation but rather as a team where each of us is responsible for the student and work together to make content comprehensible for each and every student in the class. It is ultimately making these students ready for life beyond school where they can be productive and successful.

Next, let's hear from Tracy Kocsis, elementary ENL (English as a New Language) teacher in a suburban district in western New York, as she shares her and her co-teachers' experiences with co-assessment.

A couple of things about co-assessing that my colleagues and I have found beneficial: First, you have two teachers assessing, which means that it only takes half the class time that it used to take, allowing more opportunities for teaching and learning to take place. Second, you also have two sets of eyes looking at the information and analyzing patterns in student learning. It seems like in each of my co-teaching partnerships, when we look at assessments, we each glean different information to inform teaching decisions. It's always helpful to have the other perspective from someone else who knows all the students and works with all the students. I have been very fortunate in that all of my co-teaching experiences, both current and in the past, have been with teachers who were interested in co-planning and co-teaching as a true partnership. It does take a lot of time and effort, especially at the beginning of the relationship, but once established, the benefits to all the students are without measure. For the ELs, they are so much more able to access grade-level content when I am co-teaching, both because of preplanning and just having someone there to make instant modifications and scaffolds as needed. All students benefit from increased contact time with a teacher. The benefits to instruction outweigh the drawbacks for most students. We did have one or two students at the entering level that would have benefitted from additional stand-alone ENL support, but as a building going forward, we built that time into our schedule for next year.

Let's visit Nick DiBenedetto and Dean Bourazeris's co-taught ninth-grade social studies classroom in West Hempstead, New York, where assessing and building students' background knowledge is a regular part of the assessment and instructional routines established. Most of the ELs in the class are entering- and emerging-level students, whose success heavily depends on the two teachers' coordinated efforts to understand where the students are and move them along the path of learning the content (global history) and acquiring language and literacy skills in English.

It only took a few weeks for our classroom to gain its nickname: The General Assembly of the United Nations. Although our students are primarily from Central America, they come to class with such diverse experiences that the name stuck. We quickly learned that the great majority of our students had little to no background knowledge about the historical places we would be studying. In fact, global history turned out to be a totally new subject for some of these students. Additionally, our students had literacy skills that ran the gamut from nonliterate in their native language to intermediate literacy skills in English. We decided early on that we needed to make connections to what students already knew in order to craft instruction that would meet our students where they were.

Our greatest successes have been in the anticipatory activities that we do prior to beginning a new unit of study; assessing the prior knowledge of our students has gone a long way in making our instruction successful. Typically, we begin a unit by simply projecting the name of the unit and allowing students to share anything they know. This allows us to see what preconceptions students have about specific places or periods of time. What students already know determines how we will teach the unit. For example, our students had a tremendous amount of knowledge about Mesoamerican civilizations, and students were empowered when we gave them the opportunity to share their knowledge about these civilizations. For other units, we have created galleries that demonstrate highlights such as famous people, architecture, or art from specific cultures. Students are then tasked with constructing a narrative for us based on their observations (e.g., What can you tell us about the ancient Romans? What kind of government do you think they had? What were they good at?). At this juncture, students have a fairly good understanding of what they can expect to learn about, and we then begin to help students discover how those societies arrived at those "snapshots of history."

In addition to assessing prior content knowledge, we also determine the linguistic demands of a unit and assess vocabulary knowledge before starting a unit. This often involves selecting key target words and deciding what word associations students will need to make in order to understand complex material. For example, our students learned about the concept of isolationism because of our decision that day to place a (chatty) student on the side of the room by himself. Students now have a good laugh when we move a chatty student and ask them: What concept does this demonstrate? Academic language learning is almost always visual in our class, and the words and concepts that are most memorable to students are the ones that we have the most fun teaching.

TAKEAWAYS

In this chapter, we have walked you through the process of building a comprehensive approach to co-assessment, starting from establishing shared foundational understanding to designing formative and summative assessment measures. English learners and their co-teachers must all collaborate in the entire teaching–learning cycle; thus, the types of assessments you employ and how the information gleaned from them will be used to contribute significantly to student success.

QUESTIONS FOR FURTHER DISCUSSION

1. What structures and routines do you consider to be most effective to enhance collaborative assessment?

2. What are the greatest obstacles teachers typically face when it comes to co-assessment? How can these challenges be overcome?

3. What are the most valuable resources you need to successfully co-assess?

4. How do you ensure that EL assessment yields valid, reliable, and actionable data?

11

Reflection

*Closing the Collaborative Instructional
Cycle . . . and Starting a New One*

If you have been an educator for any amount of time, you most likely have had an experience in which you planned and executed a thoughtfully prepared lesson, and the results were exceptional—your students were highly engaged, they asked pertinent questions, and the tasks set for them were completed thoroughly and accurately. After the lesson, you probably made mental notes concerning what you did and why it worked. At a later time, you take the same lesson and seemingly duplicate it with another group of students, yet the lesson falls completely flat. You may be somewhat bewildered, but there is no getting around the need for reflection in this situation. In the same way, when co-teachers either succeed or miss the mark with the delivery of instruction, it is critical for them to examine their joint practice together.

In this chapter, we explore why reflection is so very essential to co-teaching. You might be thinking, "What if we don't have time to reflect, or choose to spend our time co-planning and co-assessing? Wouldn't that be a better use of our time?" You might agree that teachers are very busy doing everything else that is expected of them, so how can they be expected to add one more thing to the already full plate? The scarcity of available time and the overwhelming demand of instructional and noninstructional collaborative and individual responsibilities might all point in one direction for reflection—*Skip it!* Herein, we make a formidable case to proceed otherwise. In other words, *don't* skip it! Rather, invest the time needed to close the collaborative instructional cycle and make *reflection in action* (while you are co-teaching) and *reflection on action* (after co-teaching) an intentional and regular part of your collaborative work (Schon, 1983).

The Importance of Reflective Practice

We recognize that reflection might be especially challenging to fit into your day for a number of reasons or that it might be difficult to convince your teaching partner of its importance, one being the notion that "the long-standing culture of teacher isolation and individualism, together with teachers' preference to preserve their individual autonomy, may hinder deep-level collaboration to occur" (Vangrieken, Dochy, Raes, & Kyndt, 2015, p. 36). Are you experiencing a culture of isolation and individualism in your school? Or are you a part of a high-performing professional learning community? Regardless of the answer, some key questions to examine for the sake of your effectiveness in a co-teaching partnership are as follows:

- How important is reflection to you and your co-teachers?
- How do you engage in such a practice in your daily or weekly routine?
- What are the impact and the outcomes of your reflection?

We have asked hundreds of co-teachers around the country to reflect on and share with us their successes and challenges. One of the most important outcomes of gathering these teacher reflections is a consistent pattern to what co-teachers attribute their success. It is not so much what is happening in the classroom, though it is critical to effectively co-deliver instruction that integrates content with language development and to share the lesson, the students, and the classroom space. It is much more what gets the co-teachers to be a team—the type of support they receive from their administrators; the structural, systemic agency that is in place; and the preparation they themselves do for the co-teaching experience. Here is a recently shared reflection by Deborah Harpine, who is an English language development (ELD) teacher at the William Walker School, Beaverton, Oregon:

We are successful because we work to actively communicate with each other, and although we sometimes have differences of opinion, they are never tied to our competence as a teacher. I feel the keys to our "success" so far lie in the steps we have taken to get to this point, although as collaborators, this is a continuous process.

Steps to our success:

1. *Administration buy-in, leadership, and support*

2. *Setting aside protected time to plan units of study in several long blocks of time to be spaced out how the team decides*

3. *Common planning time to set up weekly or bi-weekly meetings to perform the nuts and bolts of matching model choices to lesson plans*

4. *Planning the daily schedule around needs of the grade level and teacher assignments. For example, if a teacher works with more than one teacher on a grade level or multiple grade levels, the time for teaching the units of study must not be at the same time of day.*

5. *Setting a weekly or bi-weekly meeting time for teachers to plan with their co-teaching partner(s)*

6. *Teach for a while to settle in*

7. *Re-evaluate whenever necessary*

We all work to be active communicators. We listen. We think about the other's perspective. We take time to appreciate each other. We recognize that we won't agree all the time on everything. We are ok with not being the "teacher in charge" all the time. We respect each other's expertise. We don't take each other for granted or expect that every day our lessons will be perfect or that we will always be having a great day. We are flexible and are constantly working on our collaboration. In education, as in life, nothing stays the same. But we can and do use that to our advantage.

The circumstances surrounding reflection for teachers are generally rooted in their class instruction. Most teachers we have coached or mentored or who have participated in our workshops have shared with us that they either do regularly reflect on both the challenges and successes tied to the co-teaching practice or wish they had more time to do so! You can start with one small step—co-teacher reflections may range from regular, brief informal exchanges to professional dialogues driven by protocols to high-functioning inquiry communities. Read on to find a starting point for reflection or effective strategies to enhance your reflective practice. As Schmoker (2011) poignantly reminds us, "a good idea poorly implemented is a bad idea" (p. 88). Careful attention and reflection on the quality of the implementation of the integrated co-teaching approach is imperative.

THE CIRCULAR PATH TO FORMING AN INQUIRY COMMUNITY

For reflection to happen and become internalized, teachers must be engaged in it. Although this idea may sound obvious, not all people contemplate their actions. Some of us are by nature more reflective; driving home from school, we replay the events that took place, the interactions we had with others, and the choices we made during the day. Reflection is often a solitary act, yet it should be practiced in community (Farrell, 2016). However, for reflection to be transferred into a collaborative context, teachers need the purpose, time, and space to do it—"moving out from the isolation of the classroom to the shelter of inquiry communities that provided safe spaces for real dialogue, the sharing of stories, relationships with colleagues" (Waff, 2009, pp. 70–71). The place and time for reflection and inquiry must be integral to co-teachers' daily or weekly schedule so it becomes the norm rather than the exception to the rule.

Among so many others, Goodlad, Mantle-Bromley, and Goodlad (2004) have recommended teachers engage in a process of inquiry that consists of four cyclical, ongoing steps—(1) dialogue, (2) problem solving and decision making, (3) action, and (4) evaluation focused on a shared purpose. They have claimed that such collaborative inquiry is "the single-most important vehicle for school renewal" (p. 110). This collaborative inquiry may also be a highly relevant and successful approach on a smaller scale, such as for co-teaching partners to engage in on a regular basis. Thus, for collaborative reflection purposes, we have adapted Goodlad's et al. four-step framework and, in the remainder of this chapter, we are suggesting ways to apply it to co-teaching partnerships as follows:

1. **Dialogue**: Regularly engage in professional dialogue about the complex instructional issues and English learners' (ELs') academic and linguistic development and performance that co-teachers encounter daily.

2. **Problem solving and decision making**: Collectively decide what collaborative and instructional practices co-teachers wish to initiate, develop, continue, or discontinue.

3. **Action**: Based on the collaborative decisions, actively engage in initiating, developing, continuing, or discontinuing certain instructional and collaborative practices.

4. **Evaluation**: Regularly collect, analyze, and reflect on both informal and formal data about both teaching practices and EL student learning.

The ultimate goal of engaging in a reflective process like this one is to create and share an inquiry stance. "This stance becomes a professional positioning, where questioning one's own practice becomes part of an educator's work and eventually part of the district culture" (Fichtman Dana, Thomas, & Boynton, 2011, p. 11). It is not a linear, straightforward process; instead, it is one in which the steps may occur in a different order if needed, or in which participating teachers engage in continuously, in a recurring fashion. To achieve a *co-teaching inquiry stance*, let's examine how you can engage in each of the four key steps outlined above with your co-teachers and how to create a continuous reflective cycle—what tools and protocols you may use to participate in professional dialogues, problem solving and decision making, action planning, and reflecting on and evaluating the success and effectiveness of your collaboration and co-teaching.

PROFESSIONAL DIALOGUES

What is there to talk about? The better question may be phrased as what is there *not* to talk about? As co-teachers, you will be talking a lot about your students, both ELs and non-ELs, the curriculum and instructional methodologies you will be choosing to address their needs, the context in which the two of you operate including the logistics of your partnership—shared philosophy of education, scheduled planning time, the classroom space, scheduling, access to key instructional resources, student monitoring, data collection and decision-making protocols, and so on—as well as various aspects of your partnership outside of these main categories—students, curriculum and instruction, co-teaching context, and personal practice (see Figure 11.1).

While many of these reflective conversations will be informal and unplanned, and even a few minutes of engaging in them will yield a lot of information, we suggest some guiding questions for each of the following:

Figure 11.1 Professional Dialogues

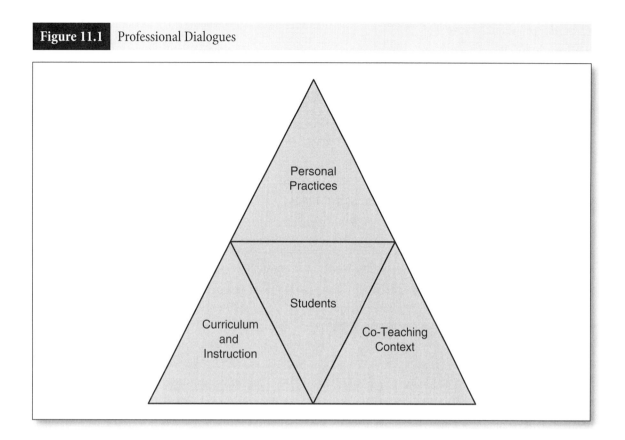

Students

- What do we know about each of our students?
- What goals have we set for them and with them?
- What do our students know and do well already?
- Are they learning what we are teaching, and what are we missing?
- Where are they today in their learning, and where do they need to be tomorrow, next week, next marking period, next year?
- What background knowledge do we need to know about our students to best support their learning?

Curriculum and Instruction

- What works and what needs adjustment in terms of the curriculum we are using?
- How effective is the instruction we are delivering?
- What aspects of our teaching are we going to continue?
- What aspects of the teaching-learning process are going to have to change?
- How might we adjust the pacing of the curriculum to better meet students' needs?
- What do students *need to know* and what information is *nice to know*?

Co-Teaching Context

- What works and what needs adjustment in the way we configure our class for instruction?
- How can we enhance the classroom environment for fully integrating ELs yet effectively differentiating for all students?
- What works and what needs adjustment regarding our time management?
- Which grouping strategies—heterogeneous or homogeneous—work best with particular students?
- How can we better establish an equitable co-teaching partnership?
- How can we better create a class environment that is equitable for all students?

Personal Context

- What works and what needs adjustment in our collaborative work prior, during, and after each lesson?
- What more do we hope to get from our co-teaching partnership?
- How do we define success for ourselves and for our students? What else do we have to do to achieve it?

Jon Nordmeyer, English language development specialist and international programs director of the World-Class Instructional Design and Assessment (WIDA) Consortium, uses a list of questions and conversation prompts to facilitate a professional dialogue between co-teachers as they reflect on their impact on student learning and work on enhancing their effectiveness during co-teaching. See Figure 11.2 for Jon's questions.

Protocols for Professional Dialogues

At times, collaborative conversations and reflections may turn into difficult dialogues. For this reason, we suggest co-teachers consider specific protocols for their conversations to focus more

Figure 11.2 Questions to Support Professional Dialogue

Could you please share some feedback as a co-teacher specifically about . . .

1) Impact on student learning:
   - Do you think our co-teaching is serving students in the class we share? If so, how?

2) Impact on teacher learning:
   - What has been most challenging?
   - What has been most rewarding?
   - What might be a new professional learning goal for our collaboration?

3) Any other feedback—observations, suggestions, or requests?
   - Please continue . . .
   - Please consider . . .

Developed by Jon Nordmeyer, used with permission.

directly on teaching practice and partnership. In our earlier work, we suggested the 2+2 formula for an immediate yet brief reflective dialogue (Honigsfeld & Dove, 2010). After each co-taught lesson, teachers offer each other two compliments and two suggestions that specifically address the needs of the students and identify aspects of planning, instructional delivery, assessments, and/or resources and materials. Using this protocol as part of your daily practice can constructively move the collaborative relationship to the next level. See how the following conversation sentence starters would be helpful to maintain a positive dialogue in the beginning of a co-teaching partnership:

Compliments

- "I appreciate your willingness to . . ."
- "I appreciated when you . . ."
- "The students really benefitted from . . ."
- "This is not my strength—can you teach me how to . . .?"
- "I noticed how engaged the students were when . . ."
- "I appreciate your expertise in . . . . I am going to try that!"

Suggestions

- "The students need our help to . . ."
- "Do you think the kids might get distracted if . . .?"
- "Based on this experience, the students would benefit if next time we planned . . ."
- "I think . . . had a hard time with this concept. Next time, we might consider . . ."

The professional dialogues co-teachers engage in may be even more structured. The teaching preference tool (Figure 11.3) developed by language development coaches and field tested by K–8 co-teachers in the Kildeer Countryside School District 96, Illinois, can help facilitate some important conversations both at the onset of a new partnership and periodically as the co-teachers begin to work together.

For co-teachers to capitalize on each other's talent and amplify their impact on students, reflection and honest conversations about their professional relationship, instructional practice, and impact on student learning are key. Try the following reflective questions based on the five disciplines of Multipliers, which Wiseman, Allen, and Foster (2013) describe as leaders bringing the best out of others:

- Do we nurture each other's talents and utilize them to benefit all our students?
- Do we create an environment with a high level of instructional intensity that requires our best thinking and work as well as those of our students?
- Do we actively seek opportunities that cause us to stretch beyond our comfort zones?
- Do we make sound decisions by welcoming differences of opinion and engaging in decision-making protocols?
- Do we give each other ownership for student progress and celebrate our success as co-teachers?

Figure 11.3	Co-Teaching: Preferences and Teaching Personalities

Purpose: *This document is a tool to help begin the discussion on each of the co-teachers' preferences and teaching personalities. The "A" and "B" options are opposites on a spectrum of personality/ preference. Therefore, most teachers will fall somewhere in the spectrum between "A" and "B," but try to select one choice. The purpose of this tool is to start a conversation, help each teacher value the unique contributions of their co-teacher, and to develop a relationship based on trust and reciprocal understanding.*

	Content Teacher	Co-teacher	I prefer to . . .	
			A	**B**
Planning	_____ _____ _____ _____ _____ _____	_____ _____ _____ _____ _____ _____	• Plan with very **specific steps** • **Create** materials together • Plan **well ahead** • Focus on **specific lessons** • Divide and conquer **independently** • Pay attention to the **details of the lesson**	• Plan with more **general ideas** • **Brainstorm** ideas together • Plan **closer to the time** of instruction • Focus on the **whole unit** • Create **everything together** • See the big picture and **overarching direction the lesson is going**
Teaching	_____ _____ _____	_____ _____ _____	• Establish **specific roles** prior to the lesson • Have "**interruptions**" during the lesson • **Stick to the plan**	• Have **flexible roles** during the lesson • Have **no interruptions** • **Adjust as necessary**
Management	_____ _____ _____	_____ _____ _____	• Have a **quiet classroom** • **Respond immediately** to off-task behavior • Use a **whole-class** visible behavior system (class chart)	• Have **some productive noise;** noise is not a problem • Stop the behavior and **discuss it later** • Use an **individual** behavior system for each student
Reflection	_____ _____ _____ _____	_____ _____ _____ _____	• Discuss lessons **ASAP** • Focus on **what to fix/ change** • Have **data-driven** conversations • Conclude reflections with **specific next steps or plans of actions**	• Take notes and **discuss later** • Emphasize **positives for** the future • Focus on **student engagement** • Conclude reflections with **overall takeaways**

Created and Field Tested by Todd Halstead and Ryan Zak, Kildeer Countryside School District 96, IL, used with permission.

Professional dialogues that center around big questions such as these pave the way to creating a context for problem solving, decision making, action planning, and many other collaborative processes necessary to support co-teaching.

PROBLEM SOLVING AND DECISION MAKING

Causton and Theoharis (2014) poignantly describe problem solving as a five-step process moving the participants from identifying the problem to finding and testing solutions. They suggest that each step center around seeking answers to some critical questions. The problems co-teachers face may be isolated incidents or issues of a more complex nature, ranging from technical difficulties of scheduling co-planning time or managing the shared classroom space to pedagogical challenges such as using new technology, or even sociocultural in nature such as preventing in-class student self-segregation of ELs speaking a shared home language. While the problems and challenges may be unique, some will be resolved through a routine conversation or a few e-mail exchanges; others will require a more structured approach. The Problem Solving Protocol in Table 11.1 offers guidance on how to approach a problem and what steps to take to successfully resolve it.

Table 11.1 Problem-Solving Protocol

From Problems to Solutions	The Search	The Questions
Problem Exploration	Fact finding	*What is the challenge or problem we co-teachers face? Who? What? When? Where? How?* *What is true and not true about this problem?*
	Problem finding	*How can we look at this challenge in a new way? Can we finish the sentence: In what ways might we . . . ? How can we clarify the problem for ourselves by taking a new angle or perspective?*
Idea Generation	Idea finding	*Can we generate as many ideas as possible without coming to a conclusion yet?*
Preparation for Action	Solution finding	*Can we compare the ideas we generated? How will we know whether our solution will work or not? What will be the criteria for success?*
	Action finding	*What is our step-by-step plan of action?*

Adapted from Causton and Theoharis (2014), pp. 50 & 138.

One clear sign of a strong partnership is the deep-rooted commitment to joint decision making. This undertaking is no small feat, considering that according to some frequently cited figures, during each 40- to 45-minute class period teachers typically make close to 30 decisions and engage in many more interactions when they teach alone. In Jackson's (1990) words:

In the small but crowded world of the classroom, events come and go with astonishing rapidity. There is evidence, as we have seen, to show that the elementary school teacher typically engages in 200 or 300 interpersonal interchanges every hour of her working day. Moreover, although that number may remain fairly stable from hour to hour, the content and sequence of those interchanges cannot be predicted or preplanned with any exactitude. In short . . . the structure underlying these kaleidoscopic events is not easily discerned, nor is it, except superficially, under the control of the teacher. (p. 149)

If so many instructional decisions and acts happen spontaneously, what can co-teachers do to ensure that important decisions are made in sync with each other? How do they handle situations when decisions are hard to make collaboratively? We invite you to review Table 11.2 for contemporary approaches to learning and classroom instruction adapted from Slavich and Zimbardo (2012) and discuss what these instructional choices represent for your co-teaching partnership, how they fit into your teaching philosophy, and how these approaches make their way into your co-taught classroom. Use this summary chart to discuss how working with ELs is aligned (or not) to teaching practices typically recommended for general education learners. Alternately, with your co-teacher, take some time to examine Table 11.2, which includes research-informed best practices for ELs also adaptable for the co-taught classroom.

Table 11.2 Contemporary Approaches to Learning and Classroom Instruction

Approach	Brief description	Example activities
Active learning	Co-teachers actively engage students in the learning process by involving them in guided activities that require students to articulate and communicate ideas, explore complex concepts, and incorporate higher-order thinking skills such as analysis, synthesis, and evaluation	One-minute paper or quick write Debating topics Role playing Daily journal Think-pair-share Analyzing/reacting to videos Collaborative group learning Whole-class discussion
Student-centered learning	Co-teachers focus on students' needs, abilities, interests, and learning styles by nurturing them to become self-directed, independent learners and giving them autonomy and control over choice of subject matter, learning methods, and pace of study, which in turn increases students' responsibility for learning and helps them develop skills to actively choose and manage their educational goals	Self-initiated assignments Self-paced learning via desktop or mobile apps or low-tech, teacher-created booklets Self-directed learning kits Action research projects Learning logs Dialogue/script writing Investigations and fieldwork Co-creating curriculum

Approach	Brief description	Example activities
Collaborative learning	Co-teachers design learning tasks that enable students to tackle problems and questions with peers; through such collaborative experiences, students develop new communicative skills and learn new problem-solving strategies as they expand their understanding of language and concepts	Jigsaw classroom Group roundtables Paired annotations Send-a-problem Numbered heads together Three-step interview Placemat activity Tea Party
Experiential learning	Co-teachers promote learning by having students directly engage in, and reflect on, personal experiences leading to increased knowledge, skill development, and extended opportunities for language use	Conducting interviews Experiments Inquiry-guided teams Participating in simulations Game-based learning Taking field trips Creative activities Building a model
Problem-based learning	Co-teachers facilitate learning by having students tackle complex, multifaceted problems in small groups while providing scaffolding, modeling experiences, and opportunities for self-directed learning, which enhances students' content knowledge and increases their academic language use, self-efficacy, problem-solving skills, collaboration skills, and self-directed learning skills	Small-group teams Clarifying concepts and terms Developing and testing hypotheses Studying privately Synthesizing and reporting new information

Adapted from Slavich, G. M., & Zimbardo, P. G. (2012). Transformational teaching: Theoretical underpinnings, basic principles, and core methods. *Educational Psychology Review, 24*, 569–608.

The Needs of English Learners in the Co-Taught Class

Discussions about best practices for English learners could fill a small library. Yet combining those practices—instructional strategies and techniques to build language and literacy competencies in English—with the teaching of content-specific material in the co-taught class prove to be challenging for many co-teachers. Identifying recommendations for instruction that focus on language-learning principles is one way to focus reflective conversations. In Table 11.3, we offer an adapted list of key practices based on the Understanding Language Framework (Stanford University, 2013) also cited in the *English Learner Toolkit* (U.S. Department of Education, 2015a) paired with reflection questions.

Table 11.3	Understanding Language Principles Applied to Co-Teaching

Recommendations	Reflection Questions Applied to Co-Teaching
Provide English learners with opportunities to develop both language and content in concert.	• Do we integrate content and language development? • Do we provide ELs with opportunities to engage in learning practices unique to our discipline? • Do we support ELs in building conceptual understanding as well as language competence?
Capitalize on English learners' prior knowledge, home language, and cultural resources and backgrounds.	• Do we value and build upon our ELs' languages, cultural assets, and prior knowledge?
Implement rigorous, grade-appropriate, standards-based lessons for English learners by differentiating instruction.	• Is our co-taught instruction aligned to grade-appropriate standards? Is our co-taught instruction rigorous in content, process, and product? • Do we prepare and provide appropriate scaffolds?
Base entry and trajectory points for the instruction of English learners according to their levels of English proficiency level(s) and previous schooling.	• Do we actively monitor and build upon ELs' English proficiency levels? • Do we activate and extend ELs' prior schooling experiences?
Advance the self-directed learning of English learners by supporting their ability to develop their language and literacy skills in various instructional settings.	• Do we equip ELs with language and literacy learning strategies? • Do we ensure that ELs comprehend our instruction? • Do we ensure that ELs use language in a variety of ways and settings?
Design formative and summative assessments to accurately measure the academic and language development of English learners.	• Do we use appropriate diagnostic, formative, and summative assessment tools? • Do we adequately measure ELs' content attainment and participation in discipline-specific activities? • Do we adequately measure ELs' academic language and literacy competence?

A Decision-Making Protocol

As co-teachers, you might have a challenging situation to face such as implementing a new co-teaching initiative, adapting new curriculum, restructuring the co-teaching program for your school or district, and so on. When important decisions have to be made, consider these four distinct steps as a guide to collaborative solutions:

1. **Brainstorming**

    Begin by generating an exhaustive list of ideas. All suggestions are welcome.

2. **Discussion**

    Recognize that the list you have just brainstormed is only the first step. Engage in a collaborative conversation by analyzing the pros and cons of each item on your list.

3. **Synthesis**

    Even if there seems to be a quick final decision, take your time to synthesize the outcome of your discussion.

4. **Consensus**

    Come to an agreement regarding the topic at hand. Remember to agree that although the final decision is going to be implemented and monitored, it can be revised at any time and a new discussion can be initiated.

Wagner et al. (2006) has recognized that there are at least two kinds of challenges we face in the educational context.

- Technical challenge is one for which a solution is already known—the knowledge and capacity exist to solve the problem. . . .
- An "adaptive" challenge, on the other hand, is one for which the necessary knowledge to solve the problem does not yet exist. It requires creating the knowledge and the tools to solve the problem in the act of working on it. (p. 10)

New and experienced co-teachers alike will face both technical and adaptive challenges. Some answers may be found in books like this one; others will require creative engagement and new knowledge building in the classroom or after a lesson through deliberate reflection and careful analysis of possible solutions.

Making coordinated in-class decisions and aligning classroom interactions with students and each other to predetermined goals require time for discussions, co-planning, and ample opportunities for negotiating some nuances prior to joint delivery of instruction. By embracing a reflective framework for joint decision making, co-teachers do not need to set aside a specific time for reflection and review; it is already built in to what they automatically or routinely do to accomplish appropriate and congruent lessons for their students. For this reason, we invite you to try the GROW model for practicing collective decision making (see Figure 11.4 for the steps to take).

| **Figure 11.4** | How to Grow Through a Reflective Practice |

G- R- O- W

Goal: Identify a shared goal. (What do you need to make a decision about?)

Reality: Examine your current reality. (Why is this change and new decision needed?)

Options and Obstacles: First, explore the obstacles to overcome to be successful, and then examine the options to take. (What are the challenges that we are facing in our collaboration and co-teaching right now? What are our options to be proactive and respond to them?)

Way Forward (5Ws+H): Establish next steps and determine action steps. (Who is going to do what, where, when, why, and how?)

Adapted from https://www.mindtools.com/pages/article/newLDR_89.htm

TAKING ACTION BASED ON REFLECTIONS

In reference to the collaborative problem-solving and decision-making conversations as well as the data gathered from your ongoing reflective practice, the next step is to actively engage in initiating, developing, continuing, or discontinuing certain practices. Hoy, Tarter, and Woolfolk Hoy (2006) have demonstrated that school faculty can come together in a collective, positive academic environment when they are committed to three properties:

- School faculty believes it can teach even the most difficult students—collective efficacy;
- School faculty trusts students and parents—faculty trust; and
- School faculty emphasizes academics—academic emphasis.

On a smaller scale, co-teachers form a partnership and come together to create a positive, collaborative academic learning environment for all. Hoy and his colleagues' (2006) research has suggested that academic optimism is a powerful force behind student achievement. Applying this research to a collaborative approach to serving ELs and building on our own extensive fieldwork with co-teachers, we infer that there are several key factors that contribute to the success of teaching partnerships that embrace academic optimism:

1. Co-teachers believe that they can teach all ELs, including new arrivals, students with limited or interrupted formal education, students who have been traumatized by their immigrant experiences or other out-of-school events, who seem unmotivated and ready to drop out of school, and so on, thus demonstrating collective efficacy.

2. Co-teachers develop a deep-rooted trust between and among themselves as well as among their students and the families they serve.

3. Co-teachers emphasize academic learning, where language and literacy development for ELs arc intertwined with ongoing challenging content instruction, and language learning is not merely a daily activity.

As you embark or continue to engage in co-teaching with your partner, periodically reflect on the degree to which these three factors are embedded in your practice and how you may enhance them for further improvement.

The academic optimism championed by Hoy et al. (2006) is well aligned to the five principles of deliberate optimism introduced by Silver, Berckemeyer, and Baenen (2015; see Figure 11.5). These five principles may serve as the foundation for a reflection tool for co-teachers to jointly implement (see Figure 11.6).

Optimism might be an innate trait you and your co-teacher already have. Or it might be one that can be cultivated by reformulating the way we think—changing our mindset and adopting the notion that people's abilities can be developed through strategizing, mentorship, and just plain hard work (Dweck, 2006). To nurture your own and your co-teacher's *deliberate optimism,* be proactive about this type of disposition toward co-teaching and try the reflection activity in Figure 11.6.

| Figure 11.5 | Five Principles of Deliberate Optimism |

1. Before acting or *reacting,* **gather as much information** from as many varied sources as possible.
2. **Determine what is beyond your control** and strategize how to minimize its impact on your life.
3. **Establish what you can control** and seek tools and strategies to help you maximize your power.
4. Actively **do something positive** toward your goal.
5. **Take ownership** of your plan and acknowledge responsibility for your choices.

Source: Silver et al., 2015, p. 38.

Effective Action Planning

Based on all the information you gather through your reflections, important decisions and next steps are determined. For effective action planning, many educators use the SMART acronym (specific, measurable, achievable, realistic, time-based; see more at https://www.projectsmart.co.uk/smart-goals.php). While many definitions and explanations of SMART goals are available, the most popular and well-known definition of the acronym is presented first, with other possible interpretations in parentheses:

S—Specific (Significant, Strategic)

M—Measurable (Meaningful, Motivating)

A—Achievable (Action Oriented, Ambitious)

R—Realistic (Rewarding, Results oriented)

T—Time-based (Tangible, Timely)

Adapted to co-teaching, the original acronym may be interpreted as follows:

- **S**pecific = Who will do what, when, where, and why?
- **M**easurable = How do we define criteria for our success and our students' success?
- **A**ttainable = What do we need to be successful with co-teaching?
- **R**ealistic = Are our goals for successful co-teaching too high, too low, or just right?
- **T**ime-based = What is our timeline to meet our goals? Do our goals have a sense of urgency?

Examples From the Field

Action planning is an effective joint task co-teachers can engage in both individually at first and then in collaboration with each other at the end of a particular time period, such as the end of semester or end of the school year. As a culminating activity of sustained professional development

Figure 11.6 Co-Teacher Reflections Based on the Principles of Deliberate Optimism

1. What is the challenge we are facing? Let's explain fully the situation we have and how we each feel about what is happening.

2. What steps are we taking to gather as much information as possible about our situation?

3. What factors are beyond our control at this time? Let's explore how we can minimize their impact on our present situation.

4. What factors could we control that would potentially make a positive impact on our situation?

5. Let's describe the things we are willing to do at this time to improve our situation. Let's be specific.

6. What steps could we take in the future? Let's reflect on why we are choosing not to control some of the variables that we could.

7. What will be our first step toward improving the situation? When will we do it? Estimate the time it will take us to put our plan into action.

8. When will we review our progress toward our goal? What indicators will we look for in order to know if we are successful or not?

Adapted from Silver et al., 2015.

| Figure 11.7 | Action Planning and Personal Reflection |

Action	Personal Reflection
STOP Things I am currently doing that I will consider STOPPING next year.	• Listening passively to other teachers' plans without offering mine also. • Worrying that other teachers won't want my ideas because I'm not an expert in their grade-level content areas. • Adhering to the collaboration schedule in cases where it doesn't make sense to stick to it. I want to reconsider how it might be possible to meet more regularly with classroom teachers, special education (SpEd) teachers, and the speech therapist, and less with grade-level or special-area teachers if we do not have students in common.
START Things I am considering STARTING next year.	• Helping set up a school collaboration book room (Collaboration Corner) with materials and resources for teaching ELs. • Collaborating regularly with SpEd teachers regarding our shared students. EL and SpEd currently only collaborate on the fly, in IEP meetings, annual reviews, and problem-solving meetings but not during the midday collaboration. I want to change that and find a time in the midday collaboration that we can meet regularly and with a structure that focuses on students' goals and content planning. • Sharing procedures or developing procedures together for co-taught classes. • Sharing student work with classroom teachers, SpEd teachers, and my EL resource partner. • Trying out all seven models of co-teaching with my EL resource partner, SpEd, speech, or anyone else that I can! • Planning roles for both teachers in a co-teaching arrangement. • Trying some co-taught lessons with the social worker, including co-planning.
CONTINUE Things I am considering CONTINUING next year.	• Collaborating with and hopefully co-teaching with my EL resource partner. • Finding and sharing resources for use with ELs or with all students. • Sharing assessment data I have. • Asking Greg, Juan, and Katie for time to plan units with classroom, SpEd, and EL resource teachers in my building and across the district. • Planning content and language objectives for lessons.

Developed by Lena Wiese; used with permission

at Woodridge School District 68, Illinois, under the leadership of Violeta Gamez, co-teaching teams worked on different types of action planning at the completion of their 10-week book study (Honigsfeld & Dove, 2010). See Figure 11.7 for a Stop, Start, and Keep Doing action planning template completed by Lena Wiese and the Action Research Project outlined by Elizabeth Epley, Daniel Wolf, and Nicole Counihan with data collection steps in Figure 11.8.

Figure 11.8	Action Plan

Background on Issue:	• There seems to be a lack of knowledge regarding co-teaching and how to effectively utilize the EL resource teacher's expertise.
Research Questions:	• How can we maximize teachers' strengths and abilities to improve student achievement?
Participants:	• EL resource teacher • Classroom teachers • Director of English learners
Data Sources:	• Formative Assessment • Teacher Observation
Data Collection Procedures:	• Teacher Surveys • Meet with EL teacher to discuss ACCESS scores as well as other data they have collected
Data Analysis:	Possibilities: • Pre/Post Tests • STAR Test
Anticipated Outcomes:	• English language learners will reach higher success in the classroom where co-teaching is implemented.
Action Plan:	• Action Step #1: The EL director will meet with the EL teachers to discuss the different co-teaching models. • Action Step #2: The team will put together items to effectively convey the different co-teaching models to general education classroom teachers. • Action Step #3: During the first month of midday collaboration, EL teachers will share the co-teaching models with teachers. • Action Step #4: The EL teachers meet with classroom teachers that have the EL cluster group. After discussing specific students (ACCESS, goals, etc.), specific lessons will be planned with co-teaching models embedded. • Action Step #5: After the lesson is taught, teachers will complete the reflection sheet found on page 157 of *Collaboration and Co-teaching* (Honigsfeld & Dove, 2010). • Action Step #6: Teachers will meet to discuss the reflection sheet and will fine tune, adjust, reevaluate strategy(ies) for the next planned lesson. • Action #7: Repeat.

Developed by Elizabeth Epley, Daniel Wolf, and Nicole Counihan; used with permission

REFLECTION AND EVALUATION

As co-teachers committed to the entire collaborative instructional cycle, you will regularly collect and analyze both informal and formal data about both your teaching practices and your students' progress (see Chapter 10 on co-assessing student progress and outcomes in content and language development). Colton, Langer, and Goff (2016) suggest "a major consequence of collaborative inquiry is collective efficacy—a sense that teachers can overcome learning challenges when they rely on one another's expertise" (p. 21). Jointly examining student data and engaging in shared reflections contribute to building such collective efficacy.

When it comes to deciding what types of reflective tools to use, there is no shortage of choices. In a comprehensive research paper, Farrell (2016) has summarized the types of procedures and tools teachers decide upon to facilitate reflection. He found that discussion, including more structured discussion groups and postobservation conferences, were the most common pathway to reflection. Other tools and practices include journaling, self and peer classroom observations, video analysis, narratives, action research, lesson study, and critical friend groups. Yet some other teachers "make use of some kind of combination of online formats for reflection such as blogs, podcasts, chats, and forum discussions" (p. 237).

We have adapted as well as designed several reflection, observation, and coaching tools that may be used both by the co-teachers who wish to reflect on their progress as partners and coaches or supervisors who work on documenting growth. These tools may be adapted—either simplified or expanded—as needed. The following examples will demonstrate how co-teaching teams have made sense of and developed ownership of these tools.

When reflecting on the co-teaching practice, coaching, or observing co-teachers, consider the following short list of look-fors that may serve as a baseline:

- **Parity:** Do both teachers participate equitably in the lesson (not equally)?
- **Integration of language skills:** Do both teachers provide instruction and support for content and language development?
- **Opportunities to talk:** Does the smaller student-teacher ratio lead to higher levels of student-to-student interaction and more student talk for academic purposes?
- **Engagement:** Do both teachers provide students with meaningful, challenging learning activities that make engagement visible?
- **Formative assessment use:** Do the co-teachers collect and respond to formative assessment data to offer interventions as needed and, as a result, maximize the benefits of co-teaching?
- **Self-Assessment/Partnership Assessment:** Self-assessment and reflection practices as well as tools to apply may be differentiated based on the implementation stage of the co-teachers. Setting realistic goals and monitoring and reflecting on implementation in the early stages of a co-teaching partnership (years 1–2) may be best supported through carefully tailored questions or prompts that establish the foundations for success. Later stage implementation is often characterized by most initial challenges being resolved, so co-teachers often look to moving from *good to great* (Collins, 2001). Figures 11.9 and 11.10 are examples of such differentiated tools for co-teachers.

Reflecting on Instructional Practices

The most frequently asked questions we receive are about serving English learners through integrated instruction in the co-taught class. Teachers in general want to know *how* they can best gauge the delivery of lessons in co-taught classes that target the learning needs of English learners. ELD/ELL teachers are often concerned whether or not they are adequately building the English language proficiency of ELs. Grade-level and content teachers want to know if they are providing sufficient academic rigor in a lesson along with scaffolding, modifications, and accommodations. Based on our fieldwork and research on co-teaching for ELs, we have developed DELIVER—an

| Figure 11.9 | A Co-Teaching Self-Assessment Checklist During Early Implementation |

Yes	No	In Our Co-Teaching Partnership
		We decide which co-teaching model we are going to use in a lesson based on the benefits to the students.
		We share ideas, information, and materials.
		We identify each other's resources and talents.
		We share responsibility for deciding what to teach.
		We agree on the curriculum standards and language development standards that will be addressed in a lesson.
		We share responsibility for deciding how to teach.
		We share responsibility for deciding who teaches what in each lesson.
		We identify student strengths and needs.
		We share responsibility for differentiating instruction.
		We share responsibility for how student learning is assessed.
		We agree on discipline procedures and carry them out jointly.
		We have regularly scheduled times to meet and discuss our work as co-teachers.
		We explain the benefits of co-teaching to the students and their families.
		We model collaboration and teamwork for our students.
		We are both viewed by our students as their teachers.
		We can use a variety of co-teaching models.
		We communicate our need for logistical support and resources to our administrators.

Adapted from Villa, R. A., Thousand J. S., & Nevin, A. I. (2008). *A guide to co-teaching: Practical tips for facilitating student learning.* Thousand Oaks, CA: Corwin. (pp. 193–94).

acronym that encompasses the seven most important aspects of a co-taught class for English learners, as follows:

- **Differentiation.** How and to what extent are the content, process, and product of the lesson adjusted for the learning needs of ELs at different levels of English language proficiency? How has curriculum for ELs been developed for integrated instruction in the co-taught class?
- **Engagement of Students.** In what ways do co-taught classes provide ELs with multiple opportunities to speak, write, interact, read, and listen (SWIRL) during one class period?
- **Language and Content Objectives.** By what method are both language and content objectives identified, reviewed with students, and given equal weight during co-taught instruction?
- **Instructional Strategies.** To what degree are tried-and-true strategies to develop the English language proficiency of ELs being incorporated into the co-taught class? What are some of those strategies being used?

- **<u>V</u>aried Co-Teaching Models.** Are co-teaching models being selected to optimally teach ELs in the co-taught class? Do the models incorporated into the lesson provide integration or segregation of ELs?
- **<u>E</u>quity and Parity Established.** Do all students perceive both educators in the room as "real" teachers instead of one as the helper or teacher's aide? How is equity promoted for all students, giving them access to the information, material, and resources they need for positive outcomes?
- **<u>R</u>igor.** To what degree do all lessons for ELs contain rigorous content (text), process (the way students learn), and/or product (the task to be completed and evaluated)?

The primary purpose of the DELIVER tool (see Figure 11.11) is observation of and reflection on co-taught lessons and to determine how the seven dimensions are implemented. Instructional

Figure 11.10 A Co-Teaching Self-Assessment Checklist During Continuous Implementation

Yes	No	In Our Co-Teaching Partnership
		We are aware of what our co-teacher(s) is (are) doing even when we are not directly in one another's presence.
		We are flexible and make changes as needed during a lesson.
		We share responsibility for differentiating instruction.
		We include other people when their expertise or experience is needed.
		We have a fair and equitable grading policy that is clearly communicated to students and parents alike.
		We can show that students are learning the content and developing language when we co-teach.
		We give feedback to one another on what goes on in the classroom.
		We make improvements in our lessons based on what happens in the classroom.
		We communicate our concerns freely and regularly.
		We have a process for resolving our disagreements and use it when faced with problems and conflicts.
		We have fun with the students and with each other when we co-teach.
		We go beyond our regularly scheduled times to meet and discuss our work.
		We use our meeting time productively.
		We can effectively co-teach even when we don't have enough time to plan.
		We showcase the benefits of, and successes with, co-teaching to the students and their families, making co-teaching visible.
		Our modeling of collaboration and teamwork translates into improved collaboration and teamwork for our students.
		We are both viewed by our students as their teachers who jointly support language and content learning.
		We depend on one another to follow through on tasks and responsibilities.
		We seek and enjoy additional training to make our co-teaching better.

(Continued)

| | Figure 11.10 | (Continued) |

Yes	No	In Our Co-Teaching Partnership
		We experiment with new co-teaching models.
		We make recommendations to our administrators based on our needs for logistical support and resources.

Adapted from Villa, R. A., Thousand J. S., & Nevin, A. I. (2008). *A guide to co-teaching: Practical tips for facilitating student learning.* Thousand Oaks, CA: Corwin. (pp. 193–94).

coaches, administrators, grade and content peers, or co-teaching partners can use it to examine and reflect on best practices for ELs in the co-taught class.

Another tool we created and named the I-TELL (Integrated Teaching for English Language Learners) Observation Tool is designed to aid administrators, instructional leaders, coaches, and peer visitors in identifying features of successful co-teaching practices for the sake of ELs. The tool in Figure 11.12 allows for direct collection of evidence on each of the collaborative indicators by a third party, thus offering objective data on the progress the co-teaching team is making. Alternately, I-TELL may serve as a self-assessment, reflection, and goal-setting tool that allows co-teachers to take a critical look at all key dimensions of a collaborative instructional cycle.

Both the DELIVER and I-TELL tools are easily adaptable: you and your teaching partner(s) or grade-level and content instructional teams might decide to reduce the dimensions of the tool to fewer elements or do just the opposite—expand the tool to offer more descriptions, more examples, or more specific guidance on how the tool may be used. Under the leadership of Glenda Harrell, members of the EL department of Wake County Public School System, North carolina, have worked extensively to adapt and pilot the I-TELL for co-teaching partners by identifying specific *look*-fors—the characteristics of the planning and instructional delivery of the co-taught class. See the two-part checklist in Figure 11.13 to be used for co-planning reflection and self-assessment of co-teaching, complete with detailed descriptors.

Noticing and Wondering

A simple yet effective reflection process is discussing the co-taught lesson (or any dimension of the collaborative instructional cycle such as co-planning and co-assessment for that matter) regarding what co-teachers have noticed and what they are wondering about in terms of next steps. *Noticings* are observations that do not contain any judgment statements; instead, they are descriptive and student-centered in nature and may focus on a variety of observations. *Wonderings* are questions and possible suggestions for next steps based on the noticings that co-teachers pose for themselves or each other. Noticings and wonderings have been a valuable approach to coaching for us as well as inviting teachers who observe their colleagues through intervisitations. See some paired examples we have overheard during these reflection sessions:

Task performance of select student:

I noticed that Gila was having a hard time with the vocabulary cards we prepared.

I wonder if we can prerecord the key words with some kid-friendly definitions and pictures using QR codes.

Figure 11.11 The DELIVER Tool

DELIVER for Integrated Instruction for English Learners

− **D**ifferentiation

  ☐ Instruction

    ○ Content _____
    ○ Process _____
    ○ Product _____

  ☐ Curriculum (for entering and developing ELs)

− **E**ngagement of Students

  ☐ Speaking _____
  ☐ Writing _____
  ☐ Interacting _____
  ☐ Reading _____
  ☐ Listening _____

− **L**anguage and Content Objectives

  ☐ Both language and content objectives are displayed and reviewed
  ☐ ELs understand what they should know and do

− **I**nstructional Strategies for ELs

  ☐ Visuals _____
  ☐ Realia _____
  ☐ Cognates _____
  ☐ Pacing _____
  ☐ Step-by-step demonstration/modeling
  ☐ Guided practice _____
  ☐ Scaffolding _____
  ☐ Use of home language(s)
  ☐ Other _____

− **V**aried Co-Teaching Models

  ☐ One group: One leads, one teaches on purpose
  ☐ One group: Two teach same content
  ☐ One group: One teaches, one assesses
  ☐ Two groups: Two teach same content
  ☐ Two groups: One preteaches, one teaches alternative content
  ☐ Two groups: One reteaches, one teaches alternative content
  ☐ Multiple groups: Teachers monitor, facilitate, and teach
  ☐ Other _____

− **E**quity and parity established

  ☐ For co-teachers _____
  ☐ For students _____

− **R**igor

  ☐ Content _____
  ☐ Process _____
  ☐ Product _____

Comments: _____
_____
_____

Participation of a group of students:

I noticed that the independent group finished the task much faster than we anticipated.

I am wondering if we could prepare a choice board that includes extension or enrichment tasks, anticipating that some groups will be fasters than others.

Language use:

I noticed our two newcomers are still in their silent periods.

I wonder if we can encourage the use of their native language for some independent tasks since they have strong native language literacy skills and we want to keep them engaged.

Figure 11.12 I-TELL Observation Tool

	No Evidence	Emerging Evidence	Adequate Evidence	Exceptional Evidence	Documentation/Comments
Co-teachers collaboratively plan and develop instructional materials for the lesson					
Equity between the co-teachers is established from the onset of the lesson and maintained throughout the lesson					
Language and content objectives are addressed by both teachers					
Teaching roles and responsibilities are shared					
Two or more co-teaching models are used: Students in one group, teachers work together: • One leads, one teaches on purpose • Two teach same content • One teaches, one assesses Students in two groups, teachers work separately: • Two teach same content • One preteaches, one teaches alternative information • One reteaches, one teaches alternative information Students in multiple groups: • Teachers monitor, facilitate, and teach					

	No Evidence	Emerging Evidence	Adequate Evidence	Exceptional Evidence	Documentation/Comments
Students are grouped purposefully in meaningful ways throughout the lesson					
Co-teachers interact with students and each other in ways that enhance student learning					
Co-teachers are familiar with and respond to the learning needs of all the students					
Co-teachers implement appropriate differentiated strategies for teaching academic language and content					
Co-teachers demonstrate respect and collegiality for each other throughout the lesson					
Co-teachers apply appropriate visual, graphic, linguistic, and interpersonal scaffolds					
Co-teachers establish high levels of engagement and ensure all four language skills are integrated: listening, speaking, reading, and writing					
Co-teachers collaboratively conduct formative and summative assessments					

Adapted from Honigsfeld & Dove (2015a)

Figure 11.13 Co-Planning Reflection Checklist

1. Co-teachers collaboratively plan and develop instructional materials for the lesson.

   - Standards-based co-planning template
   - Co-planning form for classroom and ESL instruction
   - Lesson plans (indicating both teachers' roles)
   - Parallel play checklist
   - Other

2. Language and content objectives are created by both teachers.

   - Objectives are jointly created
   - Objectives are understood by teachers
   - Other

3. Co-teachers plan or create appropriate visual, graphic, and linguistic scaffolds.

   - Realia
   - Pictures
   - Graphic organizers
   - Multimedia (video clips)
   - Sentence frames
   - Question starters
   - Other

4. Co-teachers collaboratively plan formative and summative assessments and use student data to drive instruction.

   - Create content assessments
   - Create language assessments
   - Analyze student performance
   - Utilization of student data to drive instruction
   - Other

5. Co-teachers establish high levels of engagement and ensure that all four language domains are integrated: speaking, writing, reading, listening.

   - 90% student engagement
   - Maximize instructional time
   - Lesson plans indicating SWIRL (speak, write, interact, read, listen)
   - Other

6. Co-teachers implement appropriate differentiated strategies for teaching academic language and content.

   For example:

   - SWIRL
   - Expediting Comprehension for English Language Learners (ExCELL)
   - Marzano's six-step process for building academic vocabulary
   - Blooms taxonomy
   - Other

7. Parity between the co-teachers is established from the onset of the lesson.

   - Teachers' names posted in classroom
   - Teachers maintain classroom management
   - Teachers work with all students
   - Teachers give directions
   - Teachers have space in classroom

- Teachers provide specific, immediate feedback
- Teachers talk during instruction
- Other

8. Teaching roles and responsibilities are shared.

- Leader
- Supporter
- Techie
- Scribe
- Illustrator
- Evaluator
- Other

9. Co-teaching approaches are established.

- One Group: One leads, one teaches on purpose
- One Group: Two teachers teach same content
- One Group: One teaches, one assesses
- Two Groups: Two teachers teach same content
- Two Groups: One teacher preteaches, one teaches alternative information
- Two Groups: One teacher reteaches, one teaches alternative information
- Multiple Groups: Two teachers monitor and teach

10. Students are grouped purposefully in meaningful ways throughout the lesson.

- Seating arrangement
- Classroom setup
- Other

II. Co-Teaching: Delivery

1. Parity between the co-teachers is maintained throughout the lesson.

- Lead/Supporter
- Changing of roles
- Flexibility during lesson

2. Language and content objectives are addressed by **both** teachers.

- Language and content objectives are presented
- Objectives are reviewed at least twice in the lesson
- Other

3. Teaching roles and responsibilities are shared.

- Leader
- Supporter
- Techie
- Scribe
- Illustrator
- Evaluator
- Other

4. A variety of co-teaching approaches are implemented.

- One Group: One leads, one teaches on purpose
- One Group: Two teachers teach same content

(Continued)

(Continued)

• One Group: One teaches, one assesses • Two Groups: Two teachers teach same content • Two Groups: One teacher preteaches, one teaches alternative information • Two Groups: One teacher reteaches, one teaches alternative information • Multiple Groups: Two teachers monitor and teach
5. Students are grouped purposefully in meaningful ways throughout the lesson. • Purposeful grouping • Student talk • Language practice opportunities • Flexible grouping
6. Co-teachers interact with students and each other in ways that enhance student learning. • Questioning • Answering in complete sentences • Other
7. Co-teachers implement appropriate visual, graphic, and linguistic scaffolds. • Realia • Pictures • Graphic organizers • Multimedia (video clips) • Sentence frames • Question starters • Other
8. Co-teachers establish and maintain high levels of engagement throughout the lesson and ensure that all four language domains are integrated: SWRL. • 90% student engagement • Maximize instructional time • Lesson plans indicating SWRL • Other
9. Co-teachers collaboratively implement formative and summative assessments and use student data to drive instruction. • Frequency of assessments • Evidence of data analysis
10. Co-teachers are familiar with and respond to the learning needs of all students. • Specific, immediate feedback • Awareness of in-the-moment needs of students • Other
11. Co-teachers implement appropriate differentiated strategies for teaching academic language and content. • SWIRL • ExCELL • Marzano's six-step process for building academic vocabulary • Blooms taxonomy • Other
12. Co-teachers demonstrate respect and collegiality for each other throughout lesson. • Discourse • Teaching Style • Other

Literacy:

> *I noticed that Kalie and Gurdha were reading fluently, but their comprehension is lacking.*

> *I am wondering if we could use visuals, pictures, diagrams, and some native language support as well as more frequent checks for comprehension.*

Content learning:

> *I noticed that the partially completed note-taking sheet clearly supported our developing students but was too advanced for the emerging-level students.*

> *I wonder if we can introduce tiered activities that are designed for three or even four levels rather than just two as we have been doing so far.*

Co-teaching:

> *I noticed that when I directly go to the ELs during cooperative group work, they simply wait for me to explain the task or support them rather than begin to work with their peers.*

> *I am wondering how we can help them unlearn this pattern and instead rely on their peers more and interact with them first.*

The noticing and wondering protocol may be expanded into a more structured peer observation or co-teaching technique as suggested by the Peer Observation and Coaching Conference Form (Modified Noticing and Wondering) we adapted from Thousand, Villa, and Nevin (2015) in Figure 11.14. The coach or peer observer has two different ways to use noticings and wonderings—first, with what he or she noticed, and second, discussing what the co-teachers themselves have noticed about their own lesson. The wondering dimension of this tool invites co-teachers to think about what they would do differently next time and also to identify an action plan at the closure of the session.

**VIDEO 11.1:
Reflection:
Improving
Collaborative
Practice**

http://resources
.corwin.com/
CoTeachingforELs

INSPIRATION FROM THE FIELD

Read what colleagues—ELD/ELL and classroom teachers as well as building and district administrators—shared with us from around the United States and see how they reflect or add to your own experiences.

First, consider the reflections written by Rebekah Farrell, science teacher, and Lauren Cirulli, English as a new language teacher (the equivalent of ELD/ELL), who have been co-teaching a sheltered science class consisting of only English learners for the past two years in one of the most culturally diverse high schools in central New York. Notice how intentional their work is with translanguaging (García & Li, 2014) and culturally and linguistically responsive instructional strategies (Gay, 2000; Moll, Amanti, Neff, & Gonzalez, 1992) in their co-taught science courses and beyond. The following is their reflection.

> *During our first year of co-teaching, we collaborated with the intention of looping with our English language learners (ELLs) from a survey science course to a Regents-level biology course the following*

Figure 11.14 Peer Observation and Coaching Conference Form (Modified Noticing and Wondering)

Peer Observation or Coaching Conference Form (Modified Noticing and Wondering)

Date:	Time:	Length of time co-teaching:
What went well (noticings identified by the co-teachers)	What to do differently (wonderings identified by the co-teachers)	Teacher-identified models used: _____ _____ _____ Observer-identified models used: _____ _____
		Planning Time Length _____ Frequency _____
Observer/coach noticings:	Observer/coach wonderings:	
Observer/coach suggestions:	Co-teacher(s)-identified next steps/"takeaways":	

Adapted from Thousand, Villa, and Nevin (2015)

year. Our class community was comprised of thirty ELLs representing more than five countries and eight languages. These students brought a rich array of life and learning experiences to the classroom, but their multitude of languages and various degrees of English language proficiency initially presented challenges with regard to teaching academic language and literacy development. Despite these challenges, we have found success in teaching our ELLs through a co-taught model that has worked in our classroom.

A frequent challenge with co-teaching success is a lack of time designated for common planning. Although we have encountered this obstacle as well, we have developed measures that have allowed us to be flexible within the schedule and creatively adapt to planning through e-mails, text messages, and quick "touch base" conversations. Although this is not ideal, we have designed a way to most efficiently utilize our schedules to make the system work for us, and most important, our students. Regardless of how we plan, our goal is to be intentional with our time and discuss culturally responsive opportunities for differentiation and translanguaging, a strategy wherein students can utilize their entire linguistic repertoire. This teaching technique was something that Lauren had been previously trained on, and Rebekah was eager to incorporate into the science lesson plans. Lesson plans are purposefully written to allow for not only various modalities of language but to also include multiple learning styles. In addition to thoughtful planning, we facilitate our instructional goals through the use of interactive word walls, prefix/suffix tiles, multimedia tools, bilingual glossaries/dictionaries, and personal translating devices. Students are regularly encouraged to work with their "like-language" partners in order to facilitate their acquisition of the content. During these conversations, students are also encouraged to use the literacy- and content-rich resources posted throughout every available square inch of the classroom.

Our instructional approach to designing an effective lesson begins with providing materials to our students through both a content and literacy lens. For example, we will look at an upcoming topic and analyze it from both a content and language perspective while anticipating any misconceptions students may have. Rebekah will first break down the content so that it is comprehensible to a multitude of learners, and Lauren will further adjust the modifications to help students expand their acquisition of the material. In order to help students from various backgrounds to be successful, the class is highly structured and each unit follows the same pattern. In addition to the consistent routine, the sheltered class is highly differentiated for ELLs. For example, at the start of every unit, students are provided with modified notes and a vocabulary reference sheet. They have the opportunity to either translate vocabulary into their own language or to draw pictures to help them activate prior knowledge and create personal meaning. Furthermore, students are frequently given choices as to how they want to express their understanding through their own annotations and/or justifications, allowing them to further make meaningful connections with their learning.

Our efforts at building relationships outside the school have contributed to the sense of "family" that is fostered inside the classroom. We both spend a considerable amount of time attending students' community events, family celebrations, sporting events, and cultural ceremonies. These interactions have fostered relationships wherein students feel confident in advocating for an authentic and impactful educational experience, which carries over to other classes and further promotes their future success.

Figure 11.15 Completed Noticing and Wondering Augmented with Instructional and Language Development Ideas

Noticing	Wondering	Core Instructional Ideas	Language Development Ideas
I noticed that all of the students engaged in math work before the bell rang, awesome! *Great use of instructional aide to check homework before the bell rings.* *I noticed FN is sitting alone; HL students sitting together; RJ and AN sitting together.* *I noticed that you have so many adults in the room. Wow, so many layers of support for all kiddos.* *You read the homework answers; mostly CLD kiddos asked for repeats.* *Kids are very attentive and respectful of you and the learning environment!* *Showed the problem and asked the question multiple times (gave think time for all students) before you called on everyone. SOOO MANY HANDS RAISED WITH THINK TIME!!!* *Great questions: What do I do? Why do I do it? You are asking them to explain the procedure and the why.* *Great Total Physical Response (TPR) dance for procedure/steps.* *Such crisp, quick transitions and routines!* *You complimented students that did a step (looking at recipe) that many forgot.*	*In your experience, what works best for seating charts? I have been playing around a lot recently with student choice vs. assigned seats too.* *Do you ever show the homework, or is it just a quick brain refresher?* *You gave lots of think time for the question. Do you ever allow students to briefly discuss the how/why questions before asking to share?* *Do they ever stop paying attention to you?? Seriously, you are like a magnet to their eyes :D* *Do you ever ask them to stand up and do the procedure dance too? This would be a great way to have them remember multiple steps, each move for a different step.* *I wonder if we can mix up where they complete their work so they all work next to and collaborate with a variety of students.* *I wonder if kiddos could record themselves or a partner doing and explaining their work: explain everything or video w/ a whiteboard.* *I wonder how we can facilitate these collaborative conversations for all students at the board.* *How can we get all kiddos to celebrate their own learning and their classmates' learning?*	*Total Physical Response (TPR) for procedure LOVE IT!!!!* *– maybe you can also use language/words to explain the dance when they are doing it* *– have them also say/yell/repeat the steps while they do it :D* *Number talk on the concept of fractions, improper fractions, and mixed numbers.* *Number talk on actual application of multiple fraction multiplication "A backyard has square yards (yd^2) of open space. If Patrick wants to build a vegetable garden covering the open space, how many square yards will this be?"* *Talking out their work: use video or explain everything to have them explain their thoughts as to how to solve and why they do each step.*	*Turn and talk time for challenging how/why questions to support all learners' language development to respond to complex questions/ thinking.* *Video recording or explain everything when students paired to have collaborative conversations on how they did the work, and why.*

Next, let's examine a modified noticing and wondering note-taking chart developed and implemented by language development coach Ryan Zak and his colleagues in Kildeer Countryside School District 96, Illinois.

In Kildeer Countryside, co-teachers and instructional coaches use this "Noticing and Wonderings" document to observe the strengths of the cooperating teachers and develop professional learning goals. With positive presuppositions and deep levels of mutual trust, this document helps both teachers reflect on the instruction in the classroom, the needs of the students, and a plan to bring them all together. In Figure 11.15, an ELL teacher—referred to as a Language Development Coach (LDC)— asked a teacher to complete a noticing and wonderings observation to help determine student needs in the classroom. The LDC focused on student behaviors and maintained a very professional and positive mindset while completing an observation with the purpose of understanding and developing strategies to enhance student engagement. This observation form became the shared evidence for discussion that helped both teachers determine instruction to enhance learning and language in the classroom for all students.

In the following excerpt, see how three teachers have jointly reflected about their power relationship shifting as a result of aiming for true collaboration. Read what Wendy Bresnahan, second-grade teacher, Anna Coe, ELL teacher, and Elizabeth Grenzebach, first-grade teacher at McNair Elementary School in the Hazelwood School District, Missouri, have to say about teachers' disposition toward collaboration and co-teaching:

As classroom teachers, we have found that it was difficult at the beginning to give up control of the classroom to another teacher. We were used to having teacher assistants, but they functioned differently than an ELL teacher, who has specific skills and talents to offer students. Understanding the value of an ELL teacher was not always commonplace. We've found that working together as equals has increased student engagement and achievement. Changing the attitudes of classroom teachers to become more open to the positive outcomes of co-teaching is important as co-teaching moves forward.

Finally, let's hear from a long-standing co-teacher, Nicolás Alarcón (middle school English language arts teacher), as he reflects on his partnership with Robert Thornbrough (secondary English language teacher) and their shared love for coffee and grammar:

Robert and I bonded over our love of good coffee and good grammar. We have spent four great years co-teaching and sharing our deep appreciation for simple things—a great cup of coffee, a well-written sentence—pleasing grounds for a rich co-teaching relationship.

The buzz of the grinder usually went off as the kids were hard at work on their opener, typically causing a few giggles. As the room filled with the aroma of freshly brewed coffee, I would walk across the room and serve Robert his cup. As lead teacher, I wanted our students to see me serve Robert. Robert was my elder and my respected colleague, and this small act of service sent that message.

Robert and I discovered early on that we could easily transition between the different models of co-teaching. This was a great benefit to both of us, as we got to see the learning environment from different angles. And, as time went on, these transitions happened with greater frequency and across the entire curriculum.

At the end of the lesson, Robert and I would usually debrief, sometimes for just a few minutes, sometimes longer. These moments of reflection were invaluable to me. I was able to get instant and candid feedback on how things had gone, and because I valued his perspective, I took Robert's observations to heart.

I could distill four years of coffee and grammar with Robert into two imperatives that transformed me as an educator. Robert's imperatives apply to teaching ELLs and native speakers, to co-teaching and solo-teaching, to drinking coffee and writing a good sentence. Slow down. And assume nothing.

TAKEAWAYS

This final chapter offers a closure to not only the book but to the co-planning, co-teaching, co-assessment, and reflection sequence by emphasizing the need for reflective practice as the end of the integrated, collaborative instructional cycle as well as the beginning of a new cycle. Reflection may be implemented both as an informal and highly structured formal approach to better understanding what has happened and what can be done differently in the future. While time limitations may be a deterrent to reflection, the benefits of collaborative conversations and reflective processes outweigh the perceived loss of time spent on reflecting.

VIDEO 11.2: Co-Teaching: The Instructional Cycle

http://resources
.corwin.com/
CoTeachingforELs

QUESTIONS FOR FURTHER DISCUSSION

1. What structures and routines do you consider to be most effective to help become a reflective co-teacher?

2. What are the greatest obstacles co-teachers typically face when it comes to reflecting on the collaborative instructional cycle? How can these challenges be overcome?

3. What are the most valuable tools and processes you have tried or plan to implement to successfully reflect on your co-planning, co-teaching, and co-assessment?

4. How do you ensure that reflection receives the time and attention it deserves?

References

Ajayi, L. (2008). Meaning-making, multimodal representation, and transformative pedagogy: An exploration of meaning construction instructional practices in an ESL high school classroom. *Journal of Language, Identity & Education, 7,* 206–229.

Ali, S. (2016). *Joining forces: Coteaching in the ELA department.* Retrieved from http://oraclecharterschool .org/joining-forces-co-teaching-ela-department/

Alvarez, L., Ananda, S., Walqui, A., Sato, E., & Rabinowitz, S. (2014). *Focusing formative assessment on the needs of English language learners.* Retrieved from https://www.wested.org/wp-content/files_mf/ 1391626953FormativeAssessment_report5.pdf

Anderson, R. C., Hiebert, E. H., Scott, J. A., & Wilkinson, I. A. G. (1985). *Becoming a nation of readers: The report of the Commission on Reading, U. S. Department of Education.* Champaign-Urbana, IL: Center for the Study of Reading.

Bazerman, C., Little, J., Bethel, L., Chavkin, T., Fouquette, D., & Garufis, J. (2005). *Reference guide to writing across the curriculum.* West Lafayette, IN: Parlor Press.

Beck, I. L., McKeown, M. G., & Kucan, L. (2002). *Bringing words to life: Robust vocabulary instruction.* New York, NY: Guilford.

Beck, I. L., McKeown, M. G., & Kucan, L. (2013). *Bringing words to life: Robust vocabulary instruction* (2nd ed.). New York, NY: Guilford.

Bell, A., & Baecher, L. (2012). Points on a continuum: ESL teachers reporting on collaboration. *TESOL Journal, 3*(3), 488–515.

Beninghof, A., & Leensvaart, M. (2016). Co-teaching to support ELLs. *Educational Leadership, 73*(5), 70–73.

Bessette, J. (2008). Using students' drawings to elicit general and special educators' perceptions of co-teaching. *Science Direct 24,* 1376–1396. doi:10.1016/j.tate.2007.06.007

Blair, L. (2015). *Co-teaching offers new approach to learning for Moffat County students.* Retrieved from http://www.craigdailypress.com/news/co-teaching-offers-new-approach-to-learning-for-moffat-county-students/

Blood, C. L., & Link, M. (1990). *The goat in the rug.* New York, NY: Aladdin.

Blythe, T., Allen, D., Schieffelin Powell, B. (2008). *Looking together at student work* (2nd ed.). New York, NY: Teachers College Press.

Bunch, G. C. (2013). Pedagogical language knowledge: Preparing mainstream teachers for English learners in the new standards era. *Review of Research in Education 37,* 298–341.

Bunting, E. (1989). *The terrible things: An allegory of the Holocaust.* Philadelphia, PA: Jewish Publication Society.

Calderón, M. E., Slavin, R., & Sánchez, M. (2011). Effective instruction for English learners. *Future of Our Children, 21*(1), 103–127.

Campbell, L. M., & Campbell, B. (2008). *Mindful learning: 101 proven strategies for student and teacher success* (2nd ed.). Thousand Oaks, CA: Corwin.

Carroll, K. (2007). *Linear and non-linear learning*. Retrieved from http://ken-carroll.com/2007/12/13/linear-and-non-linear-learning/

Causton, J., & Theoharis, G. (2014). *The principal's handbook for leading inclusive schools*. Baltimore, MD: Paul H. Brookes.

Chapman, C., & Hyatt, C. H. (2011). *Critical conversations in co-teaching: A problem-solving approach*. Bloomington, IN: Solution Tree.

Chingos, M. M., & Whitehurst, G. J. (2011). *Class size: What research says and what it means for state policy*. Retrieved from http://www.brookings.edu/research/papers/2011/05/11-class-size-whitehurst-chingos

Collins, J. (2001). *Good to great: Why some companies make the leap and others don't*. New York, NY: HarperCollins.

Colton, A., Langer, G., & Goff, L. (2016). *The collaborative analysis of student learning: Professional learning that promotes success for all*. Thousand Oaks, CA: Corwin.

Conderman, G., Johnston-Rodriguez, S., & Hartman, P. (2009). Communicating and collaborating in co-taught classrooms. *TEACHING Exceptional Children Plus, 5*(5). Retrieved from http://files.eric.ed.gov/fulltext/EJ967751.pdf

Conley, D. T. (2014). *A new era for educational assessment* [Deeper Learning Research Series]. Boston, MA: Jobs for the Future.

Cornell, G. (2014). *Use popular music to improve reading and inspire writing*. Retrieved from http://www.scholastic.com/teachers/top-teaching/2014/10/use-popular-music-improve-reading-and-inspire-writing

Covey, S. M. R. (2008). *The speed of trust: The one thing that changes everything*. New York, NY: Simon & Schuster.

Cunningham, P. M., Hall, D. P., & Defee, M., (1991). Non-ability-grouped, multilevel instruction: A year in a first-grade classroom. *The Reading Teacher, 44,* 566–571.

Davison, C. (2006). Collaboration between ESL and content area teachers: How do we know when we are doing it right? *International Journal of Bilingual Education and Bilingualism, 9*(4), 454–475.

Dodge, J., & Honigsfeld, A. (2014). *Core instructional routines: Go-to structures for effective literacy teaching, K–5*. Portsmouth, NH: Heinemann.

Dove, M. G., & Honigsfeld, A. (2013). *Common core for the not-so-common learner, Grades K–5: English language arts strategies*. Thousand Oaks, CA: Corwin.

Dove, M. G., Honigsfeld, A., & Cohan, A. (2014). *Beyond core expectations: A framework for servicing the not-so-common learner*. Thousand Oaks, CA: Corwin.

DuFour, R., & Eaker, R. (1998). *Professional learning communities at work: Best practices for enhancing student achievement*. Bloomington, IN: Solution Tree.

Dweck, C. S. (2006). *Mindset: The new psychology of success*. New York, NY: Random House.

Echevarria, J., Vogt, M. E., & Short, D. (2016). *Making content comprehensible for English learners: The SIOP model* (5th ed.). Boston, MA: Pearson.

Eells, R. J. (2011). *Meta-analysis of the relationship between collective teacher efficacy and student achievement* (Doctoral dissertation). Retrieved from http://ecommons.luc.edu/cgi/viewcontent.cgi?article=1132&context=luc_diss

Erickson, H. L. (2006). *Concept-based curriculum and instruction for the thinking classroom*. Thousand Oaks, CA: Sage.

Ermeling, B. A., & Graff-Ermeling, G. (2014). Teaching between the desks. *Educational Leadership, 72*(2), 55–60.

Every Student Succeeds Act, 20 U.S.C. § 1001 et seq. (2015).

Farrell, T. S. C. (2016). Anniversary article: The practices of encouraging TESOL teachers to engage in reflective practice: An appraisal of recent research contributions. *Language Teaching Research, 20,* 223–247. doi:10.1177/1362168815617335

Felder, R. M., & Brent, R. (2007). Cooperative learning. In P. A. Mabrouk (Ed.), *Active learning: Models from the analytical sciences* (pp. 34–53). Washington, DC: American Chemical Society.

Fenner, D. S. (2014). *Advocating for English learners.* Thousand Oaks, CA: Corwin.

Ferlazzo, L. (2012). *Do's & don'ts for teaching English-language learners.* Retrieved from http://www.edutopia .org/blog/esl-ell-tips-ferlazzo-sypnieski

Fichtman Dana, N., Thomas, C., & Boynton, S. (2011). *Inquiry: A districtwide approach to staff and student learning.* Thousand Oaks, CA: Corwin.

Fisher, D., & Frey, N. (2007). *Checking for understanding: Formative assessment techniques for your classroom.* Alexandria, VA: Association for Supervision and Curriculum Development.

Fisher, D., & Frey, N. (2008a). *Better learning through structured teaching: A framework for the gradual release of responsibility.* Alexandria, VA: Association for Supervision and Curriculum Development.

Fisher, D., & Frey, N. (2008b). *Wordwise and content rich: Five essential steps to teaching content vocabulary.* Portsmouth, NH: Heinemann.

Fisher, D., & Frey, N. (2012). The perils of preteaching. *Principal Leadership, 12*(9), 84–86.

Fisher, D., Frey, N., & Hattie, J. (2016). *Visible learning for literacy, grades K–12: Implementing the practices that work best to accelerate student learning.* Thousand Oaks, CA: Corwin.

Fisher, D., Frey, N., & Rothenberg, C. (2008). *Content-area conversations: How to plan discussion-based lessons for diverse language learners.* Alexandria, VA: Association for Supervision and Curriculum Development.

Fisher, D., Frey, N., & Uline, C. (2013). *Common Core English Language Arts in a PLC at work.* Bloomington, IN: Solution Tree.

Franco, B., Petrie, A., Ready, M., & Donovan, B. (2014). A system for change. *Principal Leadership,* 36–40.

Friend, M. (2008). *Co-teach! A handbook for creating and sustaining classroom partnerships in inclusive schools.* Greensboro, NC: Marilyn Friend.

Friend, M. (2014). *Co-teaching: Classroom partnerships for student success.* Retrieved from http:// wyominginstructionalnetwork.com/wp-content/uploads/2014/10/Mon-Dr-Friend-Co-Teaching-Basic.pdf

Friend, M., & Bursuck, W. D. (2014). *Including students with special needs: A practical guide for classroom teachers* (7th ed.). Upper Saddle River, NJ: Pearson.

Friend, M., & Cook, L. (1996). *Interactions: Collaboration skills for school professionals.* White Plains, NY: Longman.

Fletcher, R., & Portalupi, J. (2007). *Craft lessons: Teaching K–8 writing* (2nd ed.). Portland, ME: Stenhouse.

Fullan, M. (2007). *The new meaning of educational change* (4th ed.). New York, NY: Teachers College Press.

Fullan, M. (2016). *The new meaning of educational change* (5th ed.). New York, NY: Teacher's College Press.

Garafalo, D. (2016a). *Collaboration and co-teaching in a high school science class.* Retrieved from https://sites .google.com/site/northerneslplc/collaborating-and-co-teaching-in-a-high-school-science-class

Garafalo, D. (2016b). *An elementary ENL collaboration and co-teaching success story.* Retrieved from https:// ocmbocesis.wordpress.com/2016/05/03/an-elementary-enl-collaboration-and-co-teaching-success-story/

García, O., & Li, W. (2014). *Translanguaging: Language, bilingualism, and education.* New York, NY: Palgrave Macmillan.

Gay, G. (2000). *Culturally responsive teaching: Theory, research, and practice.* New York, NY: Teachers College Press.

Goddard, R. D. (2001). Collective efficacy: A neglected construct in the study of schools and student achievement. *Journal of Educational Psychology, 93,* 467–476.

Goldenberg, C. (2013). Unlocking the research on English learners: What we know and don't yet know about effective instruction. *American Educator, 37*(2), 4–11, 38.

Goldenberg, C. N., & Coleman, R. (2010). *Promoting academic achievement among English learners: A guide to the research.* Thousand Oaks, CA: Corwin.

Goldstein, A. (2015). *English language learners thrive in the Cherry Creek School District.* Retrieved from http://yourhub.denverpost.com/blog/2015/09/english-language-learners-thrive-in-the-cherry-creek-school-district/110243/

Goodlad, J. I., Mantle-Bromley, C., & Goodlad, S. J. (2004). *Education for everyone: Agenda for education in a democracy.* San Francisco, CA: Jossey-Bass.

Gottlieb, M. (2006). *Assessing English language learners: Bridges from language proficiency to academic achievement.* Thousand Oaks, CA: Corwin.

Gottlieb, M. (2011, November). *From academic language to academic success.* Workshop presented at the Iowa Culture & Language Conference, Coralville, IA.

Gottlieb, M. (2016). *Assessing English language learners: Bridges to educational equity.* Thousand Oaks, CA: Corwin.

Gottlieb M., & Castro, M. (2017). *Language power: Key uses for accessing content.* Thousand Oaks, CA: Corwin.

Gray, S. M. (2012). From principles to practice: Collegial observation for teacher development. *TELD/ESL Journal, 3*(2), 231–255.

Guild, P. B. (2001). *Diversity, learning style, and culture.* Retrieved from http://education.jhu.edu/PD/newhorizons/strategies/topics/Learning%20Styles/diversity.html

Guskey, T. R. (2014). *On your mark: Challenging the conventions of grading and reporting.* Bloomington, IN: Solution Tree.

Guskey, T. R., & Jung, L. A. (2013). *Answers to essential questions about standards, assessments, grading, and reporting.* Thousand Oaks, CA: Corwin.

Harvey, S., & Daniels, H. (2009). *Comprehension and collaboration: Inquiry circles in action.* Portsmouth, NH: Heinemann.

Harvey, S., & Goudvis, A. (2013). Comprehension at the core. *The Reading Teacher, 66*(6), 432–439.

Hattie, J. (2009). *Visible learning: A synthesis of over 800 meta-analyses relating to achievement.* New York, NY: Routledge.

Hattie, J. (2012). *Visible learning for teachers.* New York, NY: Routledge.

Hattic, J. (2015a). The effective use of testing: What the research says. *Education Week, 35*(10), 23, 28.

Hattie, J, (2015b). *What works best in education: The politics of collaborative expertise.* https://www.pearson.com/content/dam/corporate/global/pearson-dot-com/files/hattie/150526_ExpertiseWEB_V1.pdf

Hattie, J., & Timperley, H. (2007). The power of feedback. *Review of Educational Research, 77*(1), 81–112.

Hattie, J., & Yates, G. (2013). *Visible learning and the science of how we learn.* New York, NY: Routledge.

Hauck, M. C., Wolf, M. K., & Mislevy, R. J. (2013). *Creating a next-generation system of K–12 English learner (EL) language proficiency assessments.* Retrieved from http://www.ets.org/research/policy_research_reports/publications/paper/2013/jrld

Heritage, M. (2010). *Formative assessment and next-generation assessment systems: Are we losing an opportunity?* Washington, DC: Council of Chief State School Officers.

Hern, K. (with Snell, M.). (2013). *Toward a vision of accelerated curriculum & pedagogy.* Retrieved from http://www.learningworksca.org/wp-content/uploads/2012/02/AcceleratingCurriculum_508.pdf

Hewitt, M.B. (1998). Helping students feel like they belong. *Reclaiming Children and Youth, 7*(3), 155–159.

Honigsfeld, A., & Dodge, J. (2015). *Core instructional routines: Go-to structures for 6–12 classrooms.* Portsmouth, NH: Heinemann.

Honigsfeld, A., & Dove, M. (2008). Co-teaching in the ESL classroom. *Delta Kappa Gamma Bulletin, 74*(2), 8–14.

Honigsfeld, A., & Dove, M. G. (2010). *Collaboration and co-teaching: Strategies for English learners.* Thousand Oaks, CA: Corwin.

Honigsfeld, A., & Dove, M. G. (2013). *Common Core for the not-so-common learner, grades 6–12: English language arts strategies.* Thousand Oaks, CA: Corwin.

Honigsfeld, A., & Dove, M. G. (2015a). *Collaboration and co-teaching for English learners: A leader's guide.* Thousand Oaks, CA: Corwin.

Honigsfeld, A., & Dove, M. G. (2015b). Co-teaching ELLs: Riding a tandem bike. *Educational Leadership, 76*(4), 56–60.

Howard, L., & Potts, E. A. (2009). Using co-planning time: Strategies for a successful coteaching marriage. *TEACHING Exceptional Children Plus, 5*(4), Article 2. Retrieved from http://files.eric.ed.gov/fulltext/EJ967747.pdf

Hoy, W. K., Tarter, C. J., & Woolfolk Hoy, A. (2006). Academic optimism of schools: A force for student achievement. *American Educational Research Journal, 43*, 425–446.

Imbriano, R. (Producer, Writer, & Narrator). (2010). *A call to act: Ledbetter v. Goodyear Tire and Rubber Company.* Retrieved from http://www.annenbergclassroom.org/page/call-to-act-ledbetter

Jackson, P. W. (1990). *Life in classrooms.* New York, NY: Teachers College Press.

Johnson, D. W., Johnson, R. T., & Smith, K. A. (2006). *Active learning: Cooperation in the college classroom* (3rd ed.). Edina, MN: Interaction Book Company.

Johnson, D. W., Johnson, R. T., & Stanne, M. E. (2000). *Cooperative learning methods: A meta-analysis.* Retrieved from https://www.researchgate.net/publication/220040324_Cooperative_learning_methods_A_meta-analysis

Jung, L. A., & Guskey, T. R. (2012). *Grading exceptional and struggling learners.* Thousand Oaks, CA: Corwin.

Kagan, S., Kagan, M., & Kagan, L. (2016). *59 Kagan structures: Proven engagement strategies.* San Clemente, CA: Kagan.

Kibler, A. K., Walqui, A., & Bunch, G. C. (2015). Transformational opportunities: Language and literacy instruction for English language learners in the Common Core era in the United States. *TESOL Journal, 6*(1), 9–35.

Knowapple, J. (2015). *Equity leaders must work themselves out of a job: What collective efficacy has to do with educational equity.* Retrieved from http://corwin-connect.com/2015/12/equity-leaders-must-work-themselves-out-of-a-job-what-collective-efficacy-has-to-do-with-educational-equity/

Ko, T. (2014, January 28). *Special edition: Co-planning for success* [Web log post]. Retrieved from https://www.teachingchannel.org/blog/ausl/2014/01/28/special-edition-co-planning-for-success/

Kohn, A. (2004). Test today, privatize tomorrow: Using accountability to reform public schools to death. *Phi Delta Kappan, 85*(8), 569–577.

Kurti, R. S., Kurti, D. L., & Fleming, L. (2014). The philosophy of educational makerspaces: Part 1 of making an educational makerspace. *Teacher Librarian, 41*(5), 8–11.

Langer, G. M., Colton, A. B., & Goff, L. (2003). *Collaborative analysis of student work: Improving teaching and learning.* Alexandria, VA: Association for Supervision and Curriculum Development.

Leos, K., & Saavedra, L. (2010). *A new vision to increase the academic achievement for English language learners and immigrant students.* Retrieved from http://www.urban.org/sites/default/files/alfresco/publication-pdfs/412265-A-New-Vision-to-Increase-the-Academic-Achievement-for-English-Language-Learners-and-Immigrant-Students.PDF

Lightbown, P. M., & Spada, N. (2013). *How languages are learned* (4th ed.). Oxford, England: Oxford University Press.

Loewen, J. W. (2007*). Lies my teacher told me: Everything your American history textbook got wrong.* New York, NY: Touchstone.

Long Island Regional Bilingual Education Resource Network. (2015). *Coteaching and collaboration for teachers of ELLs.* Retrieved from http://www.esboces.org/Page/1456

Magnuson, A. (2010, September 24). Learning centers, part 1: Why they're important [Web log post]. Retrieved from http://www.scholastic.com/teachers/classroom_solutions/2010/09/learning-centers-part-1-why-theyre-important

Malefyt, T. (2016, January 6). Learning centers in the secondary classroom [Web log post]. Retrieved from https://www.edutopia.org/blog/learning-centers-in-secondary-classroom-ted-malefyt

Marietta, G., & Brookover, E. (2011). *Effectively educating PreK–3 English language learners (ELs) in Montgomery County Public Schools.* Retrieved from http://fcd-us.org/sites/default/files/FCDCase StdyMntgmryCtyELS.pdf

Martinez-Wenzl, M., Perez, K., & Gandara, P. (2012). Is Arizona's approach to educating its ELs superior to other forms of instruction? *Teachers College Record, 114*(9), 1–32.

Martinsen Holt, N. (2004). *Pull-out to collaboration: Becoming an effective ESL co-teacher* (Unpublished master's thesis). Retrieved from http://digitalcommons.hamline.edu/hse_all/304/

Marzano, R. J. (2004). *Building background knowledge for academic achievement: Research on what works in schools.* Alexandria, VA: Association for Supervision and Curriculum Development.

Marzano, R. J. (2007). *The art and science of teaching: A comprehensive framework for effective instruction.* Alexandria, VA: Association for Supervision and Curriculum Development.

Maxwell, L. (2013, October 28). *ESL and classroom teachers team up to teach the Common Core.* Retrieved from http://www.edweek.org/ew/articles/2013/10/30/10cc-eslteachers.h33.html

McTighe, J., & Wiggins, G. (1999). *Understanding by Design professional development workbook.* Alexandria, VA: Association for Supervision and Curriculum Development.

Merryweather, L. (2014, April 2). The benefits of student-led learning in international schools [Web log post]. Retrieved from https://www.teachaway.com/2014/04/02/benefits-student-led-learning-in-international-schools

Mirel, J., & Goldin, S. (2012). *Alone in the classroom: Why teachers are too isolated.* Retrieved from http://www.theatlantic.com/national/archive/2012/04/alone-in-the-classroom-why-teachers-are-too-isolated/255976/

Moll, L. C., Amanti, C., Neff, D., & Gonzalez, N. (1992). Funds of knowledge for teaching: Using a qualitative approach to connect homes and classrooms. *Theory Into Practice, 31,* 132–141.

Moskal, B. M. (2000). Scoring rubrics: What, when and how? *Practical Assessment, Research & Evaluation, 7*(3). Retrieved from http://PAREonline.net/getvn.asp?v=7&n=3

Murawski, W. W. (2009a). *Collaborative teaching in elementary schools: Making the co-teaching marriage work!* Thousand Oaks, CA: Corwin.

Murawski, W. W. (2009b). *Collaborative teaching in secondary schools: Making the co-teaching marriage work!* Thousand Oaks, CA: Corwin.

Murawski, W. W. (2010). *Collaborative teaching in elementary schools.* Thousand Oaks, CA: Corwin.

Nagel, D. (2015). *Effective grading practices for secondary teachers: Practical strategies to prevent failure, recover credits, and increase standards-based/referenced grading.* Thousand Oaks, CA: Corwin.

No Child Left Behind Act of 2001, 20 U.S.C. § 6319 (2002).

Noble, E. (2015). *Newcomer ESL program is coming to South this fall.* Retrieved from http://www.shsoutherner.net/features/2015/04/24/newcomer-esl-program-coming-to-south-this-fall/

Nobori, M. (2011). *5 strategies to ensure student learning.* Retrieved from https://www.edutopia.org/stw-differentiated-instruction-budget-assessment-how-to

Novak, K. (2014). *UDL now!: A teacher's Monday-morning guide to implementing Common Core Standards using Universal Design for Learning.* Wakefield, MA: CAST Professional Publishing.

Ntelioglou, B. Y., Fannin, J., Montanera, M., & Cummins, J. (2014). A multilingual and multimodal approach to literacy teaching and learning in urban education: A collaborative inquiry project in an urban inner city elementary school. *Frontiers in Psychology, 5,* 1–23.

Ocasio, L. (2016). *Collaborative model shows promise: District 20 pilot helps schools struggling to support English language learners.* Retrieved from http://www.uft.org/feature-stories/collaborative-model-shows-promise

O'Connell, M. J., & Vandas, K. L. (2015). *Partnering with students: Building ownership of learning.* Thousand Oaks, CA: Corwin.

Ogle, D. M. (1986). K-W-L: A teaching model that develops active reading of expository text. *The Reading Teacher, 39,* 564–570.

O'Malley, J. M., & Valdez Pierce, L. (1996). *Authentic assessment for English language learners: Practical approaches for teachers.* Reading, MA: Addison-Wesley.

Oracle Charter School. (2016). *Joining forces: Co-teaching in the ELA department.* Retrieved from http://oraclecharterschool.org/2016/05/19/joining-forces-co-teaching-ela-department/

Oxford, R. L. (1990). *Teaching and researching language learning strategies: Self-regulation in context* (2nd ed.). New York, NY: Routledge.

Oxford, R. (2017). *Teaching and researching language learning strategies: Self-regulation in context* (2nd ed.). New York, NY: Routledge.

Palmer, D., & Martínez, R. A. (2013). Teacher agency in bilingual spaces: A fresh look at preparing teachers to educate Latina/o bilingual children. *Review of Research in Education, 37,* 269–297.

Pappamihiel, N. E. (2012). Benefits and challenges of co-teaching English learners in one elementary school in transition. *The Tapestry Journal, 4*(1), 1–13.

Parris, H., Estrada, L., & Honigsfeld, A. (2016). *ELL frontiers: Using technology to enhance instruction for English learners.* Thousand Oaks, CA: Corwin.

Pawan, F., & Sietmann, G. B. (Eds.). (2007). *For all our students: Collaborative partnerships among ESL and classroom teachers.* Alexandria, VA: TELD/ESL.

Pearson, P. D., & Gallagher, M. (1983). The instruction of reading comprehension. *Contemporary Educational Psychology, 8,* 317–344.

Pillars, W. (2015). *10 ways to optimize classroom co-teaching.* Retrieved from http://www.edweek.org/tm/articles/2015/10/26/10-ways-to-optimize-classroom-co-teaching.html

Ponce, J. (2017). *The far-reaching benefits of co-teaching for ELLs.* Retrieved from https://www.teachingchannel.org/blog/2017/01/20/benefits-of-co-teaching-for-ells/

Porter-O'Donnell, C. (2004). Beyond the yellow highlighter: Teaching annotation skills to improve reading comprehension. *English Journal, 93*(5), 82–89.

Quaglia, R. J., & Corso, M. J. (2014). *Student voice: The instrument of change.* Thousand Oaks, CA: Corwin.

Rance-Roney, J. (2009). Best practices for adolescent ELs. *Educational Leadership, 66*(7), 32–37.

Reading Rockets (n.d.). *Think-alouds.* Retrieved from http://www.readingrockets.org/strategies/think_alouds

Reeves, D. B. (2000). *Accountability in action: A blueprint for learning organizations.* Denver, CO: Advanced Learning Press.

Reeves, D. (2006). *The learning leader.* Alexandria, VA: Association for Supervision and Curriculum Development.

Renner Del Nero, J. (2013). Introduction. In L. M. Morrow, K. K. Wixson, & T. Shanahan (Eds.), *Teaching with the Common Core Standards for English Language Arts, Grades 3–5* (pp. xi–xiv). New York, NY: Guilford Press.

Robles, Y. (2015). *State looking to learn from Cherry Creek's model for English learners.* Retrieved from http://www.denverpost.com/news/ci_28897474/state-looking-learn-from-cherry-creeks-model-english

Rollins, S. P. (2014). *Learning in the fast lane: 8 ways to put ALL students on the road to academic success.* Alexandria, VA: Association for Supervision and Curriculum Development.

Rothstein, D., & Santana, L. (2011). *Make just one change: Teach students to ask their own questions.* Cambridge, MA: Harvard Education Press.

Russell, F. A. (2012). A culture of collaboration: Meeting the instructional needs of adolescent English language learners. *TESOL Journal, 3,* 445–468. doi:10.1002/tesj.24

Sacks, L (2014, June 17). *It's not enough to talk the talk.* Retrieved from http://blogs.edweek.org/edweek/learning_deeply/2014/06/its_not_enough_to_talk_the_talk.html?cmp=ENL-EU-NEWS3

Sandberg, K. L., & Reschly, A.L. (2011). English learners: Challenges in assessment and the promise of curriculum-based measurement. *Remedial and Special Education, 32,* 144–154. doi:10.1177/0741932510361260

Santos, M., Darling-Hammond, L., & Cheuk, T. (2012). *Teacher development to support English language learners in the context of Common Core State Standards.* Retrieved from http://ell.stanford.edu/sites/default/files/pdf/academic-papers/10-Santos%20LDH%20Teacher%20Development%20FINAL.pdf

Schanzenbach, D. W. (2014). *Does class size matter?* Boulder, CO: National Education Policy Center. Retrieved from http://nepc.colorado.edu/publication/does-class-size-matter

Schmoker, M. (2011). *Focus: Elevating the essentials to radically improve student learning.* Alexandria, VA: Association for Supervision and Curriculum Development.

Schon, D. A. (1983). *The reflective practitioner: How professionals think in action.* New York, NY: Basic Books.

Schon, D. A. (1990). *Educating the reflective practitioner: Toward a new design for teaching and learning in the professions.* San Francisco, CA: Jossey-Bass.

Silver, D., Berckemeyer, J. C., & Baenen, J. (2015). *Deliberate optimism: Reclaiming the joy in education.* Thousand Oaks, CA: Corwin.

Silver, H. F., & Perini, M. J. (2010). The eight Cs of engagement: How learning styles and instructional design increase student commitment to learning. In R. J. Marzano (Ed.), *On excellence in teaching* (pp. 319–344). Bloomington, IN: Solution Tree.

Singer, T. W. (2014). *Opening doors to equity: A practical guide to observation-based professional learning.* Thousand Oaks, CA: Corwin.

Slavich, G. M., & Zimbardo, P. G. (2012). Transformational teaching: Theoretical underpinnings, basic principles, and core methods. *Educational Psychology Review, 24,* 569–608.

Staehr Fenner, D. (2013a). *Advocating for English learners: A guide for educators.* Thousand Oaks, CA: Corwin.

Staehr Fenner, D. (2013b). *Implementing the Common Core State Standards for English learners: The changing role of the ESL teacher.* Retrieved from http://www.tesol.org/docs/default-source/advocacy/ccss_convening_final-8-15-13.pdf?sfvrsn=8

Stanford University. (2013). *Key principles for ELL instruction.* Retrieved from http://ell.stanford.edu/sites/default/files/Key%20Principles%20for%20ELL%20Instruction%20with%20references_0.pdf

Steig, W. (2004). *Sylvester and the magic pebble.* New York, NY: Simon and Schuster.

Stein, E. (2016). *Elevating co-teaching through EDL.* Wakefield, MA: CAST Professional Publishing.

Stratton, E. (2015, December 22). *Students learn English by staying put.* Retrieved from http://www.dailyastorian.com/Local_News/20151222/students-learn-english-by-staying-put#.Vnw9F1Y-UiM.facebook

Supporting English Language Learners at Cherry Crest. (2016). Retrieved from http://www.bsd405.org/2016/03/supporting-english-language-learners-at-cherry-crest

Teachers of English to Speakers of Other Languages. (2006). *TESOL PreK–12 English language proficiency standards.* Alexandria, VA: Author.

Theoharis, G., & O'Toole, J. (2011). Leading inclusive ELL: Social justice leadership for English language learners. *Educational Administration Quarterly, 47*(4), 646–688.

Thompson, S. J., Morse, A. B., Sharpe, M., & Hall, S. (2005). *Accommodations manual: How to select, administer and evaluate use of accommodations and assessment for students with disabilities.* Washington, DC: Council of Chief State School Officers.

Thousand, J., Villa, R., & Nevin, A. (2015). *Differentiated instruction: Planning for universal design and teaching for college and career readiness* (2nd ed.). Thousand Oaks, CA: Corwin.

Tomlinson, C. A., & Imbeau, M. B. (2010). *Leading and managing a differentiated classroom.* Alexandria, VA: Association for Supervision and Curriculum Development.

Triplett, B. (2013). *The impact of separationist models of instructional support on the self-efficacy perceptions of Latino English language learners.* Unpublished doctoral dissertation. St. John Fisher College, Rochester, NY.

Tung, R., Uriarte, M., Diez, V., Gagnon, L., & Stazesky, P., with de los Reyes, E., & Bolomey, A. (2011). *Learning from consistently high performing and improving schools for English language learners in Boston Public Schools.* Boston, MA: Center for Collaborative Education. Retrieved from http://files.eric.ed.gov/fulltext/ED540998.pdf

Turkan, S., de Oliveira, L., Lee, O., & Phelps, G. (2014). Proposing the knowledge base for teaching academic content to English language learners: Disciplinary linguistic knowledge. *Teachers College Record, 116*(3), 1–30.

U.S. Department of Education. (2015a). *English learner toolkit.* Retrieved from http://www2.ed.gov/about/offices/list/oela/english-learner-toolkit/index.html

U.S. Department of Education. (2015b). *Every student succeeds act (ESSA).* Retrieved from: http://www.ed.gov/essa

U.S. Department of Justice & U.S. Department of Education. (2015). *Dear colleague letter: English learner students and limited English proficient parents.* Received from http://www2.ed.gov/about/offices/list/ocr/letters/colleague-el-201501.pdf

Valdés, G., Kibler, A., & Walqui, A. (2014). *Changes in the expertise of ESL professionals: Knowledge and action in an era of new standards.* Alexandria, VA: TESOL International Association. Retrieved from http://www.tesol.org/docs/default-source/papers-and-briefs/professional-paper-26-march-2014.pdf?sfvrsn=4

Vangrieken, K., Dochy, F., Raes, E., & Kyndt, E. (2015). Teacher collaboration: A systematic review. *Educational Research Review, 15,* 17–40.

Van Roekel, D. (2011). *NEA president shares thoughts on NCLB with* Washington Post. Retrieved from http://neatoday.org/2011/01/07/nea-president-shares-thoughts-on-esea-with-washington-post/

Venn, J. (2007). *Assessing students with special needs* (4th ed.). Upper Saddle River, NJ: Pearson.

Villa, R. A., & Thousand, J. (Eds.). (2005). *Creating an inclusive school.* Alexandria, VA: Association for Supervision and Curriculum Development.

Villa, R. A., Thousand, J. S., & Nevin, A. I. (2008). *A guide to co-teaching: Practical tips for facilitating student learning* (2nd ed.). Thousand Oaks, CA: Corwin.

Villa, R. A., Thousand, J. S., & Nevin, A. I. (2011). What is co-teaching? In T. J. Karten (Ed.), *Inclusive practices* (pp. 105–112). Thousand Oaks, CA: Corwin.

Villa, R. A., Thousand, J. S., & Nevin, A. I. (2013). *A guide to co-teaching: New lessons and strategies to facilitate student learning* (3rd ed.). Thousand Oaks, CA: Corwin.

Virginia Institute for Developmental Disabilities. (2001). *Creating collaborative IEPs: A handbook.* Richmond, VA: Author.

Waff, D. (2009). Coresearching and coreflecting: The power of teacher inquiry communities. In D. Goswami, C. Lewis, M. Rutherford, & D. Waff (Eds.), *Teacher inquiry: Approaches to language and literacy research* (pp. 69–89). New York, NY: Teachers College Press.

Wagner, T., Kegan, R., Lahey, L., Lemons, R. W., Garnier, J. Helsing, D., . . . Rasmussen, H. T. (2006). *Change leadership: A practical guide to transforming our schools.* San Francisco, CA: Jossey-Bass.

Walqui, A., & van Lier, L. (2010). *Scaffolding the academic success of adolescent English language learners: A pedagogy of promise.* San Francisco, CA: WestEd.

Wardlow, L. (2013). *Breaking the isolation of the classroom: Online teacher collaboration.* Retrieved from http://researchnetwork.pearson.com/learning-science-technology/breaking-the-isolation-of-the-classroom-teacher-online-collaboration

Wiggins, G. P. (1998). *Educative assessment: Designing assessments to inform and improve student performance.* San Francisco, CA: Jossey-Bass.

Wiggins, G. P., & McTighe, J. (2005). *Understanding by design* (2nd ed.). Alexandria, VA: Association for Supervision and Curriculum Development.

Wiggins, G. P., & McTighe, J. (2011). *The Understanding by Design guide to creating high-quality units.* Alexandra, VA: Association for Supervision and Curriculum Development.

Willner, L., Rivera, C., & Acosta, B. D. (2009). Ensuring accommodations used in content assessments are responsive to English-language learners. *The Reading Teacher, 62*(8), 696–698. doi:10.1598/RT.62.8.8

Wink, J. (2013). *The 6 C's of collaboration.* Retrieved from http://leadlearner2012.blogspot.com/2013/06/the-6-c-of-collaboration.html?m=1

Wiseman, L., Allen, L., & Foster, E. (2013). *The multiplier effect: Tapping the genius inside our schools.* Thousand Oaks, CA: Corwin.

Wlazlinski, M. (2014, Spring). From state rule to practice: How ELD/ESL push-in looks like in the classroom. *GATELD/ESL in Action, 1*(1), 1–30. Retrieved from http://georgiatesoljournal.org/ojs/index.php/GATESOL/article/download/6/18

Wood, K. D., Lapp, D., Flood, J., & Taylor, D. B. (2008). *Guiding readers through text: Strategy guides for new times.* Newark, DE: International Reading Association.

Wootton, J. (2013, February 12). *Teachers team up for English language learning.* Retrieved from http://magicvalley.com/news/local/teachers-team-up-for-english-language-learning/article_1a15e3f6-74d9-11e2-a725-001a4bcf887a.html

World-Class Instructional Design and Assessment. (2011). *Glossary of terms and expressions.* Retrieved from www.wida.us/get.aspx?id=412

World-Class Instructional Design and Assessment. (2012). *The 2012 amplification of the ELD standards, Kindergarten–Grade 12.* Retrieved from www.wida.us/get.aspx?id=540

World-Class Instructional Design and Assessment. (2013). *Essential actions: A handbook for implementing WIDA's framework for English language development standards.* Retrieved from www.wida.us

Wormcli, R. (2006). *Fair isn't always equal: Assessing & grading in the differentiated classroom.* Portland, ME: Stenhouse.

Yoon, B. (2008). Uninvited guests: The influence of teachers' roles and pedagogies on the positioning of English language learners in the regular classroom. *American Educational Research Journal, 45,* 495–522.

Zamel, V., & Spack, R. (2004). *Crossing the curriculum: Multilingual learners in college classrooms.* New York, NY: Routledge.

Zike, D. (1992). *Big book of books.* San Antonio, TX: Dinah-Might Adventures.

Zwiers, J. (2014). *Building academic language: Meeting common core standards across disciplines: Grades 5–12* (2nd ed.). San Francisco, CA: Jossey-Bass.

Index

A SAGE Publishing Company

Helping educators make the greatest impact

CORWIN HAS ONE MISSION: to enhance education through intentional professional learning.

We build long-term relationships with our authors, educators, clients, and associations who partner with us to develop and continuously improve the best evidence-based practices that establish and support lifelong learning.

Solutions you want. Experts you trust. Results you need.

Author Consulting

On-site professional learning with sustainable results! Let us help you design a professional learning plan to meet the unique needs of your school or district. www.corwin.com/pd

Institutes

Corwin Institutes provide collaborative learning experiences that equip your team with tools and action plans ready for immediate implementation. www.corwin.com/institutes

eCourses

Practical, flexible online professional learning designed to let you go at your own pace. www.corwin.com/ecourses

Read2Earn

Did you know you can earn graduate credit for reading this book? Find out how: www.corwin.com/read2earn

Contact an account manager at (800) 831-6640 or visit **www.corwin.com** for more information.